Quantitative Methods

We work with leading authors to develop the strongest educational materials bringing cutting-edge thinking and best learning practice to a global market.

Under a range of well-known imprints, including Financial Times/Prentice Hall, Addison Wesley and Longman, we craft high quality print and electronic publications which help readers to understand and apply their content, whether studying or at work.

Pearson Custom Publishing enables our customers to access a wide and expanding range of market-leading content from world-renowned authors and develop their own tailor-made book. You choose the content that meets your needs and Pearson Custom Publishing produces a high-quality printed book.

To find out more about custom publishing, visit www.pearsoncustom.co.uk

A Pearson Custom Publication

Quantitative Methods

Compiled from:

Quantitative Approaches in Business Studies
Seventh Edition
by Clare Morris

Business Statistics
by Norean R. Sharpe, Richard D. De Veaux and Paul F. Velleman

Quantitative Methods for Business
Fourth Edition
by Donald Waters

Foundation Maths
Fourth Edition
by Anthony Croft and Robert Davison

Essential Business Statistics
by Joanne Smailes and Angela McGrane

Pearson Education Limited
Edinburgh Gate
Harlow
Essex CM20 2JE

And associated companies throughout the world

Visit us on the World Wide Web at:
www.pearsoned.co.uk

First published 2010

Compiled from:

Quantitative Approaches in Business Studies Seventh Edition
by Clare Morris
ISBN 978 0 273 70889 6

Business Statistics
by Norean R. Sharpe, Richard D. De Veaux and Paul F. Velleman
ISBN 978 0 321 42659 8

Quantitative Methods for Business Fourth Edition
by Donald Waters
ISBN 978 0 273 69458 8

Foundation Maths Fourth Edition
by Anthony Croft and Robert Davison
ISBN 978 0 13 197921 5

Essential Business Statistics
by Joanne Smailes and Angela McGrane
ISBN 978 0 273 64333 3

ISBN 978 1 84959 205 5

Printed and bound by in Great Britain by Henry Ling Limited at the Dorset Press, Dorchester, DT1 1HD.

Contents

Foundation Section

Chapter 1

TOOLS OF THE TRADE: BASIC NUMERACY SKILLS

Chapter prerequisites

Before starting work on this chapter, try the short test of basic mathematical skills below; you will find the answers in Appendix 9 and, according to which questions you find difficult, you will be directed to the appropriate section of this chapter. This will save you time and prevent your having to read through a lot of things that you can already cope with. If, however, you get more than half of the test questions wrong I would advise you to read the entire chapter.

Learning outcomes

By the end of your work on this chapter you should be able to:

1. carry out the four operations of basic arithmetic (addition, subtraction, multiplication and division) with positive and negative integers, fractions and decimals;
2. round off the results of your calculations to a given number of decimal places or significant figures;
3. perform calculations involving percentages;
4. handle expressions involving powers and roots of a variable;
5. remove brackets from algebraic expressions;
6. construct a linear equation or inequality from a verbal problem;
7. solve linear equations;
8. solve a pair of simultaneous equations;
9. plot the graphs of linear equations or inequalities;
10. make efficient use of your calculator.

TEST

1 $-3 + 4 =$ 2 $-5 \div 2 =$ 3 $\frac{3}{8} + \frac{4}{5} =$ 4 $\frac{7}{8} \times \frac{3}{5} =$

5 $2 \div \frac{1}{2} =$ 6 $0.05 \times 2.5 =$ 7 $8 \div 0.2 =$

8 Convert $\frac{5}{12}$ to a decimal.

9 Express 0.28 as a fraction.

10 What is 67.469 to 3 significant figures?

11 16% of 8 = 12 18 as a percentage of 64 =

13 The price of an item including the dealer's 20 per cent mark-up is £36. What did it cost before the mark-up?

14 $x^2 \times x^4 =$ 15 $\sqrt{x^{16}} =$

16 $2(3a + b) - (a - 2b) =$

17 If it costs £6 to drive k miles then what is the cost of driving 4 miles?

18 Items priced at m pence per dozen are repacked in boxes of 100. What will the cost of such a box be, in pounds?

19 There are f female workers and m male workers in a factory. Write down an algebraic expression to show that the total workforce must be less than 150.

20 $3x - 5 = 10$; $x =$ 21 $\frac{4}{y} = \frac{7}{8}$; $y =$

22 $\begin{cases} 3p + 2q = 9 \\ 4p - 6q = 25 \end{cases}$ Find p and q.

23 Where does the graph of $s = 3t + 5$ cross the t-axis?

24 Which of these graphs, (a), (b) or (c), could be the graph of $y = x^2 + 3x - 4$?

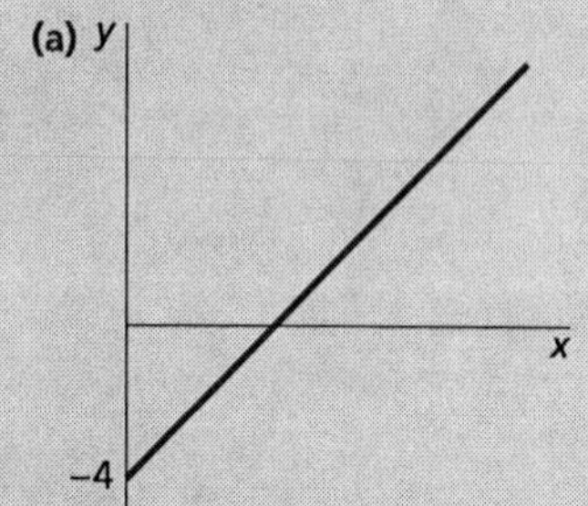

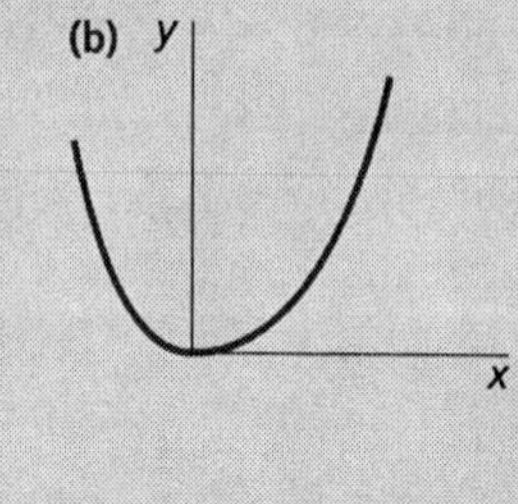

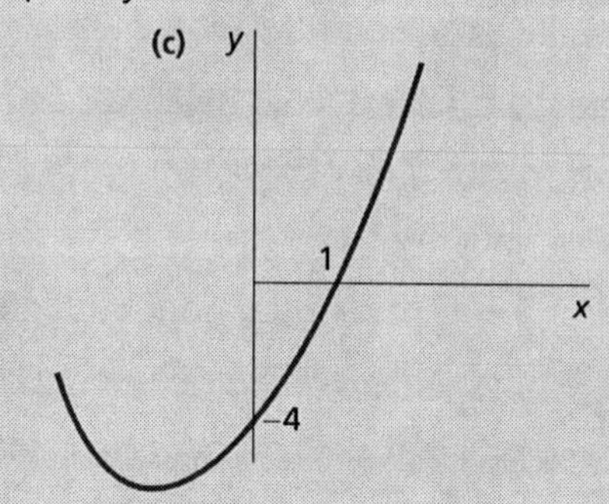

25 On which side of the line in the following diagram will inequality $x > 2y$ be satisfied?

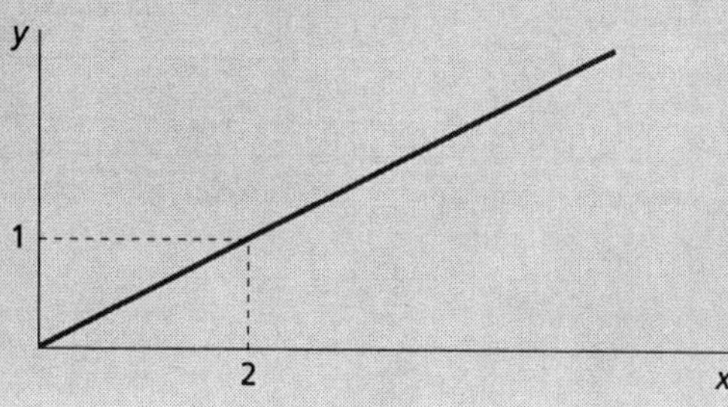

Almost everybody's problem

If you are reading this book then you are almost certainly not a mathematician. You have probably chosen to do a course in business studies, management or accounting, only to discover that among the obviously relevant and useful subjects, such as economics and law, you are expected to study mathematics (possibly disguised under the title of statistics, but that doesn't fool you).

To this news, if you are like 99 per cent of students in my experience, your reaction was close to horror. It is quite probably several years since you last studied mathematics, and your recollections of those days may not be very pleasant. But in fact your apprehension is groundless. What you will be studying in this book is not mathematics for its own sake, however appealing that may be to some of us, but *useful* mathematics – the sort of mathematics that can lead quickly and effectively to the solution of practical, business-oriented problems.

However, it would be misleading to pretend that you are not going to need to dredge up a little of what you learned at school, and this first chapter is designed to help you do just that. There is probably hardly anything that will be completely new to you; there will be some things that you once knew but have forgotten, others that you have heard about before but that may not have made much sense the first time around. You will find plenty of exercises to practise on, since practice is essential in achieving facility in the basic techniques we will be calling on later in the book.

And, in case you suspect that some topics are included just because they are good for you and cannot conceivably have any relevance to business, you will find a reference at the beginning of each section to the points at which the material of that section will be needed in later chapters.

Numbers and how we combine them

This is fundamental to all later work.

It is often helpful to think of all numbers as strung out in a straight line as follows:

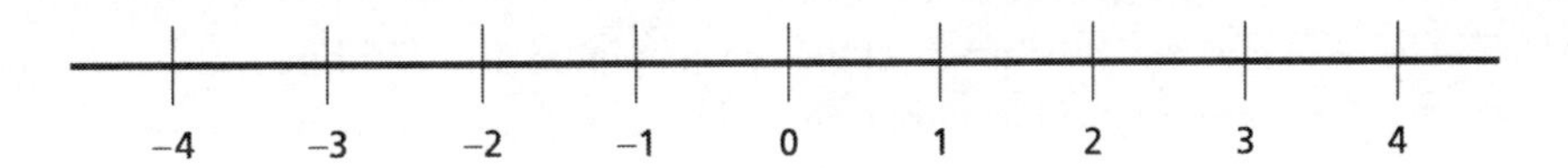

In the middle we have zero, to the right are the *positive* whole numbers +1, +2 . . . (we do not usually bother to write the + sign) and to the left are the *negative* whole numbers –1, –2 . . . The '. . .' here indicates that the numbers can be continued without limit in either direction.

An integer is a 'whole number'.

In between the integers, positive and negative, we can think of the entire line as being filled up with the remaining non-integer numbers – fractions and/or decimals which we will be returning to later.

For most people, adding positive integers is no problem; the difficulties start to appear with the minus signs. This is where the idea of the number line can be quite helpful. Consider the expression 42 – 36 + 27. Should we say '36 + 27' first, and then take the answer away from 42, or should we take '42 – 36' and then add on the 27?

In fact, with + and – signs we are safe in performing the operations from left to right, unless there are brackets telling us otherwise (of which more later). Looking at it another way, saying 'subtract 36' is exactly the same as saying 'add the negative number –36', so the whole expression can be thought of as '42 plus –36 plus 27'. In other words, subtraction means adding negative numbers. So on the number line, adding corresponds to moving to the right, subtraction to moving to the left.

Taking a simpler case, $4 - 9 + 2$ can be interpreted as: start at 4 on the line, move 9 steps to the left (which brings us to –5) and then 2 to the right, ending up at –3. Of course, after a while you will not need to use the line explicitly, but this is the basis of 'rules' you may have learned, such as 'in subtraction put the sign of the larger to the difference'.

Another example:

$$-6 - 7 + 4 = -13 + 4 = -9.$$

When it comes to multiplication and division, there are a few different ways of writing things which you should be aware of. 2×6 is often written as 2*6, especially when using a spreadsheet, and $4 \div 2$, 4/2 and $\frac{4}{2}$ all mean the same thing.

As far as multiplying or dividing negative numbers goes, this is one of the few cases where I would advise you to remember some rules (they can be proved, but in a rather long-winded way):

> Two *like* signs (two pluses or two minuses) multiplied together or divided give a positive answer.
>
> Two *unlike* signs (one plus and one minus) multiplied together or divided give a negative answer.

For example:

$$(-2) \times (-4) = 8 \qquad 12 \div (-6) = -2 \qquad -8/-2 = 4.$$

In division, if the result is not a whole number – that is, if the number being divided is not an integer multiple of the *divisor* (the dividing number) – then the remainder can be expressed as either a fraction or a decimal. To express it as a fraction, simply put the remainder over the divisor. For example, 20/7 = 2 with remainder 6, or $2\frac{6}{7}$. We will find out how to turn this into a decimal later.

One final point on the four basic rules of arithmetic: there is a standard convention about the priority which operates if you have + and – signs mixed up with × and ÷. The rule is that the multiplications and divisions are done first, unless there are brackets indicating otherwise. For instance, $2 \times 6 + 5 = 12 + 5 = 17$, **not** $2 \times 11 = 22$. If we wanted this, we would have to put $2 \times (6 + 5)$, to show that the addition is to be done first. There is, however, no difference in meaning between $\frac{-1}{2}$, $\frac{1}{-2}$ and $-\frac{1}{2}$; we usually prefer to attach the minus sign to the front of the expression, as in the last of the three expressions, but it really does not matter. It is important to remember these rules about the order of operations, since they are implicit in the way many computer packages work.

Exercise 1

1 $-5-4-7$	2 $6+4-10$	3 $2+2-2$	4 $-11+18+25$
5 $16-9+7$	6 $-8+3+2$	7 $6\times(-2)$	8 $18\div(-3)$
9 $(-4)\times(-6)$	10 $27/-3$	11 $\frac{-16}{-8}$	12 $3\times7+4$

Operations with fractions

You will need to be able to handle addition, subtraction and multiplication of fractions when we come to discuss probability in Chapter 8. Although it *is* possible using an electronic calculator to turn all your fractions into decimals and use the calculator to work out the arithmetic, doing so would waste a great deal of time, and in many cases the results are easier to interpret when expressed in fraction rather than decimal form.

There are actually three ways of writing fractions – as decimals, percentages or 'ordinary' fractions such as $\frac{1}{2}$ or $\frac{3}{4}$ – but we will concentrate in this section on the last of the three ways, leaving the first two to later sections. For addition and subtraction, the magic words are 'common denominator'. Actually there is nothing magic about it; the point is that trying to add sixths and sevenths is like trying to add apples and bananas – they are quite different things; we must express them in the same terms before we can do anything with them:

> To add or subtract fractions, express them in terms of a common denominator.

For example, to add $\frac{5}{6}$ and $\frac{2}{7}$ we must write them both with the same bottom line or *denominator* – in this case both can be written in terms of forty-seconds as:

$$\frac{35}{42}+\frac{12}{42}=\frac{47}{42}$$

(or $1\frac{5}{42}$, but we do not generally use such 'mixed' fractions).

It is easy to see why we chose 42 here – it is 6×7. Sometimes a smaller number will do, but if you find it difficult to spot this, multiplying the denominators of the fractions always works.

Another example:

$$\frac{4}{5}-\frac{1}{4}=\frac{16}{20}-\frac{5}{20}=\frac{16-5}{20}=\frac{11}{20}$$

Cancellation of fractions sometimes causes confusion but to *cancel* a fraction simply means to divide the top and bottom by the same figure; for example: $4/8 = 1/2$, $12/16 = 3/4$. It is generally preferable to express a fraction in its lowest terms, that is, to cancel it as far as possible. Notice that, as what we are really doing here is saying $12/16 = (3\times4)/(4\times4) = 3/4$, we are dividing the whole of the top and bottom of the fraction by 4. It follows that it is *not* permissible to say $(4+1)/2 = (2+1)/1 = 3$, because we have not divided the *whole* of the top by 2, but only part of it. If you are tempted to perform a cancellation like this where plus and minus signs are involved, either leave well alone, or put in some simple numbers to see whether the operation is really valid. In the example above, $(4 + 1)/2 = 2\frac{1}{2}$, whereas the 'cancelled' expression = 3, so clearly this does not work.

Multiplication is the easiest of all fraction operations:

> To multiply fractions, multiply the tops or numerators and the denominators of the fractions separately.

Examples:

$$\frac{1}{5} \times \frac{5}{7} = \frac{1 \times 5}{5 \times 7} = \frac{5}{35}; \quad \frac{2}{3} \times \frac{8}{9} = \frac{16}{27}, \text{ etc.}$$

Of course, in the first case here we could cancel by 5, to reduce the fraction to $\frac{1}{7}$.

For division, the rule is:

> Turn the divisor upside down and multiply by this number.

Example:

$$\frac{5/6}{2/3} = \frac{5}{6} \div \frac{2}{3} = \frac{5}{6} \times \frac{3}{2} = \frac{15}{12} = \frac{5}{4},$$

cancelling by 3. We could have cancelled at an earlier stage but if you are doubtful about cancellation it is safer to leave it until the end, when you have only one fraction to deal with.

Another example:

$$\frac{3}{16} \div \frac{7}{8} = \frac{3}{16} \times \frac{8}{7} = \frac{24}{112} = \frac{3}{14},$$

cancelling by 8.

A phrase you may have heard in the past is '*of* means *multiply*'. This simply means that to get a certain fraction of a number, you multiply the number by that fraction. For example, two-thirds of $12 = \frac{2}{3} \times 12 = \frac{2}{3} \times \frac{12}{1} = \frac{24}{3} = 8$. Notice too that a whole number can always be written as a fraction with 1 as the denominator, as we have done with the 12 here.

Finally, if you have to deal with negative fractions, exactly the same rules apply as for operating with negative integers.

Now try the following exercise.

Exercise 2

1 $\frac{1}{6} \times \frac{7}{8}$

2 $\frac{1}{4} - \frac{1}{3}$

3 $\frac{1}{11} + \frac{1}{22}$

4 $-\frac{1}{2} + \frac{3}{4} - \frac{1}{8}$

5 $\frac{2}{7} \times 9$

6 $\frac{2}{5} \div \frac{4}{7}$

7 $10 \div \frac{1}{2}$

8 $\frac{3}{4} \times \frac{1}{4} \div \frac{4}{5}$

9 $\left(\frac{3}{8} - \frac{3}{4}\right) \div \frac{4}{3}$

10 $\left(\frac{1}{9} + \frac{5}{6}\right) \times \frac{3}{17}$

Decimals: a special kind of fraction

Now that everyone uses calculators, nearly all the calculations you perform will be done in terms of decimals, but you cannot abdicate all responsibility for the accuracy of your calculations to the calculator because it is easy to press a wrong key in the course of entering the figures. So a familiarity with the rules for handling decimal points – in order that you can check that the answer is roughly what it should be – is, if anything, even more necessary now.

Sometimes one hears the expression 'decimal fractions' used, and the phrase gives the clue to what decimals really are – a system of fractions based on multiples of ten. When we write 0.75, for example, this is a shorthand for 'seven tenths and five hundredths' – the seven, one place to the right of the decimal point, represents tenths; the five, two places to the right, represents hundredths, and so on. But it would be tedious to have to convert back to fractions every time we wanted to operate with decimals, so there are a few simple rules to enable us to use them directly.

Addition and subtraction work much as for integers, as long as you remember to keep the decimal points lined up – that is, add tenths to tenths, hundredths to hundredths, etc. For instance, to add 2.15 and 3.4 we think of the 3.4 as 3.40, then add the 5 to the 0, the 1 to the 4 and the 2 to the 3, to get 5.55.

In multiplication, the number of decimal places in the answer is the total of the number of places in the figures being multiplied. For example:

$$3.2 \times 0.5 \times 0.2 = 1.60 \times 0.2 = 0.320$$

(notice that the final zero must be included in the count of places).

Multiplication by 10, 100, etc., is particularly easy because the decimal system is based on tens. To multiply by 10, 100, etc., move the decimal point one, two, etc., places to the right.

You may say, 'But suppose there isn't a point?' However, you can always think of a whole number such as 54 as being 54.0, so the point is there implicitly. Thus $54 \times 100 = 5400$, $3.9 \times 10 = 39$, and so on.

Division is a bit more complicated. What we do is to get rid of decimals in the denominator altogether by shifting the point the same number of places to the right in numerator and denominator – in other words, multiplying top and bottom by 10, 100 or whatever. We can do this because multiplying the top and bottom of a fraction simultaneously by the same figure makes no difference to its value. Once we have got rid of the decimals in the denominator in this way, we are back to division by an integer, and all we have to do is keep the point in the answer in the correct place:

$$3.2/0.2 = 32/2 \text{ (multiplying top and bottom by 10)} = 16$$
$$3.2/0.02 = 320/2 \text{ (multiplying by 100)} = 160$$
$$0.32/0.2 = 3.2/2 = 1.6, \text{ and so on.}$$

To divide by 10, 100, etc., we move the point (or implied point) one, two, etc., places to the left, e.g. $4.3/100 = 0.043$.

Frequently we have to turn fractions into decimals, or vice versa. To turn a fraction into a decimal, divide the denominator into the numerator according to the usual process of division, as in $4/5 = 0.8$, $5/16 = 0.3125$, etc. Sometimes the process does not stop, but repeats itself after a certain number of decimal places. For example, 1/3 = 0.333 . . . , 6/7 = 0.857 142 857 142 8 . . . This is called a *recurring* decimal. There are numbers – π is one you may have come across – that are decimals that neither repeat nor stop; they just carry on for ever with no discernible pattern!

You should remember the decimal equivalents of a few commonly used fractions: $0.5 = \frac{1}{2}$, $0.25 = \frac{1}{4}$, and so on.

The process the other way round – to write a given decimal as a fraction – is easy. If we want to turn 0.18 into a fraction, we have only to recall that this means 'one tenth and eight hundredths', that is, eighteen hundredths or 18/100. If you wish you can cancel this to 9/50.

Significant figures and rounding

Throughout all your calculations you will need to be able to round off answers to a certain number of decimal places or significant figures. Although your calculator probably spits out up to eight decimal places, it may not be sensible to quote them all – if, for instance, you are working in pounds and pence, there is no point in quoting an answer of £45.873 438. Indeed, the last few digits may not even be worth believing. There is no 'right' number of figures to quote in a given situation; you have to develop a feeling based on such things as the figures which went into the calculation, what you want to use the answer for, and so on. We will mention this at appropriate points in later chapters, but at the moment we will simply discuss the mechanics of rounding.

If we want to round a number to a given number of decimal places, the rule most commonly applied is that 5 and upwards are rounded up, everything below 5, down. So 3.675 to two decimal places is 3.68, 0.0689 to three places is 0.069, and so forth. This system does lead to slight bias in that rather more figures are rounded up than down (those ending in 5, 6, 7, 8 and 9 go up as against only 1, 2, 3 and 4 going down), but this is only important in situations where there are a lot of figures ending in 5s to be rounded. So although alternative methods have been devised to get round this problem we will stick to the common rule.

Another way to specify the accuracy required of a number is to require a certain number of *significant figures*. A figure is significant if it carries information; in this sense the zeros on the end of 15 000 or immediately after the decimal point in 0.0035 are not significant, but the zero in 7053 is. Thus 34 722 to three significant figures is 34 700; 0.002 56 to two significant figures is 0.0026, 7045 to three significant figures is 7050, and so on.

Exercise 3

1 Express 4/9 as a decimal to three places.

2 0.63/0.009 3 0.045×320 4 7.2/0.06

5 What is 16 527 to two significant figures?

6 Express 0.85 as a fraction.

7 3.5×1.2 8 0.005/0.05 9 400×0.0025

10 What is a quarter of 0.08?

Percentages

A percentage is really only a fraction in which the denominator is always 100, so that we do not bother to write it – or rather, the writing of '/100' has degenerated into the % sign. The term 'per cent' on its own means nothing, unless we specify per cent of *what*. For example, the statement 'prices are 10 per cent lower during the sale' is meaningless unless we say 'lower than list price' or 'lower than last week's price' or whatever.

The idea of expressing fractions as percentages is that for most people it is a good deal easier to visualise an amount such as 70 per cent, i.e. 70/100, than something such as 13/17. So it has become conventional to use 100 as a sort of standard denominator.

We actually use percentages in two different ways. First:

> To find a given percentage of a quantity, multiply the quantity by the percentage figure over 100.

For example:

$$16\% \text{ of } 40 = \frac{16}{100} \times 40 = \frac{640}{100} = 6.4.$$

All that we are doing here is recalling that 16 per cent means 16/100, and finding sixteen hundredths of 40.

Second:

> To express one quantity as a percentage of another, put the first over the second and multiply by 100.

For example:

$$\text{£6 as a percentage of £8: } \frac{6}{8} \times 100 = \frac{600}{8} = 75\%.$$

Again, you should remember a few common percentages as fractions and vice versa, such as $50\% = \frac{1}{2}$, $25\% = \frac{1}{4}$, and so on.

To convert decimals into percentages, or the other way round, is a matter of moving the point. For instance, 0.08 as a percentage is 8 per cent (multiply by 100, i.e. move the point two places right) and 68 per cent as a decimal is 0.68 (move point two places left).

In dealing with practical problems involving percentages, be very careful to ask, 'Percentage of what?'. As an illustration, suppose that we are told that a bill which includes $17\frac{1}{2}$ per cent VAT comes to £16. What was it before the VAT was added? The $17\frac{1}{2}$ per cent here is *not* $17\frac{1}{2}$ per cent of £16; it is $17\frac{1}{2}$ per cent of what the bill was *before* the VAT was added – the thing we are trying to find. If we call this amount x, what we can say is that $x + 17\frac{1}{2}$ per cent of x comes to £16, or in symbolic terms:

$$x + \frac{17.5x}{100} = \text{£16}.$$

$$\text{So } \frac{117.5x}{100} = £16$$

$$\text{whence } x = £16 \times \frac{100}{117.5} = £13.62.$$

Exercise 4

1. What is 8 per cent of 40?
2. Express 17 per cent as a decimal.
3. Express 45 as a percentage of 108.
4. A price of £12.50 is increased by 20 per cent. What is the new price?
5. An item now priced at £12 carries a label 'Original price reduced by 25 per cent'. What was the original price?
6. The number of customers of an online store has increased by 12 per cent since last year. If there were 850 customers last year, how many are there now?
7. In a class of 56 students, 51 pass the final assessment. What is the percentage pass rate, to the nearest whole percent?
8. What is 20 per cent of 80 per cent?
9. The amount of non-recyclable waste produced by a small factory has decreased by 30 per cent compared with last year. This year 16 tonnes were produced. What was last year's amount, to one decimal place?
10. An investment attracts 5 per cent interest per year. If you invest £200 at the start of year 1, and interest is added on the last day of the year, how much will you have in your account at the start of year 3?

Letters for numbers

As far as most people are concerned, I suppose of all the branches of mathematics they have studied at school, algebra seems the most rarefied and abstract. Certainly the higher reaches of algebra *can* be very abstract, but the kind of algebra we need to use is about as practical as it could be. The main purpose of using letters to represent numbers or quantities – which is what our kind of algebra is about – is that it enables us to express practical truths about the real world neatly, succinctly and in more general terms than we could if we insisted on sticking to definite numbers all the time.

To take a specific example: if you want to explain to someone how to find the area of a rectangle 4 cm by 3 cm, you can tell them to multiply 4 by 3. But if you call the length of the rectangle l and its width w, then you can say that the area is $l \times w$ – this will be true for *any* values of l and w. Again, consider the rule we have just encountered for expressing one quantity as a percentage of another: 'Put the first quantity on top of the second and multiply by 100'. What a mouthful! But if the first number is denoted by x and the second by y, then the rule boils down to $\frac{x}{y} \times 100$ – and once again, it holds good for whatever values of x and y we want to use.

This is the great strength in using letters to represent numbers – we are then able to write down rules, expressions and so on that are completely general, so that to find the answer in a particular case, all we need to do is substitute our particular values of x and y or whatever into the appropriate algebraic expression.

You will be coming across this application of algebra – the use of formulae to express rules – over and over in later chapters. But there are also some specific techniques that will be needed; we will begin with powers and roots, which will be referred to particularly in Chapter 17 on compound interest.

Powers and roots

We write x^2 as a shorthand for $x \times x$, x^3 to mean $x \times x \times x$, and in general x^n to mean x multiplied by itself n times. If we wish to multiply two such numbers together, say $x^m \times x^n$, where n and m are whole numbers, we will have:

$$\underbrace{(x \times x \times x \ldots \times x)}_{m \text{ times}} \times \underbrace{(x \times x \times x \ldots \times x)}_{n \text{ times}}$$

that is, x multiplied by itself $m + n$ times altogether, which can be written as x^{m+n}. So we have the first rule for operating with indices (indices is the plural of index, which means the n in x^n):

In multiplication, *add* the indices.

We can develop the rule for division in the same way. If we have x^3/x^2, we can cancel to get x^1 (this is, of course, the same as x, since we do not usually bother writing the 1). Similarly, if we have x^m/x^n, with $m > n$, cancelling gives x^{m-n}, suggesting the division rule:

In division, *subtract* the indices.

This in turn gives a meaning to a negative power of x. Consider x^2/x^3; by cancellation this becomes $1/x$, but by the division rule we have just derived it must also be equal to $x^{2-3} = x^{-1}$. So to be consistent we have to interpret x^{-1} as meaning $1/x$, and more generally x^{-n} as meaning $1/x^n$. We can also use the division rule to give x^0 a definition. Of course, x^2/x^2 is just 1, but it is also, by the division rule, $x^{2-2} = x^0$. Thus x^0 has to be equal to 1; and, there being nothing special about x, we can say:

Anything to the power 0 is 1.

Finally, what about fractional powers, such as $x^{\frac{1}{2}}$? By the multiplication rule, $x^{\frac{1}{2}} \times x^{\frac{1}{2}} = x^{\frac{1}{2}+\frac{1}{2}} = x^1$; in other words, $x^{\frac{1}{2}}$ is the thing which, when multiplied by itself, gives x. This is what we call the *square root* of x; so $x^{\frac{1}{2}}$ means $\sqrt{x}$. Similarly. $x^{\frac{1}{3}}$ means $\sqrt[3]{x}$, the cube root of x, and in general:

$x^{1/n} = \sqrt[n]{x}$, the nth root of x.

(that is, the number that, multiplied by itself n times, gives x).

To see how all these rules work in combination, we will simplify the following:

$$\frac{y^4 \times y^2}{\sqrt{y^3}} = \frac{y^{4+2}}{y^{3/2}} = \frac{y^6}{y^{3/2}} = y^{6-3/2} = y^{9/2}.$$

If you find these complicated powers a bit difficult to get hold of, try putting in numbers rather than letters. For example:

$$4^{\frac{1}{2}} = \sqrt{4} = 2, \qquad 2^{-2} = \tfrac{1}{4} \text{ or } 0.25,$$

and so on. (Strictly $\sqrt{4} = \pm 2$, since $(-2)^2 = 4$.)

Exercise 5

Simplify:

1 $y^4 \div y^2$ 2 $1/\sqrt[3]{x}$ 3 x^3/x 4 $p^2 \times pq \times q^2$ 5 $1/n^3$

6 $a \times \frac{b}{a^2}$ 7 $y^2 \times y^{-2}$ 8 $3x^2/9x$ 9 $\frac{x^2 \times x^4}{\sqrt{x}}$ 10 $\sqrt{(16x^4)}$

Note: when we write two symbols next to each other with no sign between, as in question 4 above, they are interpreted as being multiplied.

The use of brackets

In several of the formulae we shall be encountering in later chapters you will find brackets used to clarify the order in which operations are to be carried out. The basic rule for dealing with these is that operations in brackets are done first.

Suppose we want to find the value of $4(6y + 3)$ when y is 9. We must work out the $6y + 3$ first, which comes to $6 \times 9 + 3 = 54 + 3 = 57$ (remember that $\times$ comes before $+$) and then multiply this by 4 to get 228. So the 4 multiplies *everything* inside the bracket, and this applies also when we have a letter rather than a number outside. For example:

$$2p(3p - 8) = 2p \times 3p - 2p \times 8 = 6p^2 - 16p.$$

Be careful if there is a minus sign outside the brackets: remember the rules for multiplying by a negative number; for example:

$$-2x(x - 1) = -2x^2 + 2x.$$

Even if there is no number or other expression in front of a bracket, just a minus sign, the same applies:

$$8x - (x - 1)$$

means

$$8x - 1(x - 1) = 8x - x + 1 = 7x + 1.$$

It is important to realise that if we write $6x^2$ what we mean is 'square x first and then multiply by 6', whereas $(6x)^2$ means 'multiply x by 6 and then square the result'. In later statistical work we will encounter a case where this distinction is very important. Also note that xy and yx mean the same thing.

Where there are two bracketed expressions to be multiplied together, a useful mnemonic to help you ensure that you have included all the terms is FOIL, standing for First, Outer, Inner and Last:

$$(x-2)(x+3) = \underset{\text{First}}{x^2} + \underset{\text{Outer}}{3x} - \underset{\text{Inner}}{2x} - \underset{\text{Last}}{6} = x^2 + x - 6.$$

With more than two bracketed expressions, it is easiest to multiply out two at a time:

$$\begin{aligned}(x+2)(2x-1)(x+3) &= (2x^2+3x-2)(x+3)\\ &= 2x^3+9x^2+7x-6.\end{aligned}$$

Finally, if you encounter brackets within brackets, remove the inner ones first:

$$\begin{aligned}4[x+3(x-2)] &= 4(x+3x-6)\\ &= 4(4x-6)\\ &= 16x-24.\end{aligned}$$

Exercise 6

Simplify:

1 $3x(2x-6)$ 2 $(a-1)(a+2)$ 3 $x(3y+z)$

4 Find $8x^2$ and $(8x)^2$ when $x = 2$.

5 Evaluate $3pq(q-p)$ when $p = 5$ and $q = \frac{1}{2}$.

6 $(x+y)(x-y)(2x-1)$

7 $2(a+b)-3(a-b)$

8 The proprietor of a sandwich bar represents the cost of bread for each sandwich by B pence, and the cost of the filling by F pence. So the cost of making 12 sandwiches can be represented by $12(B+F)$. Explain why the brackets are needed in this expression.

9 What is wrong with this piece of algebra?

$$2(x+y) - x(x+y) = 2x + y - x^2 + xy$$

10 Simplify $x[2x-3(y-2)]$

Solving equations

Throughout the rest of this book, particularly in Chapter 13 where we discuss regression, and to a lesser extent Chapters 9 and 10, you will come across equations that have to be solved, or algebraic expressions that have to be manipulated – two very similar processes in practice.

We speak of *solving* an equation when we express an unknown quantity in terms either of other quantities or of numbers. We can only solve a single equation for *one* unknown quantity; if there is more than one, then more than one equation will be required. In this section, we will concentrate on a single equation involving a single unknown, and in fact we will deal only with *linear* equations – those that do not involve any powers of x higher than the first. You may have grappled with quadratic equations – those including x^2 terms – at school, but as we do not need those anywhere in later chapters we will not discuss them.

Our aim in solving an equation, then, is to isolate x – or whatever the unknown quantity may be called – on one side of the equals sign (usually the left, but there is no reason why it must be); we can work towards this end by all the legitimate processes of algebra – adding and subtracting things, multiplying or dividing by things – as long as we do the same to both sides of the equation at every stage. This is the only real rule in solving equations; other rules you may have learnt, such as 'change side, change sign' or 'cross multiplication', are really only special cases of this general rule.

Suppose we have the equation $3x + 2 = 9$. We want to isolate x on the left-hand side. As a first step towards this, let us get rid of the +2 by taking 2 away from each side:

$$3x + 2 - 2 = 9 - 2,$$

i.e. $3x = 7$, since $+2 - 2 = 0$.

Now get rid of the 3 from the left-hand side by dividing by 3:

$$\frac{3x}{3} = \frac{7}{3},$$

i.e. $x = \frac{7}{3}$ or $2\frac{1}{3}$.

Let us work through another example:

$$\frac{4}{y} = \frac{7}{2}.$$

The y here is on the bottom of a fraction, which we certainly do not want. Get rid of it from the bottom by multiplying through by y:

$$\frac{4}{y} \times y = \frac{7}{2} \times y, \text{ or } 4 = \frac{7y}{2}.$$

(If you find it hard to remember that $\frac{7}{2} \times y$ is the same thing as $\frac{7y}{2}$, note that y can always be thought of as $\frac{y}{1}$.) Now multiply each side of the equation by 2, obtaining $8 = 7y$. Finally, divide both sides by 7 to get $y = 8/7$.

The same sorts of processes apply if we are trying to transform a formula rather than solve an equation. For example, given the equation $A = l \times b$ for the area of a rectangle, we can get b in terms of the other two variables by dividing both sides by l, to give $b = A/l$.

Let us take a more complicated case; the formula $1/u + 1/v = 1/f$ relates the distances of object and image in a lens of a certain focal length. Suppose we want to find v in terms of u and f. First, subtract $1/u$ from each side:

$$1/v = 1/f - 1/u = \frac{u - f}{uf},$$

putting the right-hand side over a common denominator. Now invert both sides to get

$$v = \frac{uf}{u - f}.$$

We have contracted some of the steps here, as you will be able to do when you are familiar with the processes; but if in any doubt, ask yourself, 'What am I doing to *this* side of the equation? Have I done it to the *other* side too?'

A final example before you try to solve some equations yourself: if $y + z^2 = x$, find z in terms of y and x:

$$z^2 = x - y, \text{ and so } z = \pm\sqrt{x - y}.$$

Exercise 7

Solve the following equations. (Some of them look as if they might be quadratics – but they aren't!)

1 $x + 2 = -3$

2 $2 + x = 3 - x$

3 $6x^2 = 54$

4 $2x + 3 = 5$

5 If $v = u + ft$, find f.

6 $x^2 - 2 = x^2 + 4x + 8$

7 If $P = R - (F + nV)$, find V.

8 If $(a + b)^2 = 16c$, find a.

9 If $\sqrt[3]{x^2y} = 3z$, find y.

10 $x + 4 = 12 - 3x$

Equations from problems

When you are concerned not so much with handling algebraic expressions for their own sake as with using them in the course of solving practical problems, the major difficulty may well be, not solving the equation, but extracting it from the 'wordy' problem in the first place. The line of approach can best be demonstrated by an example, since this is not an area where cut-and-dried 'rules' can be laid down.

Suppose we are told that a return bus ticket for a certain trip costs half as much again as a single one, and that when a passenger books three return and two single tickets he pays £3.25. How much does each type of ticket cost?

The first step is always to give the unknown quantity a name. Here we appear to have two unknown quantities – the price of a single ticket and that of a return – but they are related in such a way that if we call the price of a single ticket £x, then a return costs $1.5 \times$ £x. Thus the statement of the problem can be reduced to

$$3 \times 1.5 \times x + 2 \times x = 3.25$$

whence

$$4.5x + 2x = 6.5x = 3.25$$

so that $x = 0.50$. A single ticket costs 50p, therefore, and a return 75p.

This was, of course, a very easy example. In more complicated cases, it can help to get to the general expression via particular figures. For example, if we are told that a firm orders items in boxes of x at a time, and are asked how many boxes will be needed to supply 500 items, we can get an idea of how to proceed by saying: 'Suppose they came in boxes of 50 at a time; how many would then be needed to supply 500 items?' The answer is clearly 10. What have we done to get this? Obviously, divided the 50 into the 500. So more generally, if the boxes contain x items, we will divide x into 500 to find that they need $500/x$ boxes.

Some unfamiliar symbols

Many of the problems we will be concerned with, especially in Chapter 18, are expressible not as equations but as inequalities: the number of workers needed to operate a production line is at least eight, we cannot spend more than £500 on this new machine, and so on.

Just as we use = to represent the fact that two quantities are equal, so we have symbols to represent these inequalities:

$a \leqslant b$ means 'a is less than or equal to b'.

So we might say $x \leqslant 100$ to express the fact that a sum of money, x pence, is never greater than £1. Or, if y denotes the number of students out of a class of 20 who pass an exam, we could say $y \leqslant 20$, because obviously 20 is the maximum number who can pass.

In a similar way,

$p \geqslant q$ means 'p is greater than or equal to q'.

If I am manufacturing p items in a week and already have advance orders for 16, I might say $p \geqslant 16$ to express the fact that I must make at least 16 items.

If you find it confusing to recall which symbol is which, notice that the bigger end of the symbol points to the bigger quantity.

There are also two other symbols, related to these but not quite so widely used, $<$ and $>$. These mean 'less than (or greater than) but not equal to'. So if you have got only enough raw material to make 20 items, you could write 'number of items < 21'.

Exercise 8

1 The cost of a journey is reckoned to be 50p plus 5p per mile. Write down an expression for the cost of travelling m miles.

2 I am buying handkerchiefs and socks for my family's Christmas presents – a box of handkerchiefs costs £1.50 and a pair of socks £1.25. I don't want to spend more than £12 altogether. If I buy h boxes of handkerchiefs and s pairs of socks, write down an expression representing my financial limitation.

3 A spoon costs twice as much as a fork, and six forks and ten spoons cost £20.80. How much does a spoon cost?

4 Balloons can be bought in packets of 12 for 25p, or separately for 3p each. Write down an expression for the cost of buying y balloons ($12 < y < 23$).

Simultaneous equations

You will need to be able to solve simultaneous equations – a pair of linear equations with two unknowns – to cope with material in Chapter 18. The equations are called simultaneous because we have to consider them both at once if we are to be able to solve them.

There are two methods that may be used to solve a pair of simultaneous linear equations with two unknowns, often called x and y. If you have studied this topic before, then continue to use the method with which you are familiar; if you are coming to the subject with no prior knowledge, I recommend you to read the explanation of both methods and then choose the one which you find easiest.

Both methods are best illustrated using an example:

$$2x + y = 4, \qquad (1)$$

$$3x - 2y = 7. \qquad (2)$$

Both methods involve moving from two equations with two unknowns to one equation with one unknown, which we already know how to solve. However, the process by which this is achieved varies between the two approaches.

Method A

In this method we use one equation to express one of the variables in terms of the other, and then substitute this into the other equation. We will choose to use equation (1) above to express y in terms of x, as this is the easiest option. (Can you see why? It's because we only have a single y in Equation 1.)

Manipulation of equation (1) gives

$$y = 4 - 2x. \qquad (3)$$

Now we replace the y in equation (2) by $4 - 2x$, to get:

$$3x - 2(4 - 2x) = 7.$$

Removing the brackets gives

$$3x - 8 + 4x = 7,$$

so

$$7x - 8 = 7,$$

and hence

$$7x = 7 + 8 = 15,$$

so that $x = 15/7$. Now we use equation (3) to tell us the value of y:

$$y = 4 - 2 \times (15/7) = 4 - 30/7 = 28/7 - 30/7 = -2/7.$$

So the solution is $x = 15/7$, $y = -2/7$. It is always a good idea to check your answer by putting the x and y values you have found back into the original equations. Here we have, from (1):

$$2x + y = 30/7 - 2/7 = 28/7 = 4,$$

and from (2):

$$3x - 2y = 45/7 - (-4/7) = 45/7 + 4/7 = 49/7 = 7,$$

so that both equations are satisfied by the solution.

This method will always work except in two special situations:

(i) where the original equations are *inconsistent* – that is, they just cannot both be true at once (for example, $x + y = 9$ and $x + y = 7$);

(ii) where the original equations are really the *same* equation – for example, $2x - y = 4$ and $x = 2 + \frac{1}{2}y$.

You might like to try solving these equations, to see where the method breaks down.

Method B

In the second method, we aim to get the same number either of *x*s or of *y*s in the two equations, so that we can get rid of one variable by either adding or subtracting the equations, to give a single equation in one variable which we already know how to solve. To achieve this end, we may operate on either or both of the equations according to the rules of algebra, as long as we remember the cardinal rule that we must perform an operation *throughout* an equation – that is, to both sides.

Here, if we multiply the top equation by 2 and leave the bottom one alone, we get:

$$4x + 2y = 8$$

$$3x - 2y = 7$$

which, added, give:

$$7x = 15, \text{ since } +2y - 2y = 0.$$

Thus $x = 15/7$, and we can now substitute this value in either of the *original* two equations to find y. Choosing the original first equation, because it is slightly simpler:

$$\begin{aligned} &2 \times 15/7 + y = 4 \\ &\text{i.e. } 30/7 + y = 4 \\ &\text{i.e. } \quad y = 4 - 30/7 \\ &\qquad\quad = -2/7. \end{aligned}$$

This agrees with the result obtained by method A.

Exercise 9

Solve, where possible, the following pairs of equations:

1 $2x + y = 3$; $x - y = 6$.

2 $7x + 2y = 11$; $4x + 3y = 10$.

3 $x - y = 4$; $2x = 2y + 8$.

4 $2x + y = 1$; $2x - 3y = 9$.

5 $x + y = 3$; $x - 2y = 3$.

6 Find two numbers, one of which is twice the other, and whose sum is 18.

7 $a + 2b = 14$; $2a - b = 13$.

8 $2x + y = 7$; $4x + 2y = 3$.

9 Peter is three years older than Ahmed, and their combined ages add up to 31. How old is Peter?

10 $x/y = 5$; $2x + y = 33$.

Straight line graphs

In Chapters 13, 15 and 18, there will be quite a lot of graphical work, so it is important that you should be able to plot or sketch simple graphs without too much trouble.

The idea behind almost all graphs is to show pictorially the relationship between two quantities, often called x and y, though it is a good idea not to get too attached to this notation. Graphs that result in straight lines are going to be particularly important to us, since a straight line is the only form one can be quite definite about; plotting it accurately is simply a matter of using a ruler, whereas plotting any kind of curve involves some degree of skill and judgement (or the use of a computer package, as we will see in the next chapter). Moreover, to plot a straight line graph we need know only two points on the line (three if we want an extra point for checking purposes), whereas to obtain a reasonably accurate curve, a whole set of points is needed.

It is therefore useful, and saves wasting time, if you are able to recognise when an equation will result in a straight line graph. Consider the case of a manufacturer who, in producing some commodity, has fixed costs of £300 plus a variable cost of £2 per item. We will call the number of items being made n, and will construct a graph to show the relationship between the number of items made and the total cost of making them.

If no items at all are made, there will still be the fixed costs of £300 to pay, so when $n = 0$, cost = £300. The total cost will then increase by £2 for every extra item that is made; so 10 items will cost £320, 20 items will cost £340, and so on. It is clear that the graph representing the relationship will climb at a steady rate – that is, it will be a straight line. The graph is shown in Figure 1.1 and illustrates a number of general points about graph-plotting.

First, we have chosen to put the number of items being made on the horizontal axis, and the costs on the vertical axis. This is in accordance with the convention that the *independent* quantity goes horizontally and the dependent one vertically; in this case cost depends on the numbers of items being made. Of course it is not always totally clear which is the dependent quantity, so in some cases there may be scope for alternative ways of plotting. However, it is fairly safe to say that amounts of money – costs, profits, revenues and so on – are nearly always plotted on the vertical axis.

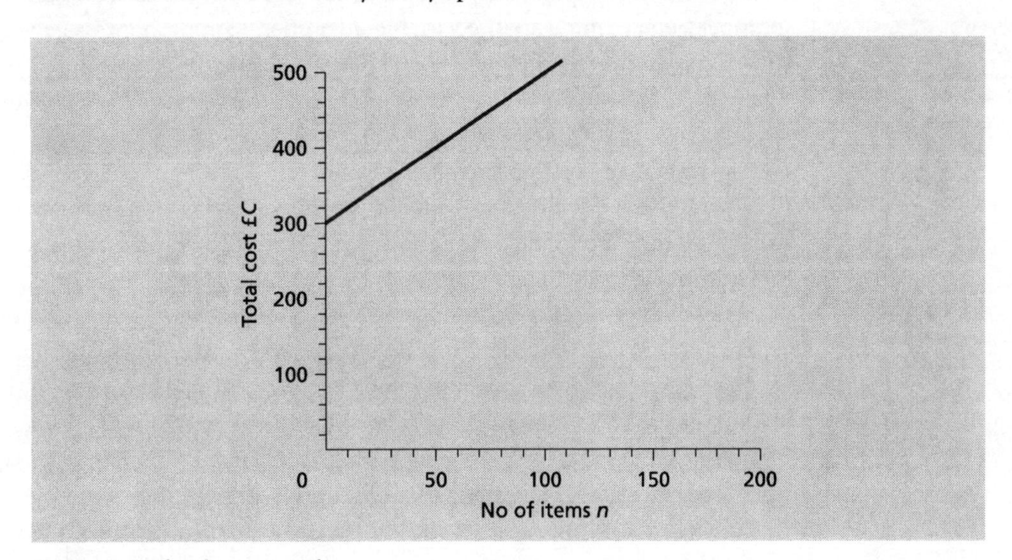

Figure 1.1 Plotting a graph

The second thing to notice is the choice of scales. The question of the *range* of n-values we choose to plot is one to which we will return later, but for now you should notice that the n-scale goes up in steps of 10, and the cost-scale in steps of £20. When you are using graph paper that is divided into multiples of ten squares, it is asking for trouble to choose a scale that goes in multiples of seven, or three, or some other amount not easily related to ten; you are very likely to go wrong in trying to estimate intermediate values by eye. It is much safer, therefore, to use steps of 5, 10 and so on which are easily related to the subdivisions on your graph paper.

I hope it is hardly necessary to point out that the scales on both axes increase by *equal* steps; it would be quite wrong, and could result in some very funny-shaped graphs, if we started off with one large division on the scale representing ten items, and then suddenly changed half-way along the axis to one division representing twenty.

If we now look at the graph line itself, we see that it commences when no items are being made at a cost of £300, as already calculated, and then climbs by £20 for every ten items made. We can relate these facts to the equation representing the line, as follows. The total cost, £C say, is given by the fixed cost of £300 plus £2 per item made – that will be £$2n$ for n items. Thus $C = 300 + 2n$ is the equation of the cost line. Now, comparing this with the graph, you can see that the 300 – the 'fixed' part that does not change with n – is represented by the point where the graph crosses the vertical axis. This point is known as the *intercept*:

> The intercept is the value of C where $n = 0$.

As for the £2 per item, that gives us the *slope* of the line:

> The slope of the line is the amount by which C increases for each increase of one unit in n.

We could find this slope by taking any convenient increase in n, and dividing it into the corresponding increase in C.

In fact, any straight line equation will have the form $y = a + bx$, where a and b are some numbers, and x and y are the variable quantities. Comparing this general equation with the cost equation just discussed, which had values of 300 for a and 2 for b, you can see that a is going to tell us where the graph crosses the vertical axis (assuming that the horizontal scale starts from zero) and b tells us the slope. By giving a and b different values, we can obtain all possible straight lines.

For example, equations in which a is zero will pass through the origin of the graph; particular cases would be $y = 2x$ and $C = \frac{1}{2}n$. If we wish to have a line which slopes *downhill* from left to right, then we must give the slope a negative value, expressing the fact that as x increases, y gets smaller. So, for instance, the graph of $y = 20 - 2x$ is as shown in Figure 1.2.

It is easy to see why equations involving powers of x higher than 1 cannot result in straight lines. If we had $y = x^2$, then as x increases from 1 to 2, y will increase from 1 to 4 – an increase of 3. But as x goes from 2 to 3, the corresponding y-increase is from 4 to 9, a change of 5 units. In fact the bigger x gets, the faster y increases, so we no longer have the steady rate of increase that would produce a straight line.

Having said this, however, I should warn you that sometimes straight line equations may arise in a form which does not immediately look like $y = a + bx$. For example,

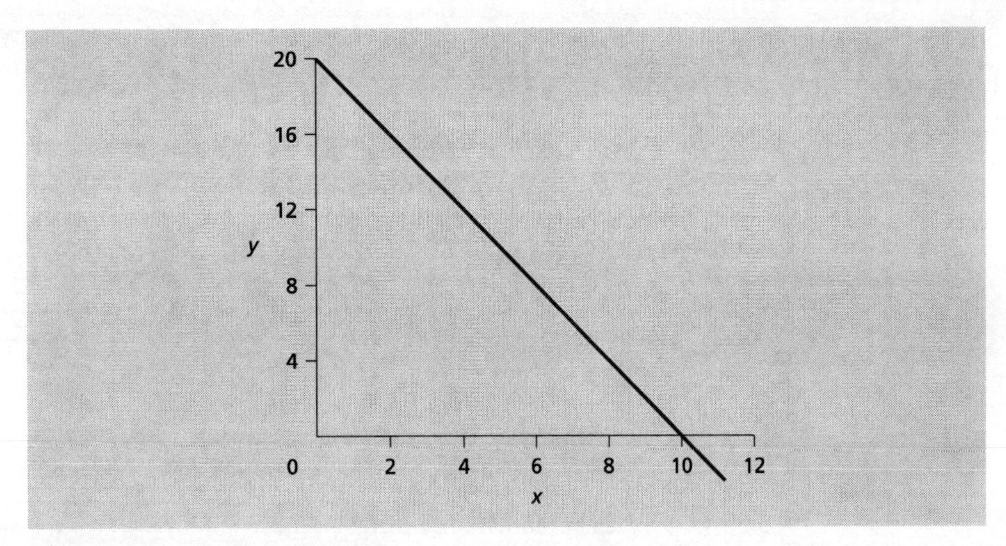

Figure 1.2 Graph of $y = 20 - 2x$

$x/y = 6$ looks as if it involves a y on the bottom of a fraction – a y^{-1}, in fact – but a bit of algebraic juggling turns the equation into $x = 6y$, or $y = \frac{1}{6}x$, the equation of a line through the origin with a slope of $\frac{1}{6}$. So you must be prepared for such possibilities.

Having recognised an equation as giving a straight line, how should you go about plotting it? It is safest to find three points on the line, two for plotting and one for checking. Take $y = 20 - 2x$, and suppose we want to plot it for values of x from 0 to 10. We could use $x = 0$, 1 and 2 as our three points, but it is much safer to use values as far apart as possible, since this will minimise the effect of any errors in plotting, as is shown by Figure 1.3. So we choose $x = 0$, which gives $y = 20$; $x = 5$, giving $y = 10$; and $x = 10$, for which $y = 0$. We plot points at 0 on the horizontal scale and 20 on the vertical; and at 10 on the horizontal and 0 on the vertical; join them together and then verify that the third point, $x = 5$ and $y = 10$, does indeed lie on the line we have plotted.

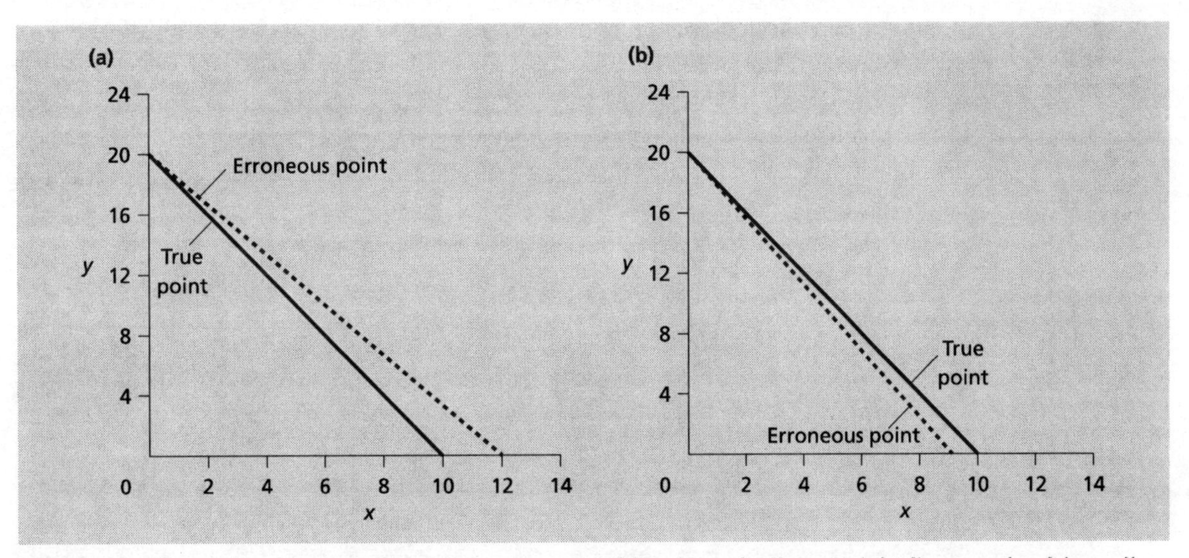

Figure 1.3 The need to use points as far apart as possible when plotting straight line graphs: (a) small error in plotting gives large errors as x increases; (b) small error in plotting gives only small errors throughout

Other types of graph

If for some reason you have to plot a graph which you recognise will *not* give a straight line, the process is not dissimilar, but you need to use a lot more points in order to be able to draw a smooth curve through them. In this case it is easier to set out the calculation of points as a table. To plot $y = x^2 + 3x$, for example, I would recommend a layout as follows:

	x	0	1	2	3	4	...
	x^2	0	1	4	9	16	...
+	$3x$	0	3	6	9	12	...
	y	0	4	10	18	28	...

Points would then be plotted at $x = 0$ and $y = 0$, $x = 1$ and $y = 4$, etc., and as smooth a curve as possible drawn through them. If you find it very difficult to get your curve to go through one particular point, go back to check your calculation – the point might be in the wrong place!

Graphing inequalities

Before we end this section, we will take a brief look at how inequalities, introduced on page 22, can be shown graphically. Taking a very easy case first, consider $y \geqslant 6$.

We want to identify the region of the graph in which the value of y is equal to, or bigger than, 6, regardless of what is happening to x. It is not hard to see that that will be true everywhere on and above the horizontal line through $y = 6$. We generally choose to indicate this on the graph by shading the side of the line where the inequality is *not* satisfied, as shown in Figure 1.4.

A more complicated case would be $3x + 5y \leqslant 15$. We begin by plotting the line $3x + 5y = 15$; the easiest way to do that is to note that x is 5 when y is zero, and y is 3 when x is zero. Then we must decide on which side of this line the inequality is satisfied. Take some simple point below the line, such as the origin. Here $3x + 5y$ is zero, which is certainly less than or equal to 15, so the side of the line including the origin satisfies the inequality but points above the line do not (see Figure 1.5).

We have been concentrating throughout this section on what is called the *positive quadrant* – the region of graphs in which both x and y are positive. In many of the

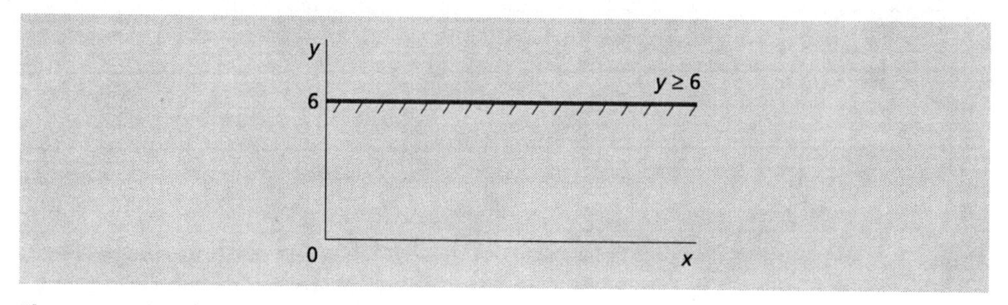

Figure 1.4 Graphing a simple inequality

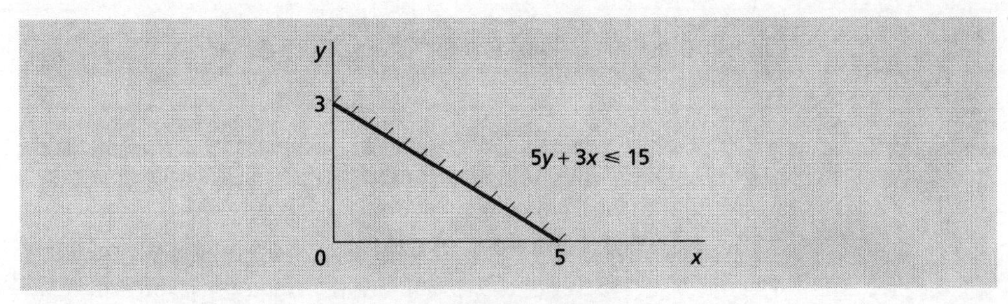

Figure 1.5 Graphing a more complicated inequality

practical applications we are concerned with, that will be the region of interest, because real variables such as costs, quantity produced, numbers of employees and so on cannot be negative. Nevertheless, you should not forget that there *are* cases where we might need to extend our graphs to cover negative regions; an example would be the profit graph of a firm making a loss – that is to say, a negative profit.

Sketching graphs

Don't imagine that you necessarily have to plot a graph using graph paper in order to get an idea of the relationship between two quantities. Very often it's sufficient to identify a few key facts – such as whether the graph passes through the origin and whether its slope is positive or negative – and then roughly sketch the overall shape of the graph. You need only worry about plotting points accurately if you need to be able to read off precise values from the graph, or if you are using it to find the exact solution of a problem.

We've spent quite a long time discussing graphs, because they are fundamental to many topics later in the book. Try the following exercise to make sure you have understood the sections.

Exercise 10

1. Which of the following equations would give straight line graphs: (a) $y = 2x - 17$; (b) $xy = 4$; (c) $p = 6q + 44$; (d) $2/x = 5/y$?
2. Find the slope of the graphs in 1 above which give straight lines.
3. Plot the graph of $R = 200n - 8n^2$ for values of n between 0 and 30.
4. Show on a single graph the regions satisfying $x > 4$ and $3x + 2y > 12$.
5. Sketch the graph of $y = 2x + 1$.
6. Where does the graph of $6x - 7y = 21$ cross the x-axis?
7. Does the graph of $y = x(x - 3)$ pass through the origin?
8. The equation $n = 20(200 - p)$ relates the price of an item in pence, p, to the number of items sold per week, n. Where does this graph cross the n-axis? What does this represent in practical terms?
9. Describe the region defined by the inequality $2x + 5y < 20$.
10. Draw up the table needed to plot the graph of $C = 4n(n - 10)$ for values of n from 0 to 20.

Making use of graphs

In the previous sections we discussed plotting graphs and inequalities without reference to what practical situation they might represent. We will now take a brief look at the applications to which they may be put.

One of the most important of these is in the solution of equations. For instance, if we have the graph of $y = 2x + 3$ (a straight line) then the point where this crosses the x-axis – that is, where $y = 0$ – gives the solution of the equation $0 = 2x + 3$, or, as we would more usually express it, $2x + 3 = 0$. This is a very simple equation which could easily be solved without the use of a graph, but the same method works for the more complex equations, such as quadratics, which give rise to curves.

To find the solution of the quadratic $x^2 + 2x - 15 = 0$, as an example, we would plot the graph $y = x^2 + 2x - 15$ as explained on page 28, and then look for the points at which the curve crosses the x-axis (where $y = 0$). These turn out to be $x = 3$ and $x = -5$, which are exactly the values satisfying the quadratic, as you can check for yourself.

Perhaps even more important is the use of graphs to solve two equations simultaneously. The points at which two equations are simultaneously satisfied are the points at which their graphs cross, as you can verify by plotting the graphs of one of the pairs of simultaneous equations you solved in Exercise 9. This gives us a method for solving two simultaneous equations even when one of them is not linear and the methods of the section on simultaneous equations (page 23) will not work.

A business application

All these points are best illustrated by taking a look at one of the major applications of graphical methods in business – the *break-even graph*. The idea behind this is simple: a firm is said to break even when costs are just balanced by revenues. The break-even point is, in fact, the point at which they begin to make a profit.

Suppose that we return to the item whose production costs were discussed on pages 25–6, giving rise to the straight line cost equation $C = 300 + 2n$ where n was the number produced. We will now imagine that the demand for the product is related to the price being charged for it by the equation $n = 600 - 50p$, where n is the number sold at a price p pounds. This means that if a price of £2 is charged, 500 items will be sold; at £3 each, the number sold will be 450, and so on.

We can manipulate this expression to give price in terms of number sold, using the processes discussed on page 20, to get $p = (600 - n)/50$, or $p = 12 - 0.02n$. This is the price at which n items could be sold, so the revenue generated by the sale of these n items will be price × quantity. The revenue equation is thus $R = n(12 - 0.02n)$, or $R = 12n - 0.02n^2$. Notice here how we use meaningful notation – R for revenue, n for number – rather than x and y.

To find the output at which the firm will break even, then, all we need do is plot, on the same pair of axes, the revenue and cost graphs. A point that often causes problems in cases of this kind, though, is what sort of range of values of n we should be looking at. Should we draw up tables of values for C and R with $n = 1, 2, 3 \ldots$, or with $n = 1000$,

2000, 3000 . . . ? Well, it is pretty clear that since we are talking about a commodity where the fixed costs of production are £300, while prices, as we have just seen, are of the order of a few pounds, we are going to have to sell a fair number before we even cover the fixed costs, let alone start making a profit.

So we try a couple of values of n of the order of several hundreds, to get a better idea what sort of range we should be considering. If $n = 500$ then the costs are $300 + 2 \times 500 = £1300$, while the revenue generated is $12 \times 500 - 0.02 \times 500 \times 500 = £1000$, so a loss is being made. If $n = 300$, then in a similar way the costs are £900 and the revenue £1800 (you should check these calculations), so a profit of £900 is made. Thus the change from profit to loss comes somewhere between $n = 300$ and $n = 500$.

Knowing this, we choose to set up a table as follows:

n	50	100	150	200	250	300	350	400	450	500
C(£)	400	500	600	700	800	900	1000	1100	1200	1300
$12n$	600	1200	1800	2400	3000	3600	4200	4800	5400	6000
$0.02n^2$	50	200	450	800	1250	1800	2450	3200	4050	5000
R(£)	550	1000	1350	1600	1750	1800	1750	1600	1350	1000

It is clear from the table that the firm begins to make a profit at some output below 50 items; there is already a profit at $n = 50$, but we know there must be a loss at $n = 0$, where there is no revenue to offset costs of £300. A profit ceases to be made between 450 and 500 items. To determine the values more exactly, the two curves, one for revenue and one for costs, are plotted as shown in Figure 1.6, from which the approximate break-even

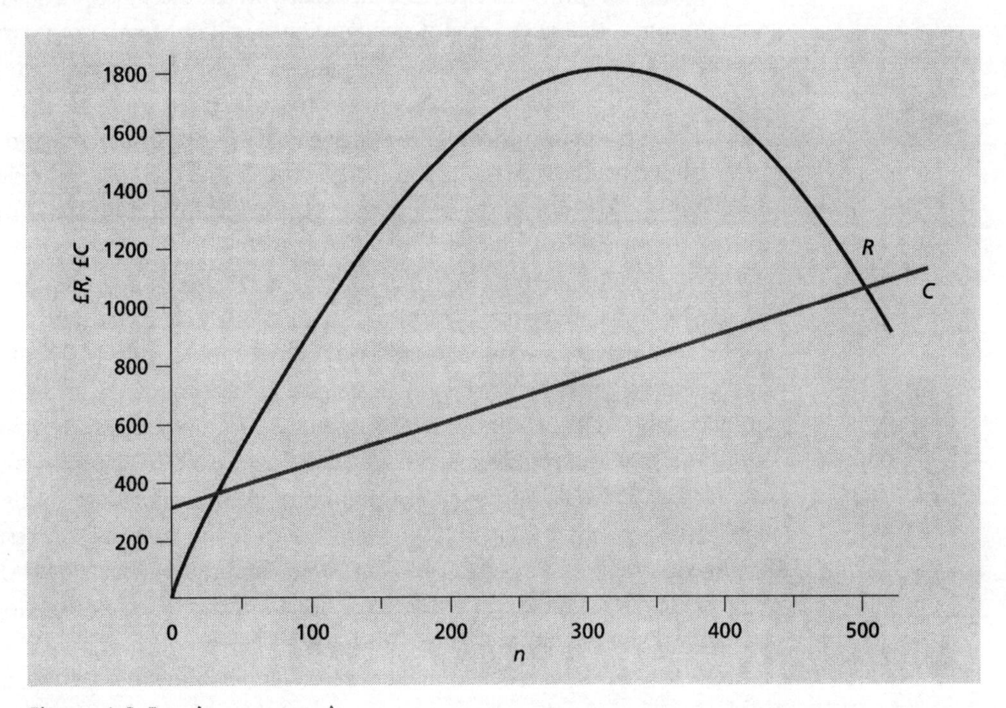

Figure 1.6 Break-even graph

points can be read off as $n = 32$ and $n = 468$. Strictly speaking, only the first of these is called a break-even, though of course it is as important to know where you stop making a profit as where you start to make one!

Exercise 11

1 A firm has fixed costs of £500 and a variable cost of 50p per item. It sells its product at a price of 80p per item, regardless of the number sold. Draw a graph to find at what output the firm breaks even.

2 Draw a suitable graph to determine the solution of the equation $x^2 - 6x + 5 = 0$.

3 A firm has the choice of two machines; machine A will give a fixed cost of £20 plus £1 for every 100 items produced; machine B has no fixed costs, but will incur variable costs at a rate of £1 multiplied by the square of the number of hundreds of items produced. At what output does machine A become cheaper than machine B?

A word about calculators

Although it is important that you should be happy with the basic mathematical skills described in this chapter, it would be silly to ignore the fact that the great majority of calculations are now carried out using either a calculator or a computer package such as a spreadsheet. The topic of computer packages for carrying out statistical calculations will be discussed in the next chapter; here I mention a few points concerned with getting the most out of your calculator.

I will not constantly mention the fact that you should be using a calculator for your computations – that goes without saying. What I will do is point out particular processes that can be speeded up by making efficient use of such things as the constant key or the memory on your calculator. It would be impossible to tell you what key sequences to use, since there are so many different models of calculator on the market, and each has its own quirks of operation. It is up to you to read the booklet that came with your calculator when you bought it, and make sure you exploit to the full all those buttons you have paid for.

If you are about to buy a calculator before embarking on your course, the minimum you need is a machine with the four basic functions (+, –, ×, ÷) plus a memory (preferably one with both M+ and M– facilities) and a square root. Many of you will already have scientific calculators, which can compute means, standard deviations and so on automatically – that is, without requiring the user to understand the details of the calculation. You should certainly know how to use these facilities, and they come in very handy for checking answers, but many examinations, particularly those set by external bodies such as the accountancy institutes, will not permit you to quote the results from such a machine in isolation. They preface exam papers by a statement such as 'All workings must be shown to obtain full credit'. Be careful, therefore, not to become too dependent on your calculator if you are doing a course of this kind.

Below is a set of exercises to make sure you are comfortable with your calculator and get the best out of it. If you get stuck on any of them, go back to the instruction manual!

Exercise 12

You should be able to perform all these calculations on a four-function, single memory calculator with per cent key and square root, *without* having to write down any intermediate steps.

1 17×82

2 $83 + 66 + 947$

3 $54 - 76 + 12$

4 $95 \div 8.3$

5 $0.002 \times 10\,304$

6 $12 \times 8 + 13 \times 11$

7 $11/7 + 5/3 + 9/13$

8 $16 \times 16 + 17 \times 17 + 18 \times 18$

9 $14 \div \sqrt{2}$

10 $\sqrt{8} \times 4$

11 Find the total cost of 3 loaves at 58p each, 2 kg of cheese at £4.20 per kg, and 6 lettuces at 65p each.

12 There are 2.54 cm in one inch. Convert the following set of lengths to inches: 8 cm, 27 cm, 33 cm, 49 cm, 72 cm.

13 An examination is marked out of 80. What is the percentage mark of a student who gets 66 out of 80?

14 In the same exam, five students gain 23, 37, 44, 59, 73 out of 80. Convert all these marks to percentages (nearest whole per cent).

15 What is 33 per cent of £900?

16 Find the cost inclusive of $17\frac{1}{2}$ per cent VAT of an item that without VAT costs £17.

17 $\sqrt{\dfrac{8 \times 13 + 517}{86}}$

18 $\dfrac{11 + 17.3}{2.8 \times 4.3 + 3.6 \times 9}$

19 $1.1 + 1.1^2 + 1.1^3 + 1.1^4$

For calculators with an M– key:

20 $2.3 \times 6 - 1.9 \times 4.$

21 $\sqrt{\dfrac{263}{7} - 4.9^2}$

22 $\dfrac{16}{8 \times 18.2 - 4 \times 13.7}$

23 $2 \times 3 + 4 \times 5 - 6 \times 7$

24 A shopkeeper pays his wholesaler for a dozen items at £1.72 each, 40 at £8.84 each, and 200 at 63p each, and receives a refund for 60 items costing 52p each which he returns. How much does he pay when 8 per cent cash discount has been deducted?

Further reading

If you have worked carefully through the material of this chapter, plus the exercises, and not had too much difficulty, you should be well equipped to tackle the rest of the book. However, if you feel your difficulties need a more thorough revision of basic maths, you may find the following book helpful:

Morris, C. (with Thanassoulis, E.) (2007), *Essential Maths*, Palgrave.

SECTION 1
DATA ANALYSIS

CHAPTER 2

Data

Amazon.com

Amazon.com opened for business in July 1995, billing itself even then as "Earth's Biggest Bookstore," with an unusual business plan: They didn't plan to turn a profit for four to five years. Although some shareholders complained when the dotcom bubble burst, Amazon continued its slow, steady growth, becoming profitable for the first time in 2002. Since then, Amazon has remained profitable and has continued to grow. By 2004, they had more than 41 million active customers in over 200 countries and were ranked the 74th most valuable brand by *Business Week*. Their selection of merchandise has expanded to include almost anything you can imagine, from $400,000 necklaces, to yak cheese from Tibet, to the largest book in the world. In 2006, profits were $190 million—even after a $662 million charge for Research and Development.

Amazon R&D is constantly monitoring and evolving their website to best serve their customers and maximize their sales performance. To make changes to the site, they experiment by collecting data and analyzing what works best. As Ronny Kohavi, former director of Data Mining and Personalization, said, "Data trumps intuition. Instead of using our intuition, we experiment on the live site and let our customers tell us what works for them."

Amazon.com has recently stated "many of the important decisions we make at Amazon.com can be made with data. There is a right answer or a wrong answer, a better answer or a worse answer, and math tells us which is which. These are our favorite kinds of decisions."[1] While we might prefer that Amazon refer to these methods as Statistics instead of math, it's clear that data analysis, forecasting, and statistical inference are the core of the decision making tools of Amazon.com.

"Data is king at Amazon. Clickstream and purchase data are the crown jewels at Amazon. They help us build features to personalize the website experience."

—*Ronny Kohavi, Former Director of Data Mining and Personalization, Amazon.com*

Many years ago, stores in small towns knew their customers personally. If you walked into the hobby shop, the owner might tell you about a new bridge that had come in for your Lionel train set. The tailor knew your dad's size, and the hairdresser knew how your mom liked her hair. There are still some stores like that around today, but we're increasingly likely to shop at large stores, by phone, or on the Internet. Even so, when you phone an 800 number to buy new running shoes, customer service representatives may call you by your first name or ask about the socks you bought six weeks ago. Or the company may send an e-mail in October offering new head warmers for winter running. This company has millions of customers, and you called without identifying yourself. How did the sales rep know who you are, where you live, and what you had bought?

The answer to all these questions is data. Collecting data on their customers, transactions, and sales lets companies track inventory and know what their customers prefer. These data can help them predict what their customers may buy in the future so they know how much of each item to stock. The store can use the data and what they learn from the data to improve customer service, mimicking the kind of personal attention a shopper had 50 years ago.

THE W'S:
WHO
WHAT
WHEN
WHERE
WHY

2.1 What *Are* Data?

We bet you thought you knew this instinctively. Think about it for a minute. What exactly *do* we mean by "data"? Do data even have to be numbers? The amount of your last purchase in dollars is numerical data, but some data record names or other labels. The names in Amazon.com's database are data, but are not numerical.

Sometimes, data can have values that look like numerical values but are just numerals serving as labels. This can be confusing. For example, the ASIN

[1] Amazon.com 2005 Annual Report

(Amazon Standard Item Number) of a book may have a numerical value, such as 978-0321426592, but it's really just another *name* for the book *Business Statistics*.

Data values, no matter what kind, are useless without their context. Newspaper journalists know that the lead paragraph of a good story should establish the "Five W's": *Who, What, When, Where*, and (if possible) *Why*. Often, we add *How* to the list as well. Answering these questions can provide a **context** for data values. The answers to the first two questions are essential. If you can't answer *Who* and *What*, you don't have data, and you don't have any useful information.

Here's an example of some of the data Amazon might collect:

10675489	B0000010AA	10.99	Chris G.	902	Boston	15.98	Kansas	Illinois
Samuel P.	Orange County	10783489	12837593	N	B000068ZVQ	Bad Blood	Nashville	Katherine H.
Canada	Garbage	16.99	Ohio	N	Chicago	N	11.99	Massachusetts
B000002BK9	312	Monique D.	Y	413	B00000I5Y6	440	15783947	Let Go

Table 2.1 *An example of data with no context. It's impossible to say anything about what these values might mean without knowing their context.*

Try to guess what they represent. Why is that hard? Because these data have no *context*. We can make the meaning clear if we add the context of *Who* and *What* and organize the values into a **data table** such as this one.

Purchase Order Number	Name	Ship to State/Country	Price	Area Code	Previous CD Purchase	Gift?	ASIN	Artist
10675489	Katherine H.	Ohio	10.99	440	Nashville	N	B00000I5Y6	Kansas
10783489	Samuel P.	Illinois	16.99	312	Orange County	Y	B000002BK9	Boston
12837593	Chris G.	Massachusetts	15.98	413	Bad Blood	N	B000068ZVQ	Chicago
1578397	Monique D.	Canada	11.99	902	Let Go	N	B0000010AA	Garbage

Table 2.2 *Example of a data table. The variable names are in the top row. Typically, the* Who *of the table are found in the leftmost column.*

Now we can see that these are four purchase records, relating to CD orders from Amazon. The column titles tell *What* has been recorded. The rows tell us *Who*. But, be careful. Look at all the variables to see *Who* the variables are about. Even if people are involved, they may not be the *Who* of the data. For example, the *Who* here are the purchase orders (not the people who made the purchases) because each row refers to a different purchase order, not necessarily a different *person*. A common place to find the *Who* of the table is the leftmost column. The other W's might have to come from the company's database administrator.[2]

In general, the rows of a data table correspond to individual **cases** about *Whom* (or about which—if they're not people) we record some characteristics. These cases go by different names, depending on the situation. Individuals who answer a survey are referred to as **respondents.** People on whom we experiment are **subjects** or (in an attempt to acknowledge the importance of their role in the experiment) **participants,** but animals, plants, website, and other inanimate subjects are often called **experimental units.** In a database, rows are called **records**—in this example, purchase records. Perhaps the most generic term is **cases.** In the table, the cases are the individual CD purchase orders.

Sometimes people refer to data values as *observations*, without being clear about the *Who*. Be sure you know the *Who* of the data, or you may not know what the

[2] In database management, this kind of information is called "metadata" or data about data.

data say. The *characteristics* recorded about each individual or case are called **variables.** These are usually shown as the columns of a data table, and they should have a name that identifies *What* has been measured.

A general term for a data table like this is a **spreadsheet,** a name that comes from bookkeeping ledgers of financial information. The data were typically spread across facing pages of a bound ledger, the book used by an accountant for keeping records of expenditures and sources of income. For the accountant, the columns were the types of expenses and income, and the cases were transactions, typically invoices or receipts. Since the advent of computers, use of spreadsheet programs has become a common skill, and the programs have become some of the most successful applications in the computer industry. It is usually easy to move a data table from a spreadsheet program to a program designed for statistical graphics and analysis, either directly or by copying the data table and pasting it into the statistics program.

Although data tables and spreadsheets are great for relatively small data sets, they are cumbersome for the complex data sets that companies must maintain on a day-to-day basis. Various other database architectures are used to store data. The most common is a relational database. In a **relational database**, two or more separate data tables are linked together so that information can be merged across them. Each data table is a *relation* because it is about a specific set of cases with information about each of these cases for all (or at least most) of the variables ("fields" in database terminology). For example, a table of customers, along with demographic information on each, is such a relation. A data table with information about a different collection of cases is a different relation. For example, a data table of all the items sold by the company, including information on price, inventory, and past history, is a relation as well (for example, as in Table 2.3). Finally, the day-to-day transactions may be held in a third database where each purchase of an item by a customer is listed as a case. In a relational database, these three relations can be

Customers

Customer Number	Name	City	State	Zip Code	Customer since	Gold Member?
473859	R. De Veaux	Williamstown	MA	01267	2007	No
127389	N. Sharpe	Wellesley	MA	02481	2000	Yes
335682	P. Velleman	Ithaca	NY	14580	2003	No
...						

Items

Product ID	Name	Price	Currently in Stock?
SC5662	Sliver Cane	43.50	Yes
TH2839	Top Hat	29.99	No
RS3883	Red Sequined Shoes	35.00	Yes
...			

Transactions

Transaction Number	Date	Customer Number	Product ID	Quantity	Shipping Method	Free Ship?
T23478923	9/15/08	473859	SC5662	1	UPS 2nd Day	N
T23478924	9/15/08	473859	TH2839	1	UPS 2nd Day	N
T63928934	10/20/08	335473	TH2839	3	UPS Ground	N
T72348299	12/22/08	127389	RS3883	1	Fed Ex Ovnt	Y

Table 2.3 A relational database shows all the relevant information for three separate relations linked together by customer and product numbers.

linked together. For example, you can look up a customer to see what he or she purchased or look up an item to see which customers purchased it.

In statistics, all analyses are performed on a single data table. But often the data must be retrieved from a relational database. Retrieving data from these databases often requires specific expertise with that software. In the rest of the book, we'll assume that all data have been downloaded to a data table or spreadsheet with variables listed as columns and cases as the rows.

2.2 Variable Types

It is wise to be careful. The *What* and *Why* of area codes are not as simple as they may first seem. When area codes were first introduced, AT&T was still the source of all telephone equipment, and phones had dials.

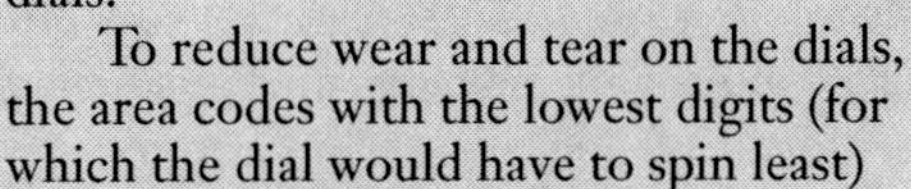

To reduce wear and tear on the dials, the area codes with the lowest digits (for which the dial would have to spin least) were assigned to the most populous regions—those with the most phone numbers and thus the area codes most likely to be dialed. New York City was assigned 212, Chicago 312, and Los Angeles 213, but rural upstate New York was given 607, Joliet was 815, and San Diego 619. For that reason, at one time, the numerical value of an area code could be used to guess something about the population of its region. Since the advent of push-button phones, area codes have finally become just categories.

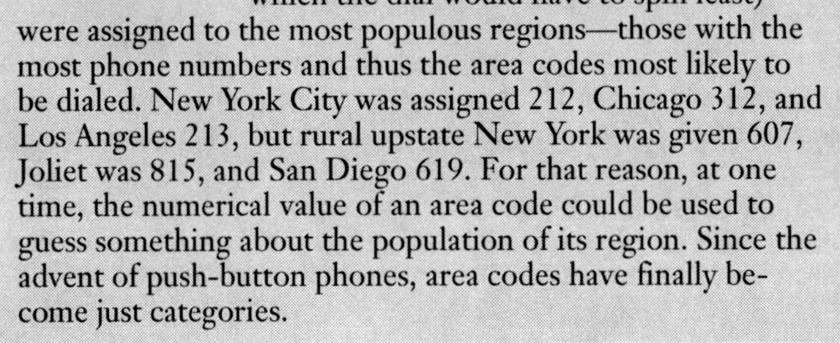

Variables play different roles, and knowing the variable's *type* is crucial to knowing what to do with it and what it can tell us. When a variable names categories and answers questions about how cases fall into those categories, we call it a **categorical variable.**[3] When a variable has measured numerical values with *units* and the variable tells us about the quantity of what is measured, we call it a **quantitative variable.** Sometimes, the variable may be viewed as categorical or quantitative depending on the situation. It's more a decision about what we hope to learn from a variable than a quality of the variable itself. It's the questions we ask of a variable (the *Why* of our analysis) that shape how we think about it and how we treat it.

Descriptive responses to questions are often categories. For example, the responses to the questions "What type of mutual fund do you invest in?" or "What kind of advertising does your firm use?" yield categorical values. An important special case of categorical variables is one that has only two possible responses (usually "yes" or "no"), which arise naturally from questions like "Do you invest in the stock market?" or "Do you make online purchases from this website?"

One tradition that hangs on in some quarters is to name variables with cryptic abbreviations written in uppercase letters. This can be traced back to the 1960s, when the very first statistics computer programs were controlled with instructions punched on cards. The earliest punch card equipment used only uppercase letters, and the earliest statistics programs limited variable names to six or eight characters, so variables were called things like PRSRF3. Modern programs do not have such restrictive limits, so there is no reason for variable names that you wouldn't use in an ordinary sentence.

Be careful. If you treat a variable as quantitative, be sure the values have units and measure a quantity of something. For example, area codes are numbers, but do we use them that way? Is 610 twice 305? Of course it is, but that's not really the point. We don't care that Allentown, PA (area code 610), is twice Key West, FL (305). The numerical values of area codes are completely arbitrary (well, not quite—see the side bar). The numbers assigned by the area codes are codes that *categorize* the phone number into a geographical area. So, we treat area code as a categorical variable.

For quantitative variables, the **units** tell how each value has been measured. Even more important, units such as yen, cubits, carats, angstroms, nanoseconds, miles per hour, or degrees Celsius tell us the *scale* of measurement. The units tell us how much of something we have or how far apart two values are. Without units, the values of a measured variable have no meaning. It does little good to be promised a raise of 5,000 a year if you don't know whether it will be paid in euros, dollars, yen, or Estonian krooni. An essential part of a quantitative variable is its units.

Sometimes the type of the variable is clear. Some variables can answer questions *only* about categories. If the values of a variable are words rather than numbers, it's a good bet that it is categorical. But

[3] You may also see them called *qualitative* variables.

some variables can answer both kinds of questions. For example, Amazon could ask for your *Age* in years. That seems quantitative, and would be if they want to know the average age of those customers who visit their site after 3 A.M. But suppose they want to decide which CD to offer you in a special deal—one by Raffi, Blink182, Carly Simon, or Mantovani—and need to be sure they have adequate supplies on hand to meet the demand. Then thinking of your age in one of the categories child, teen, adult, or senior might be more useful. If it isn't clear whether to treat a variable as categorical or quantitative, think about *Why* you are looking at it and what you want it to tell you.

A typical course evaluation survey asks:

"How valuable do you think this course will be to you?"

1 = Not valuable; 2 = Slightly valuable; 3 = Moderately valuable; 4 = Extremely valuable.

Is this variable categorical or quantitative? Once again, we'll look to the *Why*. A teacher might simply count the number of students who gave each response for her course, treating *Educational Value* as a categorical variable. When she wants to see whether the course is improving, she might treat the responses as the *amount* of perceived value—in effect, treating the variable as quantitative. But what are the units? There is certainly an *order* of perceived worth; higher numbers indicate higher perceived worth. A course that averages 3.5 seems more valuable than one that averages 2, but we should be careful about treating *Educational Value* as purely quantitative. To treat it as quantitative, she'll have to imagine that it has "educational value units" or some similar arbitrary construction. Because there are no natural units, she should be cautious.

Question	Categories or Responses
Do you invest in the stock market?	___ Yes ___ No
What kind of advertising do you use?	___ Newspapers ___ Internet ___ Direct mailings
What is your class at school?	___ Freshman ___ Sophomore ___ Junior ___ Senior
I would recommend this course to another student.	___ Strongly Disagree ___ Slightly Disagree ___ Slightly Agree ___ Strongly Agree
How satisfied are you with this product?	___ Very Unsatisfied ___ Unsatisfied ___ Satisfied ___ Very Satisfied

Table 2.4 *Some examples of categorical variables*

Counts

In Statistics, we often count things. When Amazon considers a special offer of free shipping to customers, they might first analyze how purchases have been shipped in the recent past. They might start by counting the number of purchases shipped in each category: ground transportation, second-day air, and overnight air. Counting is a natural way to summarize the categorical variable *Shipping Method*. So *every* time we see counts, does that mean that the associated variable is categorical? Actually, no.

We also use counts to *measure* the amounts of things. How many songs are on your digital music player? How many classes are you taking this semester? To measure these quantities, we'd naturally count. The variables (*Songs*, *Classes*) are quantitative, whose units are the "number of," or generically, just "counts" for short.

Shipping Method	Number of Purchases
Ground	20,345
Second-day	7,890
Overnight	5,432

Table 2.5 *A summary of the categorical variable* Shipping Method *that shows the counts, or number of cases for each category.*

So we use counts in two different ways. When we have a categorical variable, we count the cases in each category to summarize what the variable tells us. The counts themselves are not the data, but are something we use to summarize the data. For example, Amazon counts the number of purchases in each category of the categorical variable *Shipping Method*.

At other times, our focus is on the amount of something, which we measure by counting. Amazon might track the growth in the number of teenage customers each month to forecast CD sales. *Teen* was a category when we looked at the categorical variable *Age*. But now it's a quantitative variable in its own right whose amount is measured by counting the number of customers as shown in Table 2.6.

Month	Number of Teenage Customers
January	123,456
February	234,567
March	345,678
April	456,789
May	...
...	...

Table 2.6 *A summary of the quantitative variable* Teenage Customers *that shows the counts, or how many teenage customers made purchases, for each month of the year.*

Identifiers

What's your student ID number? It may be numerical, but is it a quantitative variable? No, it doesn't have units. Is it categorical? Yes, but a special kind. Look at how many categories there are and at how many individuals there are in each category. There are exactly as many categories as individuals and only one individual in each category. While it's easy to count the totals for each category, it's not very interesting. This is an **identifier variable**. Amazon wants to know who you are when you sign in again and doesn't want to confuse you with some other customer. So they assign you a unique identifier.

Identifier variables themselves don't tell us anything useful about the categories because we know there is exactly one individual in each. However, they are crucial in this era of large data sets because by uniquely identifying the cases, they make it possible to combine data from different sources, protect confidentiality, and provide unique labels. Most company databases are, in fact, relational databases. The identifier is crucial to linking one data table to another in a relational database. The identifiers in Table 2.3 are the *Customer Number, Product ID*, and *Transaction Number*. Variables like *UPS Tracking Number, Social Security Number*, and Amazon's *ASIN* are other examples of identifiers.

You'll want to recognize when a variable is playing the role of an identifier so you won't be tempted to analyze it. Knowing that Amazon's average ASIN number increased 10% from 2007 to 2008 doesn't really tell you anything—any more than analyzing any categorical variable as if it were quantitative would.

Be careful not to be inflexible in your typing of variables. Variables can play different roles, depending on the question we ask of them, and classifying variables rigidly into types can be misleading. For example, in their annual reports, Amazon refers to its database and looks at the variables *Sales* and *Year*. When analysts ask how many books Amazon sold in 2005, what role does *Year* play? There's only one row for 2005, and *Year* identifies it, so it plays the role of an identifier variable. In its role as an identifier, you might match other data from Amazon, or the economy in general, for the same year. But analysts also track sales growth over time. In this role, *Year* measures time. Now it's being treated as a quantitative variable with units of years. The difference lies in the consideration of the *Why* of our question.

Other Data Types

Categorical variables used only to name categories are sometimes called **nominal variables.** Sometimes all we want to know about a variable is the order of its values. For example, we may want to pick out the first, the last, or the middle value. In such cases, we can say that our variable has **ordinal** values. Values can be individually ordered (e.g., the ranks of employees based on the number of days they've worked for the company) or ordered in classes (e.g., Freshman, Sophomore, Junior, Senior). But the ordering always depends on our purpose. Are the categories Infant, Youth, Teen, Adult, and Senior ordinal? Well, if we are ordering on age, they surely are. But if we are ordering (as Amazon might) on purchase volume, it is likely that either Teen or Adult will be the top group.

Some people differentiate quantitative variables according to whether their measured values have a defined value for zero. This is a technical distinction and usually not one we'll need to make. (For example, it isn't correct to say that a temperature of 80°F is twice as hot as 40°F because 0° is an arbitrary value. On the Celsius scale those temperatures are 26.6°C and 4.44°C—a ratio of 6.) The term *interval scale* is sometimes applied to data such as these, and the term *ratio scale* is applied to measurements for which such ratios are appropriate.

Cross-Sectional and Time Series Data

The quantitative variable *Teenage Customers* in Table 2.6 is an example of a **time series** because we have the same variable measured at regular intervals over time. Time series are common in business. Typical measuring points are months, quarters, or years, but virtually any consistently-spaced time interval is possible. Variables collected over time hold special challenges for statistical analysis, and Chapter 20 discusses these in more detail. By contrast, most of the methods in this book are better suited for **cross-sectional data**, where several variables are measured at the same time point.

For example, if we collect data on sales revenue, number of customers, and expenses for last month at each Starbucks (more than 13,000 locations as of 2007), this would be cross-sectional data. If we expanded our data collection process to include sales revenue and expenses each day over a time span of several months, we would now have a time series for sales and expenses. Because different methods are used to analyze these different types of data, it is important to be able to identify both time series and cross-sectional data sets.

2.3 Where, How, and When

We must know *Who*, *What*, and *Why* to analyze data. Without knowing these three, we don't have enough to start. Of course, we'd always like to know more. The more we know, the more we'll understand. If possible, we'd like to know the *When* and *Where* of data as well. Values recorded in 1803 may mean something different than similar values recorded last year. Values measured in Tanzania may differ in meaning from similar measurements made in Mexico.

How the data are collected can make the difference between insight and nonsense. As we'll see later, data that come from a voluntary survey on the Internet are almost always worthless. In a recent Internet poll, 84% of respondents said "no" to the question of whether subprime borrowers should be bailed out. While it may be true that 84% of those 23,418 respondents did say that, it's dangerous to assume that that group is representative of any larger group. Chapter 3 discusses sound methods for collecting data from surveys and polls so that you can make inferences from the data you have at hand to the world at large.

You may also collect data by performing an experiment in which you actively manipulate variables (called factors) to see what happens. Most of the "junk mail" credit card offers that you receive are actually experiments done by marketing groups in those companies. Chapter 23 discusses both the design and the analysis of experiments like these.

Sometimes, the answer to the question you have may be found in data that someone, or more typically, some organization has already collected. Companies, nonprofit organizations, and government agencies collect a vast amount of data that is becoming increasingly easy to access via the Internet, although some organizations may charge a fee for accessing or downloading their data. The U.S. government through its various agencies collects information on nearly every aspect of life in the United States, both social and economic (see for example www.census.gov), as the European Union does for Europe (see ec.europa.eu/eurostat). International organizations such as the World Health Organization (www.who.org) and polling agencies such as Gallup (www.gallup.com) offer information on a variety of topics as well.

There's a world of data on the Internet

These days, one of the richest sources of data is the Internet. With a bit of practice, you can learn to find data on almost any subject. Many of the data sets we use in this book were found in this way. The Internet has both advantages and disadvantages as a source of data. Among the advantages are the fact that often you'll be able to find even more current data than we present. The disadvantage is that references to Internet addresses can "break" as sites evolve, move, and die.

Our solution to these challenges is to offer the best advice we can to help you search for the data, wherever they may be residing. We usually point you to a website. We'll sometimes suggest search terms and offer other guidance.

Some words of caution, though: Data found on Internet sites may not be formatted in the best way for use in statistics software. Although you may see a data table in standard form, an attempt to copy the data may leave you with a single column of values. You may have to work in your favorite statistics or spreadsheet program to reformat the data into variables. You will also probably want to remove commas from large numbers and such extra symbols as money indicators ($, ¥, £, €); few statistics packages can handle these.

Throughout this book, whenever we introduce data, we will provide a margin note listing the W's of the data. It's a habit we recommend. The first step of any data analysis is to know why you are examining the data (what you want to know), whom each row of your data table refers to, and what the variables (the columns of the table) record. These are the *Why*, the *Who*, and the *What*. Identifying them is a key part of the *Plan* step of any analysis. Make sure you know all three before you spend time analyzing the data.

JUST CHECKING

An insurance company that specializes in commercial property insurance has a separate database for their policies that involve churches and schools. Here is a small portion of that database.

Policy Number	Years Claim Free	Net Property Premium ($)	Net Liability Premium ($)	Total Property Value ($1,000)	Median Age of Zip Code	School?	Territory	Coverage
4000174699	1	3107	503	1036	40	FALSE	AL580	BLANKET
8000571997	2	1036	261	748	42	FALSE	PA192	SPECIFIC
8000623296	1	438	353	344	30	FALSE	ID60	BLANKET
3000495296	1	582	339	270	35	TRUE	NC340	BLANKET
5000291199	4	993	357	218	43	FALSE	OK590	BLANKET
8000470297	2	433	622	108	31	FALSE	NV140	BLANKET
1000042399	4	2461	1016	1544	41	TRUE	NJ20	BLANKET
4000554596	0	7340	1782	5121	44	FALSE	FL530	BLANKET
3000260397	0	1458	261	1037	42	FALSE	NC560	BLANKET
8000333297	2	392	351	177	40	FALSE	OR190	BLANKET
4000174699	1	3107	503	1036	40	FALSE	AL580	BLANKET

1 List as many of the W's as you can for this data set.
2 Classify each variable as to whether you think it should be treated as categorical or quantitative (or both); if quantitative, identify the units.

WHAT CAN GO WRONG?

- **Don't label a variable as categorical or quantitative without thinking about the data and what they represent.** The same variable can sometimes take on different roles.
- **Don't assume that a variable is quantitative just because its values are numbers.** Categories are often given numerical labels. Don't let that fool you into thinking they have quantitative meaning. Look at the context.
- **Always be skeptical.** One reason to analyze data is to discover the truth. Even when you are told a context for the data, it may turn out that the truth is a bit (or even a lot) different. The context colors our interpretation of the data, so those who want to influence what you think may slant the context. A survey that seems to be about all students may in fact report just the opinions of those who visited a fan website. The question that respondents answered may be posed in a way that influences responses.

ETHICS IN ACTION

Sarah Potterman, a doctoral student in educational psychology, is researching the effectiveness of various interventions recommended to help children with learning disabilities improve their reading skills. Among the approaches examined is an interactive software system that uses analogy-based phonics. Sarah contacted the company that developed this software, RSPT Inc., in order to obtain the system free of charge for use in her research. RSPT Inc. expressed interest in having her compare their product with other intervention strategies and was quite confident that their approach would be the most effective. Not only did the company provide Sarah with free software, but RSPT Inc. also generously offered to fund her research with a grant to cover her data collection and analysis costs.

ETHICAL ISSUE *Both the researcher and company should be careful about the funding source having a vested interest in the research result (related to Item H, ASA Ethical Guidelines).*

ETHICAL SOLUTION *RSPT Inc. should not pressure Sarah Potterman to obtain a particular result. Both parties should agree on paper before the research is begun that the research results can be published even if they show that RSPT's interactive software system is not the most effective.*

Jim Hopler is operations manager for a local office of a top-ranked full service brokerage firm. With increasing competition from both discount and online brokers, Jim's firm has redirected attention to attaining exceptional customer service through its client-facing staff, namely brokers. In particular, they wish to emphasize the excellent advisory services provided by their brokers. Results from surveying clients about the advice received from brokers at the local office revealed that 20% rated it *poor*, 5% rated it *below average*, 15% rated it *average*, 10% rated it *above average*, and 50% rated it *outstanding*. With corporate approval, Jim and his management team instituted several changes in an effort to provide the best possible advisory services at the local office. Their goal was to increase the percentage of clients who viewed their advisory services as *outstanding*. Surveys conducted after the changes were implemented showed the following results: 5% *poor*, 5% *below average*, 20% *average*, 40% *above average*, and 30% *outstanding*. In discussing these results, the management team expressed concern that the percentage of clients who considered their advisory services *outstanding* fell from 50% to 30%. One member of the team suggested an alternative way of summarizing the data. By coding the categories on a scale from 1 = poor to 5 = outstanding and computing the average, they found that the average rating increased from 3.65 to 3.85 as a result of the changes implemented. Jim was delighted to see that their changes were successful in improving the level of advisory services offered at the local office. In his report to corporate, he only included average ratings for the client surveys.

ETHICAL ISSUE *By taking an average, Jim is able to show improved customer satisfaction. However, their goal was to increase the percentage of outstanding ratings. Jim redefined his study after the fact to support a position (related to Item A, ASA Ethical Guidelines).*

ETHICAL SOLUTION *Jim should report the percentages for each rating category. He can also report the average. He may wish to include in his report a discussion of what those different ways of looking at the data say and why they appear to differ. He may also want to explore with the survey participants the perceived differences between "above average" and "outstanding."*

What have we learned?

We've learned that data are information in a context.

- The W's help nail down the context: *Who, What, Why, Where, When.*
- We must know at least the *Who, What,* and *Why* to be able to say anything useful based on the data. The *Who* are the *cases*. The *What* are the *variables.* A variable gives information about each of the cases. The *Why* helps us decide which way to treat the variables.

We treat variables in two basic ways, as *categorical* or *quantitative*.

- Categorical variables identify a category for each case. Usually we think about the counts of cases that fall in each category. (An exception is an identifier variable that just names each case.)
- Quantitative variables record measurements or amounts of something; they must have *units*.
- Sometimes we treat a variable as categorical or quantitative depending on what we want to learn from it, which means some variables can't be pigeonholed as one type or the other. That's an early hint that in Statistics we can't always pin things down precisely.

Terms

Case A case is an individual about whom or which we have data.

Categorical variable A variable that names categories (whether with words or numerals) is called categorical.

Context The context ideally tells *Who* was measured, *What* was measured, *How* the data were collected, *Where* the data were collected, and *When* and *Why* the study was performed.

Cross-sectional data Data taken from situations that vary over time but measured at a single time instant is said to be a cross-section of the time series.

Data Systematically recorded information, whether numbers or labels, together with its context.

Data table An arrangement of data in which each row represents a case and each column represents a variable.

Experimental unit An individual in a study for which or for whom data values are recorded. Human experimental units are usually called subjects or participants.

Identifier variable A categorical variable that records a unique value for each case, used to name or identify it.

Nominal variable The term "nominal" can be applied to data whose values are used only to name categories.

Ordinal variable The term "ordinal" can be applied to data for which some kind of order is available but for which measured values are not available.

Participant A human experimental unit. Also called a subject.

Quantitative variable A variable in which the numbers are values of measured quantities with units.

Record Information about an individual in a database.

Relational database A relational database stores and retrieves information. Within the database, information is kept in data tables that can be "related" to each other.

Respondent Someone who answers, or responds to, a survey.

Spreadsheet A spreadsheet is layout designed for accounting that is often used to store and manage data tables. Excel is a common example of a spreadsheet program.

Subject A human experimental unit. Also called a participant.

Time series Data measured over time. Usually the time intervals are equally-spaced (e.g., every week, every quarter, or every year).

Units A quantity or amount adopted as a standard of measurement, such as dollars, hours, or grams.

Variable A variable holds information about the same characteristic for many cases.

Skills

- Be able to identify the *Who*, *What*, *When*, *Where*, *Why*, and *How* of data, or recognize when some of this information has not been provided.
- Be able to identify the cases and variables in any data set.
- Know how to treat a variable as categorical or quantitative depending on its use.
- For any quantitative variable, be able to identify the units in which the variable has been measured (or note that they have not been provided).

REPORT

- Be sure to describe a variable in terms of its *Who*, *What*, *When*, *Where*, *Why*, and *How* (and be prepared to remark when that information is not provided).

Technology Help

Most often we find statistics on a computer using a program, or *package*, designed for that purpose. There are many different statistics packages, but they all do essentially the same things. If you understand what the computer needs to know to do what you want and what it needs to show you in return, you can figure out the specific details of most packages pretty easily.

For example, to get your data into a computer statistics package, you need to tell the computer:

- Where to find the data. This usually means directing the computer to a file stored on your computer's disk or to data on a database. Or it might just mean that you have copied the data from a spreadsheet program or Internet site and it is currently on your computer's clipboard. Usually, the data should be in the form of a data table. Most computer statistics packages prefer the *delimiter* that marks the division between elements of a data table to be a *tab* character and the delimiter that marks the end of a case to be a *return* character.

- Where to put the data. (Usually this is handled automatically.)
- What to call the variables. Some data tables have variable names as the first row of the data, and often statistics packages can take the variable names from the first row automatically.

Mini Case Study Project

Like all credit and charge card companies, this company makes money on each of its cardholders' transactions. Thus, its profitability is directly linked to card usage. To increase customer spending on its cards, the company sends many different offers to its cardholders, and market researchers analyze the results to see which offers yield the largest increases in the average amount charged.

On your disk (in the file **ch02_MCSP_Credit_Card_Bank**) is a small part of a database like the one used by the researchers. For each customer, it contains several variables in a spreadsheet.

Examine the data in the data file. List as many of the W's as you can for these data and classify each variable as categorical or quantitative. If quantitative, identify the units.

EXERCISES

For each description of data in Exercises 1 to 26, identify the W's, name the variables, specify for each variable whether its use indicates it should be treated as categorical or quantitative, and for any quantitative variable identify the units in which it was measured (or note that they were not provided).

1. The news. Find a newspaper or magazine article in which some data are reported (e.g., see *The Wall Street Journal*, *Financial Times*, *Business Week*, or *Fortune*). For the data discussed in the article, answer the questions above. Include a copy of the article with your report.

2. Investments. In the U.S., 401(k) plans permit employees to shift part of their before-tax salaries into investments such as mutual funds. One company, concerned with what it believed was a low employee participation rate in its 401(k) plan, sampled 30 other companies with similar plans and asked for their 401(k) participation rates.

3. Oil spills. After several major ocean oil spills by oil tankers, Congress passed the 1990 Oil Pollution Act, which requires all tankers to have thicker hulls. Further improvements in the structural design of a tanker have been proposed since then, each with the objective of reducing the likelihood of an oil spill and decreasing the amount of outflow in the event of a hull puncture. Infoplease (www.infoplease.com) reports the date, the spillage amount and cause of puncture for 50 recent major oil spills from tankers and carriers.

4. Sales. A major U.S. company is interested in seeing how various promotional activities are related to domestic sales. Analysts decide to measure the money spent on different forms of advertising ($ thousand) and sales ($ million) on a monthly basis for three years (2004–2006).

5. Food store. A food retailer that specializes in selling organic food has decided to open a new store. To help determine the best location in the United States for the new store, researchers decide to examine data from existing stores, including weekly sales ($), town population (thousands), median age of town, median income of town ($), and whether or not the store sells wine and beer.

6. Sales II. The company in Exercise 4 is also interested in the impact of national indicators on their sales. It decides to obtain measurements for unemployment rate (%) and inflation rate (%) on a quarterly basis to compare to their quarterly sales ($ million) over the same time period (2004–2006).

7. Arby's menu. A listing posted by the Arby's restaurant chain gives, for each of the sandwiches it sells, the type of meat in the sandwich, number of calories, and serving size in ounces. The data might be used to assess the nutritional value of the different sandwiches.

8. MBA admissions. A school in the northeastern United States is concerned with the recent drop in female students in its MBA program. It decides to collect data from the admissions office on each applicant, including: sex of each applicant, age of each applicant, whether or not they were accepted, whether or not they attended, and the reason for not attending (if they did not attend). The school hopes to find commonalities among the female accepted students who have decided not to attend the business program.

9. Climate. In a study appearing in the journal *Science*, a research team reports that plants in southern England are flowering earlier in the spring. Records of the first flowering dates for 385 species over a period of 47 years indicate that flowering has advanced an average of 15 days per decade, an indication of climate warming according to the authors.

10. MBA admissions II. An internationally recognized MBA program in London intends to also track the GPA of the MBA students and compares MBA performance to standardized test scores over a 5-year period (2000–2005).

11. Schools. A State Education Department requires local school districts to keep records on all students, recording: age, race or ethnicity, days absent, current grade level, standardized test scores in reading and mathematics, and any disabilities or special educational needs the student may have.

12. Pharmaceutical firm. Scientists at a major pharmaceutical firm conducted an experiment to study the effectiveness of an herbal compound to treat the common cold. They exposed volunteers to a cold virus, then gave them either the herbal compound or a sugar solution known to have no effect on colds. Several days later they assessed each patient's condition using a cold severity scale ranging from 0–5. They found no evidence of the benefits of the compound.

13. Start-up company. A start-up company is building a database of customers and sales information. For each customer, it records name, ID number, region of the country (1 = East, 2 = South, 3 = Midwest, 4 = West), date of last purchase, amount of purchase, and item purchased.

14. Cars. A survey of autos parked in executive and staff lots at a large company recorded the make, country of origin, type of vehicle (car, van, SUV, etc.), and age.

15. Vineyards. Business analysts hoping to provide information helpful to grape growers compiled these data about vineyards: size (acres), number of years in existence, state, varieties of grapes grown, average case price, gross sales, and percent profit.

16. Environment. As research for an ecology class, students at a college in upstate New York collect data on streams each year to study the impact of the environment. They record a number of biological, chemical, and physical variables, including the stream name, the substrate of the stream (limestone, shale, or mixed), the acidity of the water (pH), the temperature (°C), and the BCI (a numerical measure of biological diversity).

17. Gallup Poll. The Gallup Poll conducted a representative telephone survey of 1180 American voters. Among the reported results were the voter's region (Northeast, South, etc.), age, political party affiliation, whether the respondent owned any shares of stock, and their attitude (on a scale of 1 to 5) toward unions.

18. FAA. The Federal Aviation Administration (FAA) monitors airlines for safety and customer service. For each flight the carrier must report the type of aircraft, number of passengers, whether or not the flights departed and arrived on schedule, and any mechanical problems.

19. EPA. The Environmental Protection Agency (EPA) tracks fuel economy of automobiles. Among the data EPA analysts collect from the manufacturer are the manufacturer (Ford, Toyota, etc.), vehicle type (car, SUV, etc.), weight, horsepower, and gas mileage (mpg) for city and highway driving.

20. Consumer Reports. In 2002, Consumer Reports published an article evaluating refrigerators. It listed 41 models, giving the brand, cost, size (cu ft), type (such as top-freezer), estimated annual energy cost, overall rating (good, excellent, etc.), and repair history for that brand (percentage requiring repairs over the past 5 years).

21. Lotto. A study of state-sponsored Lotto games in the United States (*Chance*, Winter 1998) listed the names of the states and whether or not the state had Lotto. For states that did, the study indicated the number of numbers in the lottery, the number of matches required to win, and the probability of holding a winning ticket.

22. L.L. Bean. L.L. Bean is a large U.S. retailer that depends heavily on its catalog sales. It collects data internally and tracks the number of catalogs mailed out, the number of square inches in each catalog, and the sales ($ thousands) in the 4 weeks following each mailing. The company is interested in learning more about the relationship (if any) among the timing and space of their catalogs and their sales.

23. Stock market. An online survey of students in a large MBA Statistics class at a business school in the northeastern United States asked them to report their total personal investment in the stock market ($), total number of different stocks currently held, total invested in mutual funds ($), and the name of each mutual fund in which they have invested. The data were used in the aggregate for classroom illustrations.

24. Theme park sites. A study on the potential for developing theme parks in various locations throughout Europe in 2008 collects the following information: the country where the proposed site is located, estimated cost to acquire site (in euros), size of population within a one hour drive of the site, size of the site (in hectares), mass transportation within 5 minutes of the site. The data will be used to present to prospective developers.

25. Indy. The 2.5-mile Indianapolis Motor Speedway has been the home to a race on Memorial Day nearly every year since 1911. Even during the first race there were controversies. Ralph Mulford was given the checkered flag first but took three extra laps just to make sure he'd completed 500 miles. When he finished, another driver, Ray Harroun, was being presented with the winner's trophy, and Mulford's protests were ignored. Harroun averaged 74.6 mph for the 500 miles. Here are the data for the first few and three recent Indianapolis 500 races.

Year	Winner	Car	Time (hrs)	Speed (mph)	Car #
1911	Ray Harroun	Marmon Model 32	6.7022	74.602	32
1912	Joe Dawson	National	6.3517	78.719	8
1913	Jules Goux	Peugeot	6.5848	75.933	16
...					
...					
2005	Dan Wheldon	Dallara/ Honda	3.1725	157.603	26
2006	Sam Hornish, Jr.	Dallara/ Honda	3.1830	157.085	6
2007	Dario Franchitti	Dallara/ Honda	2.7343	151.774	27

26. Kentucky Derby. The Kentucky Derby is a horse race that has been run every year since 1875 at Churchill Downs, Louisville, Kentucky. The race started as a 1.5-mile race, but in 1896 it was shortened to 1.25 miles because experts felt that 3-year-old horses shouldn't run such a long race that early in the season. (It has been run in May every year but one—1901—when it took place on April 29.) The table at the bottom of the page shows the data for the first few and a few recent races.

When you organize data in a spreadsheet, it is important to lay it out as a data table. For each of these examples in Exercises 27 to 30, show how you would lay out these data. Indicate the headings of columns and what would be found in each row.

27. Mortgages. For a study of mortgage loan performance: amount of the loan, the name of the borrower.

28. Employee performance. Data collected to determine performance-based bonuses: employee ID, average contract closed (in $), supervisor's rating (1–10), years with the company.

29. Company performance. Data collected for financial planning: weekly sales, week (week number of the year), sales predicted by last year's plan, difference between predicted sales and realized sales.

30. Command performance. Data collected on investments in Broadway shows: number of investors, total invested, name of the show, profit/loss after one year.

For the following examples in Exercises 31 to 34, indicate whether the data are a time series or a cross section.

31. Car sales. Number of cars sold by each salesperson in a dealership in September.

Date	Winner	Margin (lengths)	Jockey	Winner's Payoff ($)	Duration (min:sec)	Track Condition
May 17, 1875	Aristides	2	O. Lewis	2850	2:37.75	Fast
May 15, 1876	Vagrant	2	B. Swim	2950	2:38.25	Fast
May 22, 1877	Baden-Baden	2	W. Walker	3300	2:38.00	Fast
May 21, 1878	Day Star	1	J. Carter	4050	2:37.25	Dusty
May 20, 1879	Lord Murphy	1	C. Shauer	3550	2:37.00	Fast
...						
May 5, 2001	Monarchos	4 3/4	J. Chavez	812000	1:59.97	Fast
May 4, 2002	War Emblem	4	V. Espinoza	1875000	2:01.13	Fast
May 3, 2003	Funny Cide	1 3/4	J. Santos	800200	2:01.19	Fast
May 1, 2004	Smarty Jones	2 3/4	S. Elliott	854800	2:04.06	Sloppy

32. Motorcycle sales. Number of motorcycles sold by a dealership in each month of 2008.

33. Cross sections. Average diameter of trees brought to a sawmill in each week of a year.

34. Series. Attendance at the third World Series game recording the age of each fan.

JUST CHECKING ANSWERS

1 Who—policies on churches and schools
What—policy number, years claim free, net property premium ($), net liability premium ($), total property value ($000), median age in zip code, school?, territory, coverage
How—company records
When—not given

2 Policy number: identifier (categorical)
Years claim free: quantitative
Net property premium: quantitative ($)
Net liability premium: quantitative ($)
Total property value: quantitative ($)
School?: categorical (true/false)
Territory: categorical
Coverage: categorical

CHAPTER 5

Diagrams for presenting data

Contents

Chapter outline

The amount of detail in raw data obscures the underlying patterns. Data reduction and presentation clears away this detail and highlights the overall features and patterns. It gives a view of the data that is concise, but still accurate. There are two approaches to summarising data. In this chapter we describe some diagrams, and Chapter 6 continues the theme by looking at numerical summaries.

After finishing this chapter you should be able to:

- Discuss the aims of data reduction and presentation
- Design tables of numerical data
- Draw frequency distributions of data
- Use graphs to show the relationship between two variables
- Design pie charts
- Draw different kinds of bar chart
- Consider pictograms and other formats
- Draw histograms for continuous data
- Draw ogives and Lorenz curves for cumulative data.

Data reduction and presentation

In the last chapter we saw that data are the basic numbers and facts that we process to give useful information. So 78, 64, 36, 70 and 52 are data that we process to give the information that the average mark of five students sitting an exam is 60%.

Most people can deal with small amounts of numerical data. We happily say, 'this building is 60 metres tall', 'a car travels 15 kilometres on a litre of petrol', and '16% of people use a particular product'. But we have problems when there is a lot of data. For instance, the weekly sales of a product from a website over the past year are:

51 60 58 56 62 69 58 76 80 82 68 90 72
84 91 82 78 76 75 66 57 78 65 50 61 54
49 44 41 45 38 28 37 40 42 22 25 26 21
30 32 30 32 31 29 30 41 45 44 47 53 54

This gives the raw data – which you probably skipped over with hardly a glance. If you put such figures in a report, people would find it boring and skip to something more interesting – even though the figures could be very important. To make them less daunting we could try putting them in the text, starting with 'In the first week sales were 51 units, and they rose by nine units in the second week, but in the third week they fell back to 58 units, and fell another two units in the fourth week . . .'. Clearly, this does not work with so many numbers, and we need a more convenient format.

The problem is that raw data swamps us with detail, obscuring the overall patterns and shape of the data – we cannot see the wood for the trees. Usually we are not interested in the minute detail, but really want only the overall picture. So imagine that you have put a lot of effort into collecting data and now want to show it to other people. You have two jobs – data reduction to reduce the amount of detail, and data presentation to give the results in a useful format.

- **Data reduction** gives a simplified and accurate view of the data, showing the underlying patterns but not overwhelming us with detail.
- **Data presentation** shows clearly and accurately the characteristics of a set of data and highlights the patterns.

Now we have the sequence of activities for analysing data, which starts with data collection, moves to data reduction and then data presentation. In practice, there is no clear distinction between data reduction and data presentation, and we usually combine them into a single activity. This combined activity of summarising – or more broadly processing or managing – data has the advantages of:

- showing results in a compact form
- using formats that are easy to understand
- allowing diagrams, graphs or pictures
- highlighting underlying patterns
- allowing comparisons of different sets of data
- using quantitative measures.

On the other hand, summarising data has the major disadvantage that it loses details of the original data and is irreversible.

Diagrams for presenting data

When you look around, there are countless examples of diagrams giving information. A newspaper article adds a diagram to summarise its story; an advertisement uses a picture to get across its message; a company's financial performance is summarised in a graph. Diagrams attract people's attention, and we are more likely to look at them than read the accompanying text – hence the saying, 'One picture is worth a thousand words'. Good diagrams are attractive, they make information more interesting, give a clear summary of data, emphasise underlying patterns, and allow us to extract a lot of information in a short time. But they do not happen by chance, and need careful planning.

If you look at a diagram and cannot understand what is happening, it means that the presentation is poor – and the fault is with the presenter rather than the viewer. Sometimes there is a more subtle problem – when you look at a diagram quickly and immediately see one pattern, but then look more closely and see that your initial impression was wrong. To be generous, this might be a simple mistake in presenting the data poorly, but the truth is that people often make a deliberate decision to present data in a form that is misleading and dishonest. Advertisements are notorious for presenting data in a way that gives the desired impression, rather than accurately reflecting a situation, and politicians might be more concerned with appearance than with truth. Huff[1] developed this theme in the 1950s with his classic descriptions of 'How to lie with statistics' and this has been followed by similar descriptions, such as those of Kimble in the 1970s[2] and more recently Wainer.[3,4] The problem is that diagrams are a powerful means of presenting data, but they give only a summary – and this summary can easily be misleading. In this chapter we show how to use diagrams to present information properly, giving a fair and honest summary of the raw data.

There are many types of diagram for presenting data, with the most common including:

- tables of numerical data and frequency distributions
- graphs to show relationships between variables
- pie charts, bar charts and pictograms showing relative frequencies
- histograms that show relative frequencies of continuous data.

The choice of best format is often a matter of personal judgement and preference. But remember that we want to give people information as fairly and efficiently as possible – and we are not just looking for the prettiest picture. Some guidelines for choosing the type of diagram include the following, where appropriate:

- Choose the most suitable format for the purpose
- Always present data fairly and honestly
- Make sure any diagram is clear and easy to understand
- State the source of data
- Use consistent units and say what these are
- Include totals, sub-totals and any other useful summaries
- Give each diagram a title
- Add notes to highlight assumptions and reasons for unusual or atypical values.

Review questions

5.1 What is the difference between data and information?

5.2 What is the purpose of data reduction?

5.3 'Data presentation always gives a clear, detailed and accurate view.' Is this true?

5.4 What are the two main methods of presenting data?

Tables of numerical data

Tables are probably the most common way of summarising data. We have already used several in this book, and you can see more whenever you pick up a newspaper, a magazine, a books or a report. Table 5.1 shows the weekly sales of the product mentioned above, and this gives the general format for tables.

Table 5.1 Weekly sales of product

Week	Quarter 1	Quarter 2	Quarter 3	Quarter 4	Total
1	51	84	49	30	214
2	60	91	44	32	227
3	58	82	41	30	211
4	56	78	45	32	211
5	62	76	38	31	207
6	69	75	28	29	201
7	58	66	37	30	191
8	76	57	40	41	214
9	80	78	42	45	245
10	82	65	22	44	213
11	68	50	25	47	190
12	90	61	26	53	230
13	72	54	21	54	201
Totals	882	917	458	498	2,755

Now you can see that sales are higher in the first two quarters and lower in the second two. But the table is still only a presentation of the raw data – and it does not really give a feel for a typical week's sales, it is difficult to find the minimum or maximum sales, and patterns are not clear. We can emphasise the underlying patterns by reducing the data. To start with, we can find that minimum sales are 21, and then count the number of weeks with sales in a range of, say, 20 to 29. There are six weeks in this range, and counting the number of weeks with sales in other ranges gives the summary shown in Table 5.2.

Tables that show the number of values in different ranges are called frequency tables, and the 'ranges' are called classes. Then we can talk about the 'class of 20 to 29', where 20 is the lower class limit, 29 is the upper class limit, and the class width is 29 – 20 = 9. We arbitrarily chose classes of 20 to 29, 30 to 39, and so on, but could have used any other reasonable values.

Table 5.2 Frequency table of sales

Range of sales	Number of weeks
20 to 29	6
30 to 39	8
40 to 49	10
50 to 59	9
60 to 69	7
70 to 79	6
80 to 89	4
90 to 99	2

This is largely a choice that is guided by the structure of the data and the use of the table. Two guidelines are as follows:

- The classes should all be the same width.
- There should be enough classes to make patterns clear, but not too many to obscure them; this usually suggests a minimum of four classes, and a maximum around ten.

If the eight classes in Table 5.2 seem too many, we could divide the data into, say, four classes and add a note about the source to give the final result shown in Table 5.3.

Table 5.3 Frequency table of weekly sales

Range	Number of weeks
20 to 39	14
40 to 59	19
60 to 79	13
80 to 99	6

Source: Company Weekly Sales Reports.

Tables 5.1 to 5.3 show an inevitable effect of data reduction – the more data is summarised, the more detail is lost. For instance, Table 5.3 shows the distribution of weekly sales, but it gives no idea of the seasonal variations. We can accept this loss of detail if the result still shows all the information we want and is easier to understand – but not if the details are important. If we want to plan the number of seasonal employees, we could not use Table 5.3 but would have to return to Table 5.1.

You can obviously present a set of data in many different tables – and you always have to compromise between making them too long (when they show lots of detail, but are complicated and obscure underlying patterns) and too short (when they show patterns clearly, but lose most of the detail). Another guideline says that if you repeatedly present data over some period, you should always keep the same format to allow direct comparisons (and you see this effect in company reports and government publications).

WORKED EXAMPLE 5.1

Carlson Industries has collected the following monthly performance indicators over the past five years. How would you summarise these in a different table?

	Year 1	2	3	4	5
January	136	135	141	138	143
February	109	112	121	117	118
March	92	100	104	105	121
April	107	116	116	121	135
May	128	127	135	133	136
June	145	132	138	154	147
July	138	146	159	136	150
August	127	130	131	135	144
September	135	127	129	140	140
October	141	156	137	134	142
November	147	136	149	148	147
December	135	141	144	140	147

Solution

There are many different ways of summarising these, with some options shown in the spreadsheet of Figure 5.1.

	A	B	C	D	E	F	G	H
1	**Carlson Industries**							
2								
3	**Range**	**Frequency**		**Monthly averages**			**Annual averages**	
4								
5	< 99	1		January	138.6		Year 1	128.3
6	100–109	5		February	115.4		Year 2	129.8
7	110–119	5		March	104.4		Year 3	133.7
8	120–129	8		April	119		Year 4	133.4
9	130–139	19		May	131.8		Year 5	139.2
10	140–149	18		June	143.2			
11	> 150	4		July	145.8			
12				August	133.4			
13				September	134.2			
14				October	142			
15				November	145.4			
16				December	141.4			

Figure 5.1 Table of results for Carlson Industries

Frequency distributions

The results shown in a frequency table form a frequency distribution. For example, the following table shows the frequency distribution for the number of weekly deliveries to a logistics centre during a year.

Number of deliveries	20 to 39	40 to 59	60 to 79	80 to 99
Number of weeks	14	19	13	6

As you can see, there are six observations in the highest class of deliveries, 80 to 99. But suppose that there had been one unusual week with 140 deliveries. In this table it would be in a class of its own some distance away from the others.

Number of deliveries	20 to 39	40 to 59	60 to 79	80 to 99	100 to 119	120 to 139	140 to 169
Number of weeks	14	19	13	5	0	0	1

Sometimes it is important to highlight outlying values – but usually it is just confusing, so we define the highest class to include all outliers. Here we do this by defining the top class as '80 or more'. Similarly, it is better to replace the precise '20 to 39' for the bottom class by the less precise '39 or fewer'.

An obvious point is that you have to define boundaries between classes so that there is no doubt about which class an observation is in. Here you could not define adjacent classes of '20 to 30' and '30 to 40', as a value of 30 could be in either one. Using '20 to 29' and '30 to 39' avoids this problem for discrete data, but fails with continuous data. For instance, you could not classify people's ages as '20 to 29' and '30 to 39', as this would leave no place for people who are 29.5. Instead you have to use more precise – but rather messy – phrases like 'aged 20 or more and less than 30'.

WORKED EXAMPLE 5.2

The weights of materials (in kilograms) needed for 30 projects are as follows. Draw a frequency distribution of this data.

202 457 310 176 480 277 87 391 325 120 554
94 362 221 274 145 240 437 404 398 361 144
429 216 282 153 470 303 338 209

Solution

The first decision is the best number of classes. The range is between 87 kg and 554 kg, so a reasonable solution is to use six classes of 'less than 100 kg', '100 kg or more and less than 200 kg', '200 kg or more and less than 300 kg', and so on. Notice that we are careful not to phrase these as 'more than 100 kg and less than 200 kg', as a project needing exactly 100 kg would not fit into any class. Adding the number of observations in each class gives the frequency distribution in Figure 5.2.

	A	B	C
1	**Frequency distribution**		
2			
3	**Class**	**Frequency**	**Percentage frequency**
4	**less than 100 kg**	2	6.7
5	**100 kg or more, and less than 200 kg**	5	16.7
6	**200 kg or more, and less than 300 kg**	8	26.7
7	**300 kg or more, and less than 400 kg**	9	30.0
8	**400 kg or more, and less than 500 kg**	5	16.7
9	**500 kg or more**	1	3.3
10	**Totals**	**30**	**100.0**

Figure 5.2 Frequency distribution for worked example 5.2

	A	B	C	D	E
1	**Different types of frequency distribution**				
2					
3	**Class**	**Frequency**	**Cumulative frequency**	**Percentage frequency**	**Cumulative percentage frequency**
4	**less than 100 kg**	2	2	6.7	6.7
5	**100 kg or more, and less than 200 kg**	5	7	16.7	23.3
6	**200 kg or more, and less than 300 kg**	8	15	26.7	50.0
7	**300 kg or more, and less than 400 kg**	9	24	30.0	80.0
8	**400 kg or more, and less than 500 kg**	5	29	16.7	96.7
9	**500 kg or more**	1	30	3.3	100.0
10	**Total**	**30**		**100.0**	

Figure 5.3 Different types of frequency distribution

Frequency distributions show the number of observations in each class, but in Figure 5.2 we also calculated a **percentage frequency distribution**, which shows the percentage of observations in each class. Another useful extension shows the cumulative frequencies. Instead of recording the number of observations in a class, **cumulative frequency distributions** add all observations in lower classes. In Figure 5.2 there were two observations in the first class, five in the second class and eight in the third. The cumulative frequency distribution shows two observations in the first class, 2 + 5 = 7 in the second class, and 2 + 5 + 8 = 15 in the third. In the same way, we can also draw a **cumulative percentage frequency distribution**, as shown in Figure 5.3.

Review questions

5.5 What are the advantages of using tables of data?

5.6 What is a frequency distribution?

5.7 What is the best number of classes for a table of data?

5.8 Tables of data can seem very dull – so why are they so widely used?

IDEAS IN PRACTICE UK cereal production

Tables range from the very simple to the very complex. For example, we can show the percentages of wheat, barley, oats and other cereals grown in the UK in the following simple table:

Cereal	Percentage of cereal-growing land
Wheat	64%
Barley	32%
Oats	3%
Others	1%

Or we can add a lot more detail to get the result in Table 5.4 – and we could continue adding more data until the tables become very complex.

Ideas in practice continued

Table 5.4 Main cereal crops grown in the United Kingdom

	1990	1995	2000	2005
Wheat				
Area ('000 hectares)	2,014 (55.0)	1,859 (58.4)	2,086 (62.3)	1,869 (63.8)
Harvest ('000 tonnes)	14,033 (62.1)	14,312 (65.4)	16,708 (69.7)	14,877 (70.6)
Yield (tonnes per hectare)	7.0	7.7	8.0	8.0
Barley				
Area ('000 hectares)	1,517 (41.4)	1,193 (37.5)	1,128 (33.7)	944 (32.2)
Harvest ('000 tonnes)	7,911 (35.0)	6,842 (31.3)	6,492 (27.1)	5,533 (26.3)
Yield (tonnes per hectare)	5.2	5.7	5.8	5.9
Oats				
Area ('000 hectares)	107 (2.9)	112 (3.5)	109 (3.3)	91 (3.1)
Harvest ('000 tonnes)	530 (2.3)	617 (2.8)	640 (2.7)	534 (2.5)
Yield (tonnes per hectare)	5.0	5.5	5.9	5.9
Totals				
Area ('000 hectares)	3,660	3,182	3,348	2,928
Harvest ('000 tonnes)	22,582	21,870	23,988	21,060

Sources: adapted from Department for the Environment, Farming and Rural Affairs, *Agriculture in the UK Annual Report 2005*, London, and website at www.defra.gov.uk.

Notes: figures in brackets are percentages of annual totals, 2005 figures are current estimates. Rounding means that percentages may not add to 100%.

Diagrams of data

Tables are good at presenting a lot of information, but it can still be difficult to identify underlying patterns. We can see these more clearly in other kinds of diagram, such as the graphs we described in Chapter 3. These graphs show the relationship between two variables on a pair of Cartesian axes, with the x-axis showing the independent variable and the y-axis showing corresponding values of a dependent variable. If we are plotting sales of ice cream against temperature, there is clearly an independent variable (the temperature) and a dependent variable (the consequent sales of ice cream). But if we are plotting sales of ice cream against sales of sausages, there is no clear relationship and we can choose to draw the axes either way round.

Formats for graphs

As with tables, there are many different formats for graphs. Returning to the weekly sales of a product described earlier, we can start by plotting sales (the dependent variable) against the week (the independent variable). Then the simplest graph shows the individual points in a scatter diagram, shown in Figure 5.4(a).

You can see the general pattern here, but this becomes even clearer when we join the points, as shown in Figure 5.4(b). The sales clearly follow a

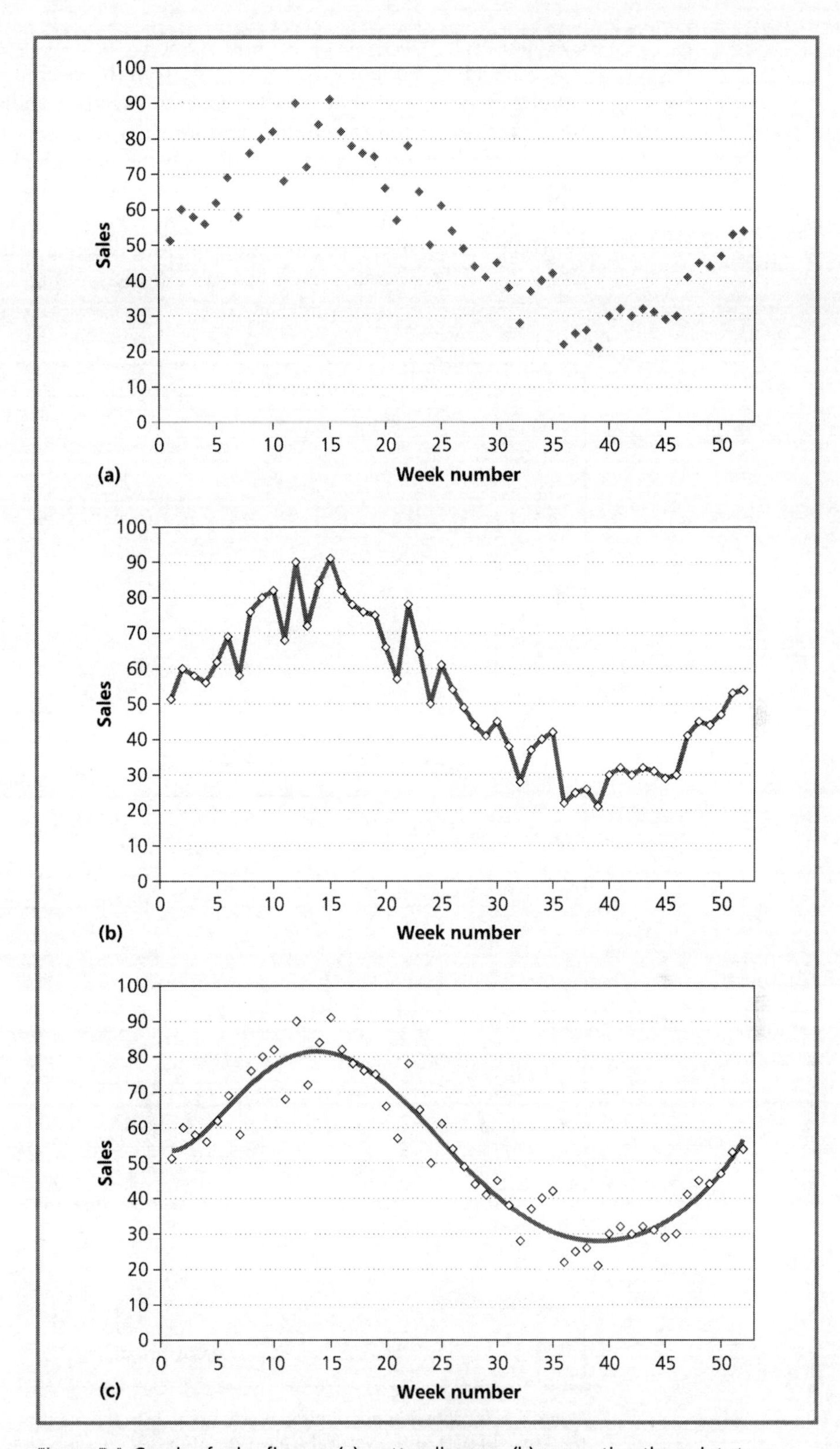

Figure 5.4 Graph of sales figures: (a) scatter diagram, (b) connecting the points to emphasise the pattern, (c) showing the underlying pattern

seasonal cycle, with a peak around week 12 and a trough around week 38. There are small random variations away from this overall pattern, so the graph is not a smooth curve but is rather jagged. We are usually more interested in the underlying patterns than the random variations, so we can emphasise this by drawing a smooth trend line through the individual points, as shown in Figure 5.4(c).

The most common difficulty with graphs is choosing the scale for the y-axis. We could redraw the graphs in Figure 5.4 with different scales for the y-axis, and give completely different views. Figure 5.5(a) has a long scale for the y-axis, so

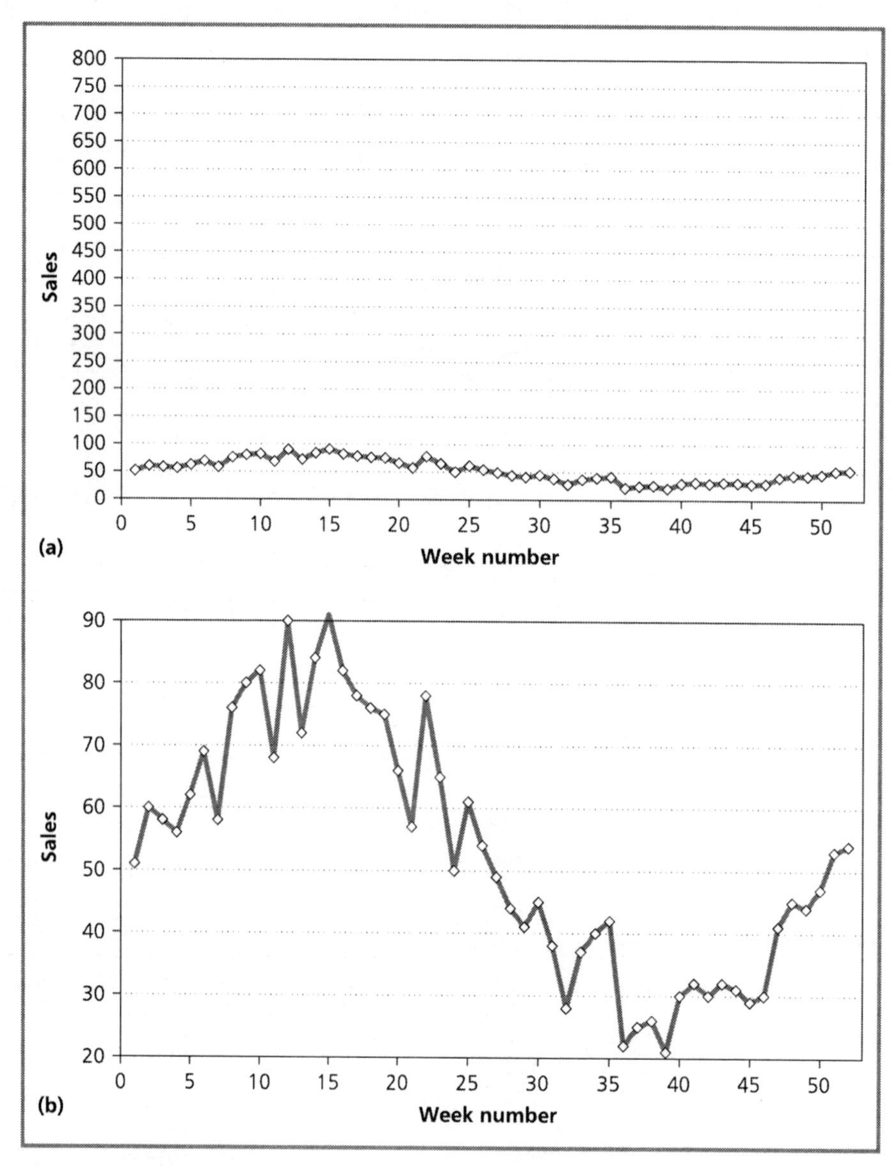

Figure 5.5 (a) Showing poorly drawn graphs: a vertical scale that is too long hides the patterns, (b) part of the vertical scale is omitted, giving a false impression

the graph appears to show stable sales with only small variations; Figure 5.5(b) has a broken scale (omitting values 0 to 20), so the graph suggests high sales in the first half and almost no sales in the second half. Both of these views are misleading.

Graphs have a very strong initial impact, so it is important to choose the right scales, and some guidelines for good practice include the following:

- Always label both axes clearly and accurately
- Show the scales on both axes
- The maximum of the scale should be slightly above the maximum observation
- Wherever possible, the scale on axes should be continuous from zero; if this is too difficult, or hides patterns, show any break clearly in the scale
- Where appropriate, give the source of data
- Where appropriate, give the graph a title.

Drawing several graphs on the same axes makes it easy to compare different sets of data. For example, we can plot the price of electricity, gas, oil and coal on the same axes to see how they have varied over the past year – or we could compare the price of a single commodity over different years. Figure 5.6 shows the average monthly price of a commodity over five years. As the price differences are small, we have highlighted the pattern by plotting only the relevant part of the y-axis.

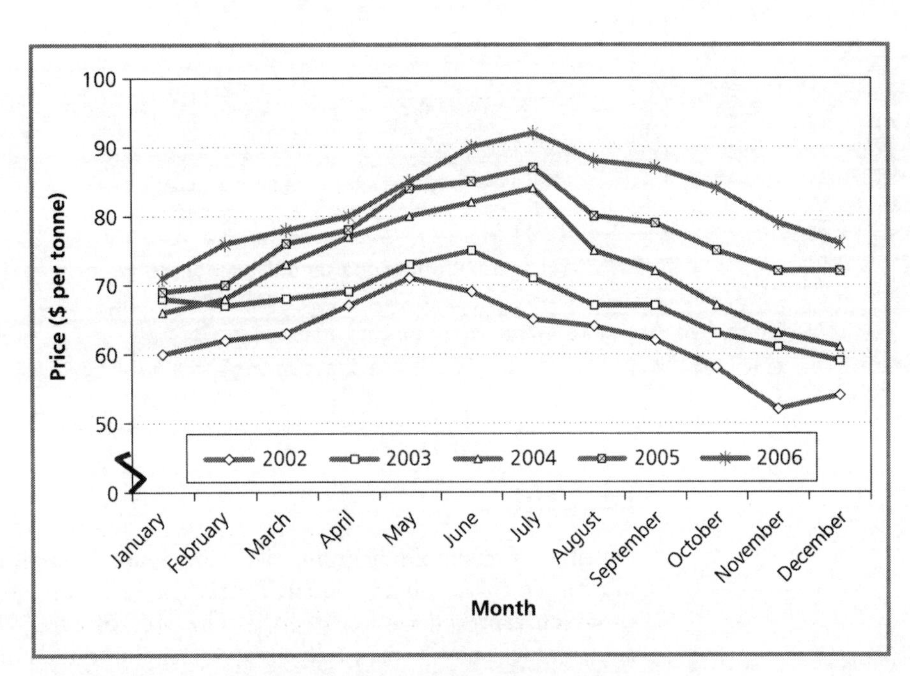

Figure 5.6 Average monthly price of a commodity over five years

WORKED EXAMPLE 5.3

Table 5.5 shows the profit reported by Majestica, Inc. and the corresponding share price. Draw a graph of this data.

Solution

Here there are three variables – quarter, profit and share price – but we can plot only two of these on a graph. There are several options for graphs, such as the variation in share price (or profit) against quarter. The most interesting is the relationship between profit (as the independent variable) and share price (as the dependent variable) shown in Figure 5.7. Here we have chosen the scales to highlight the main areas of interest, and drawn a trend line to suggest the underlying relationship.

Table 5.5 Quarterly company profit and average share price

	Year 1				Year 2				Year 3			
Quarter	1	2	3	4	1	2	3	4	1	2	3	4
Profit	12.1	12.2	11.6	10.8	13.0	13.6	11.9	11.7	14.2	14.5	12.5	13.0
Share price	122	129	89	92	132	135	101	104	154	156	125	136

Source: Company financial reports, New York Stock Exchange and the *Wall Street Journal*.

Note: Profits are in millions of dollars and share prices are in cents.

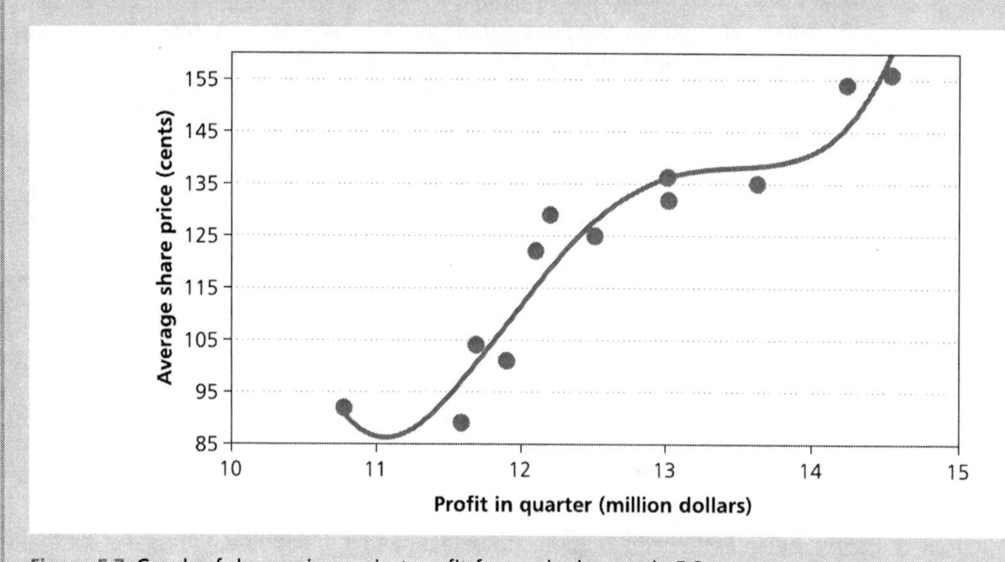

Figure 5.7 Graph of share price against profit for worked example 5.3

Pie charts

Pie charts are simple diagrams that give a summary of categorical data. To draw a pie chart you draw a circle – the pie – and divide this into slices, each of which represents one category. The area of each slice – and hence the angle at the centre of the circle – is proportional to the number of observations in the category.

WORKED EXAMPLE 5.4

Hambro GmbH has operations in four regions of Europe, with annual sales in millions of euros given in the following table. Draw a pie chart to represent these.

Region	North	South	East	West	Total
Sales	25	10	35	45	115

Solution

There are 360° in a circle, and these represent 115 observations. So each observation is represented by an angle of 360/115 = 3.13° at the centre of the circle. Then the sales in the North region are represented by a slice with an angle of 25 × 3.13 = 78.3° at the centre; sales in the South region are represented by a slice with an angle of 10 × 3.13 = 31.3° at the centre, and so on. Figure 5.8(a) shows a basic chart for this data. Of course, you do not really have to do these calculations, as many standard packages draw pie charts automatically. They can also improve the presentation, and Figure 5.8(b) shows the same data when it is sorted into order, rotated to put the biggest slice at the back, labelled and given a three-dimensional effect.

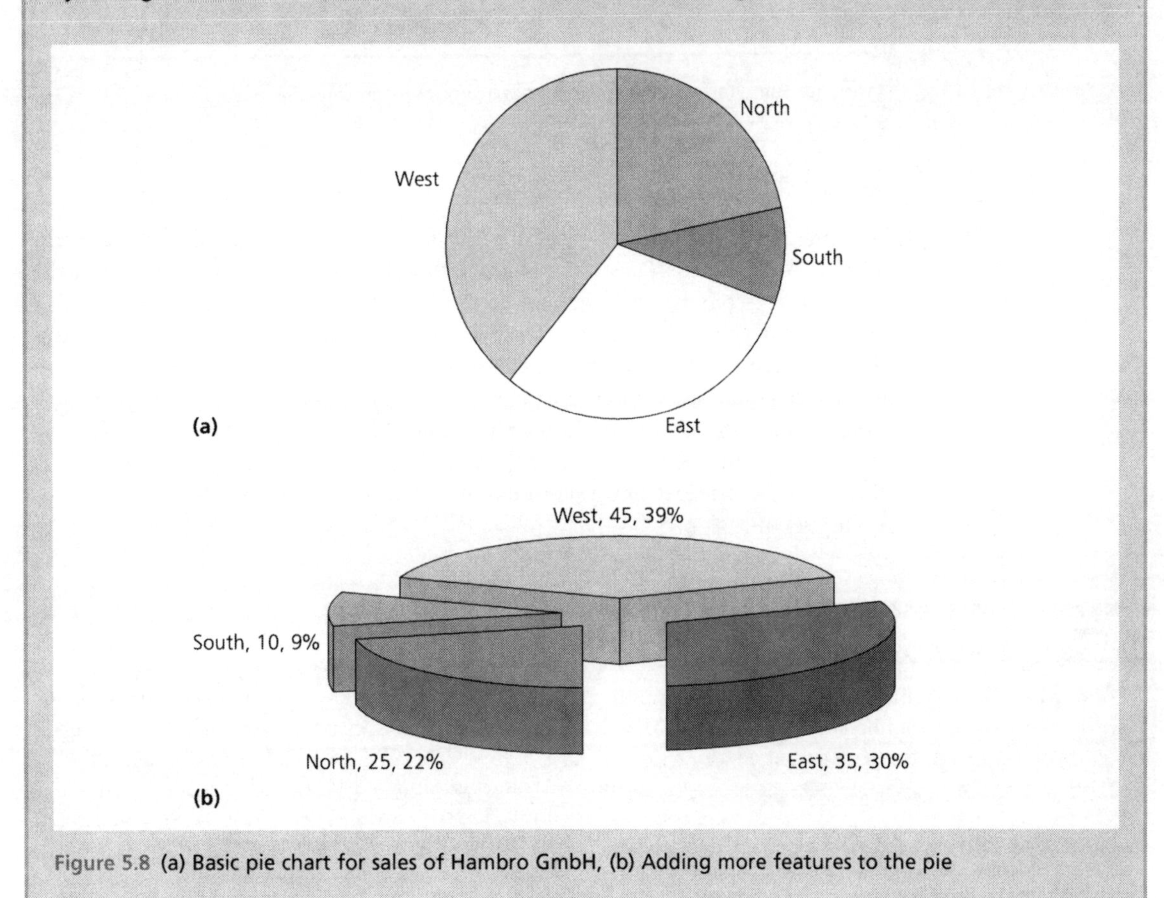

Figure 5.8 (a) Basic pie chart for sales of Hambro GmbH, (b) Adding more features to the pie

Pie charts are very simple and can make an impact, but they show only very small amounts of data. When there are more than, say, six or seven slices they become too complicated and confusing. There is also some concern about whether people really understand data presented in this format or whether it gives a misleading view.[5,6]

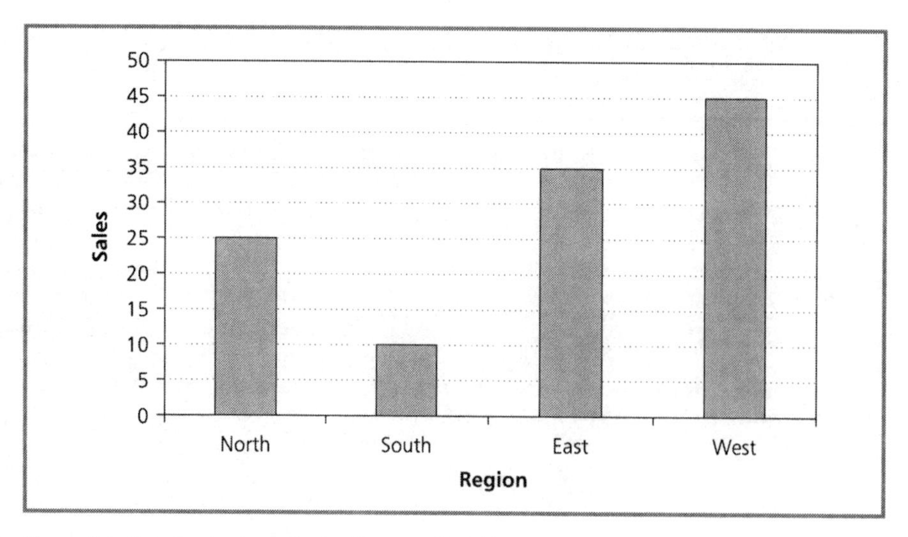

Figure 5.9 Bar chart of results for Hambro GmbH

Bar charts

Like pie charts, bar charts show the number of observations in different categories. But here each category is represented by its own line or bar, and the length of this bar is proportional to the number of observations. Figure 5.9 shows a bar chart for the data from Hambro GmbH given in worked example 5.4. Here the bars are vertical, but they could equally be horizontal and – as with pie charts – we can add many variations to enhance the appearance. One constant rule, though, is that you should always start the scale for the bars at zero, and never be tempted to save space by omitting the lower parts of bars. This is sometimes unavoidable in graphs, but in bar charts the result is simply confusing.

WORKED EXAMPLE 5.5

South Middleton Health District has five hospitals, with the following numbers of beds in each. How could you represent this data in bar charts?

	Hospital				
	Foothills	General	Southern	Heathview	St John
Maternity	24	38	6	0	0
Surgical	86	85	45	30	24
Medical	82	55	30	30	35
Psychiatric	25	22	30	65	76

Solution

There are many possible formats here. One shows the number of surgical beds in each hospital – illustrated in Figure 5.10(a). A particular strength of bar charts is that we can show several sets of data in the same diagram to make direct comparisons. For example, Figure 5.10(b) compares the number of beds of each type in each hospital. If we want to highlight the relative sizes of the hospitals, we could combine the bars by 'stacking' them, as shown in Figure 5.10(c). If we want to emphasise type of beds in each hospital, we could describe the percentages of beds, as shown in Figure 5.10(d).

Worked example 5.5 continued

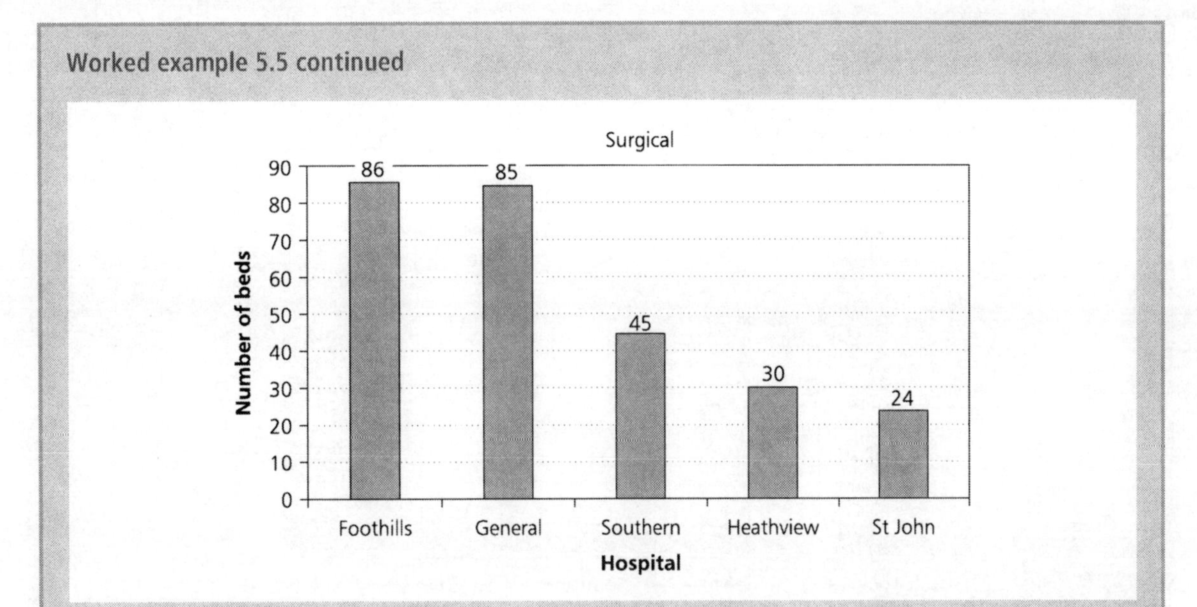

Figure 5.10(a) Bar chart for South Middleton Health District hospitals: number of surgical beds

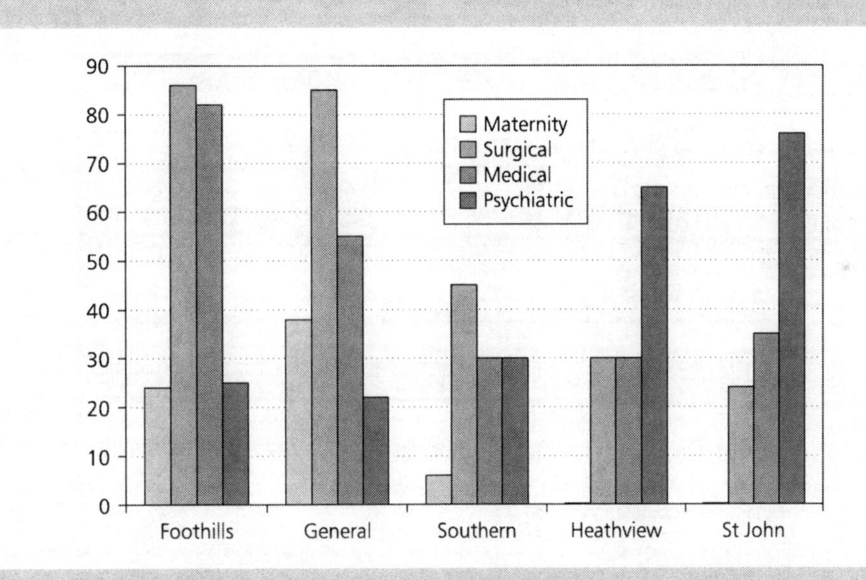

Figure 5.10(b) Comparison of the number of beds in each hospital

Worked example 5.5 continued

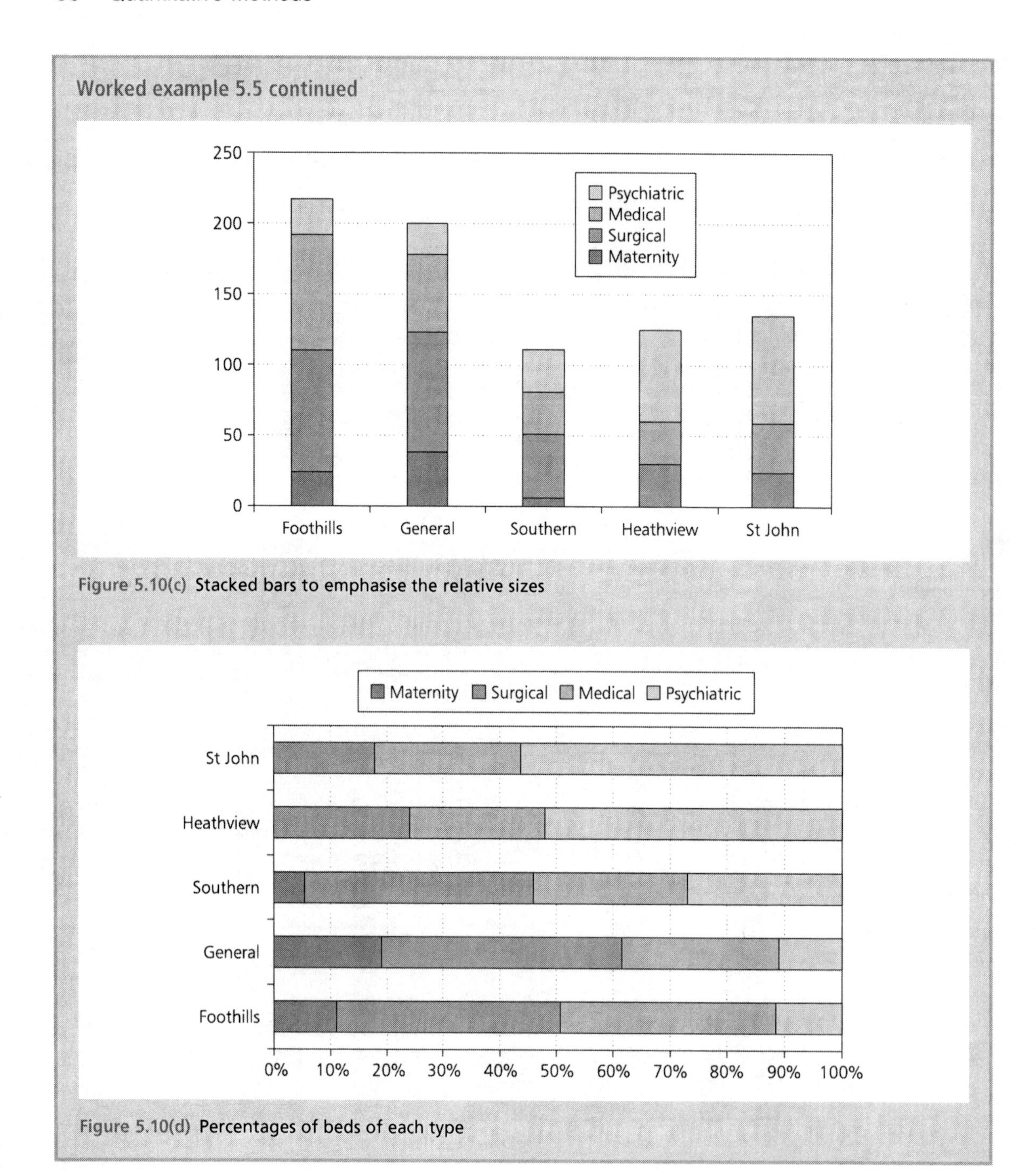

Figure 5.10(c) Stacked bars to emphasise the relative sizes

Figure 5.10(d) Percentages of beds of each type

WORKED EXAMPLE 5.6

Draw a frequency distribution for the following discrete data:

150 141 158 147 132 153 176 162 180 165
174 133 129 119 133 188 190 165 157 146
161 130 122 169 159 152 173 148 154 171
136 155 141 153 147 168 150 140 161 185

Solution

This illustrates one of the main uses of bar charts, which is to show frequency distributions. We start by defining suitable classes. The values range from 119 to 190, so a class width of 10 gives nine classes. As the values are discrete, we can arbitrarily use 110 to 119, 120 to 129, 130 to 139, and so on. Figure 5.11 shows a spreadsheet calculating a frequency distribution, percentage frequency, and cumulative frequencies – and then drawing these in a bar chart.

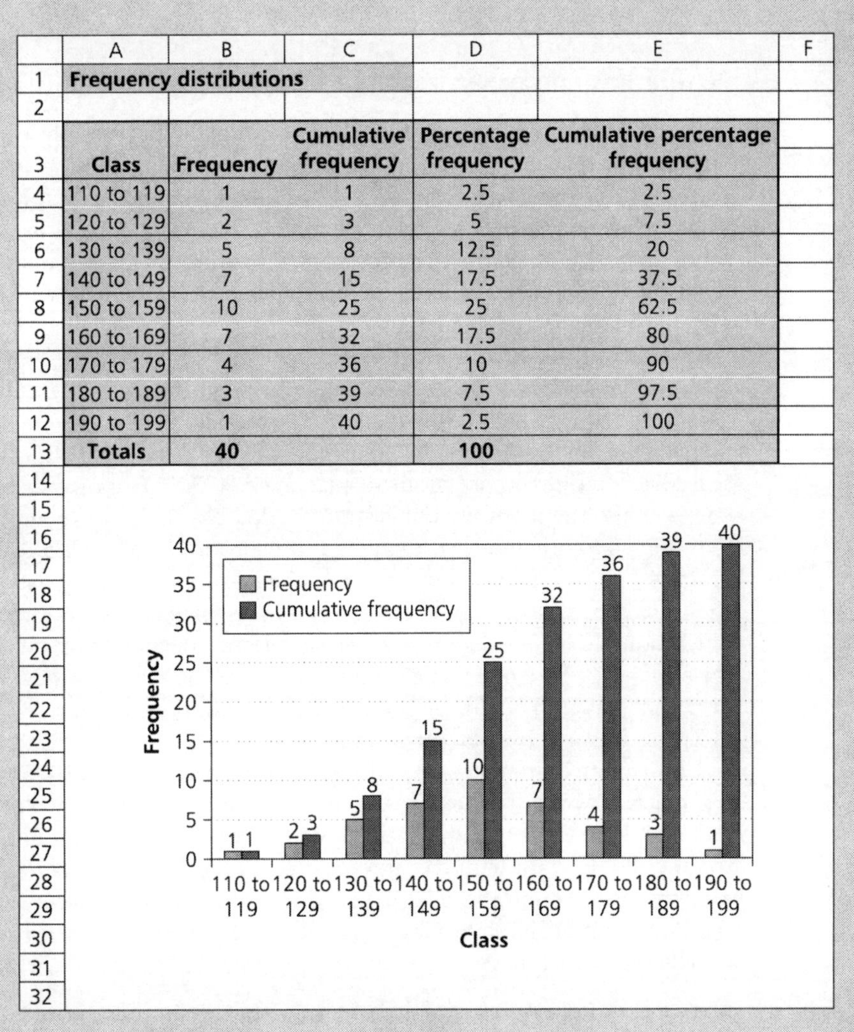

	A	B	C	D	E	F
1	**Frequency distributions**					
2						
3	**Class**	**Frequency**	**Cumulative frequency**	**Percentage frequency**	**Cumulative percentage frequency**	
4	110 to 119	1	1	2.5	2.5	
5	120 to 129	2	3	5	7.5	
6	130 to 139	5	8	12.5	20	
7	140 to 149	7	15	17.5	37.5	
8	150 to 159	10	25	25	62.5	
9	160 to 169	7	32	17.5	80	
10	170 to 179	4	36	10	90	
11	180 to 189	3	39	7.5	97.5	
12	190 to 199	1	40	2.5	100	
13	**Totals**	**40**		**100**		

Figure 5.11 Frequency distribution with a spreadsheet

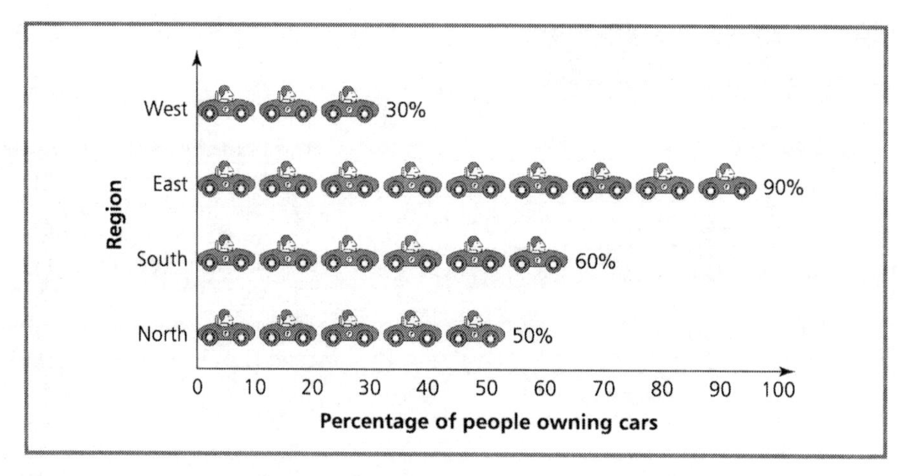

Figure 5.12 Pictogram of percentages of people owning cars in different regions

Pictograms and other images

Basic diagrams can have a considerable impact, but people often want to enhance this by adding even more features. One way of doing this is through pictograms, which are similar to bar charts, except the bars are replaced by sketches of the things being described. For example, Figure 5.12 shows the percentage of people owning cars in different regions by a pictogram. Instead of plain bars, we have used pictures of cars, each of which represents 10% of people.

Pictograms are very eye-catching and good at conveying general impressions, but they not always accurate. An obvious problem comes with fractional values: if 53% of people owned cars in one region of Figure 5.12, a line of 5.3 cars would be neither clear not particularly attractive (although it would still give the right impression of 'just over 50%'). A more serious problem comes when the pictures, images and added effects become more important than the charts themselves. Imagine a mushroom farmer who uses the pictogram in Figure 5.13 to show that sales have doubled in the past year. Rather than draw a row of small mushrooms, the farmer uses sketches of single mushrooms. The problem is that we should be concentrating on the height of the sketches, where one is quite rightly twice as high as the other – but it is the area that has immediate impact, and doubling the number of observations increases the area by a factor of four.

Unfortunately, the meaning of many diagrams is hidden by poor design or too much artwork. The unnecessary decoration is sometimes called 'chartjunk' and people refer to the 'ink ratio' – which compares the amount of ink used to describe the data with the amount used in decoration. Remember that the aim of data presentation is not to draw the prettiest picture, but to give the best view of the data. Some useful guidelines for this refer to 'graphical excellence'[6] which has:

- a well-designed presentation of data that combines significant content, statistical description, and design
- clarity, giving results that are easy to understand

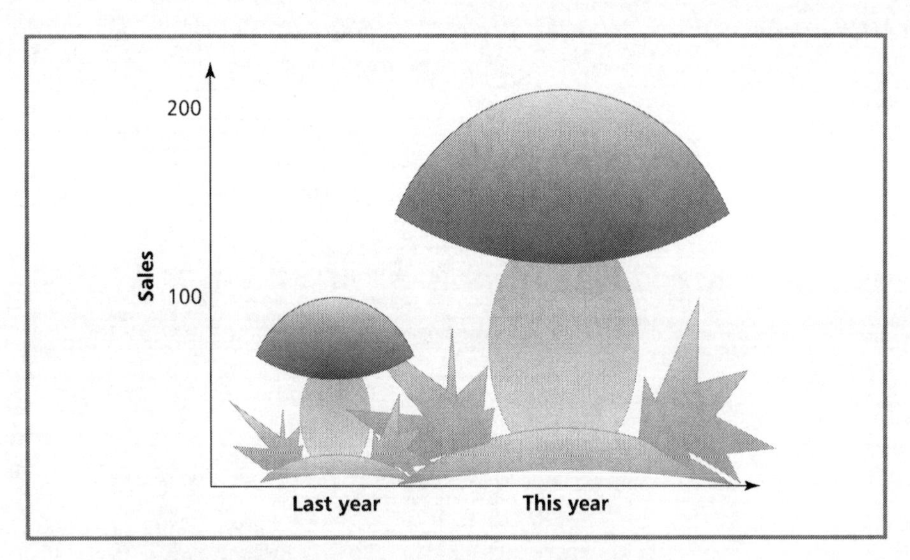

Figure 5.13 Misleading pictogram of increasing mushroom sales

- efficiency, with a precise presentation transmitting the largest number of ideas in the shortest possible time
- accuracy, giving a fair and honest representation of the data.

Review questions

5.9 You should always try to find the best diagram for presenting data. Do you think this is true?

5.10 Why must you label the axes of graphs?

5.11 'There is only one bar chart that accurately describes a set of data.' Is this true?

5.12 If you wanted to make an impact with some data, what format would you consider?

5.13 What are the problems with pictograms?

5.14 Give some examples of diagrams where the added artwork has hidden or distorted the results.

Continuous data

Bar charts are easy to use for discrete data, but with continuous data we have already mentioned the messiness of defining classes as '20 units or more and less than 30 units'. This affects the way we draw frequency distributions of continuous data – and it is sometimes easier to use histograms.

Histograms

Histograms are frequency distributions for continuous data. They look similar to bar charts, but there are important differences. The most important is that histograms are used only for continuous data, so the classes are joined and form a continuous scale. When we draw bars on this scale, their width – as well as

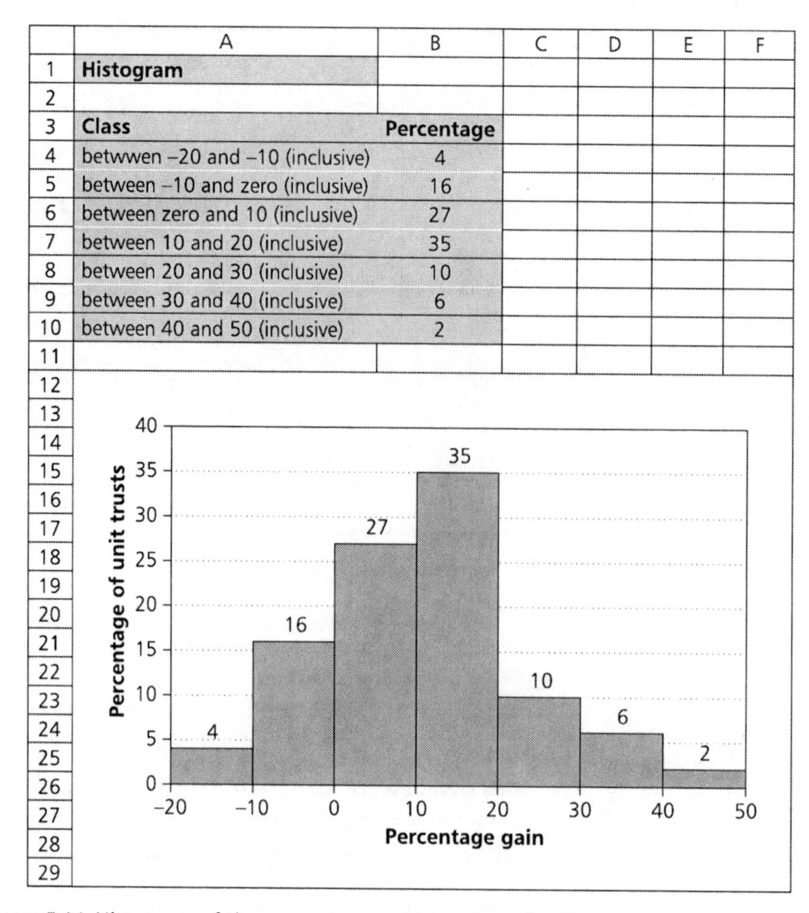

	A	B	C	D	E	F
1	**Histogram**					
2						
3	**Class**	**Percentage**				
4	betwwen −20 and −10 (inclusive)	4				
5	between −10 and zero (inclusive)	16				
6	between zero and 10 (inclusive)	27				
7	between 10 and 20 (inclusive)	35				
8	between 20 and 30 (inclusive)	10				
9	between 30 and 40 (inclusive)	6				
10	between 40 and 50 (inclusive)	2				
11						

Figure 5.14 Histogram of the percentage gain in value of unit trusts

their length – has a definite meaning. The width shows the class size, and the area of the bar shows the frequency.

Figure 5.14 shows a frequency distribution for the percentage gain in value of certain unit trusts over the past five years, and the associated histogram. Here there is a continuous scale along the x-axis for the percentage gain, and each class is the same width, so both the heights of the bars and their areas represent the frequencies.

WORKED EXAMPLE 5.7

Draw a histogram of the following continuous data.

Class	Frequency
Less than 10	8
10 or more, and less than 20	10
20 or more, and less than 30	16
30 or more, and less than 40	15
40 or more, and less than 50	11
50 or more, and less than 60	4
60 or more, and less than 70	2
70 or more, and less than 80	1
80 or more, and less than 90	1

Worked example 5.7 continued

Solution

Figure 5.15(a) shows this distribution as a histogram. This has a rather long tail with only eight observations in the last four classes, and you might be tempted to combine these into one class with eight observations. But you have to be careful here. You cannot change the scale of the *x*-axis as it is continuous, so the single last class will be four times as wide as the other classes. Then you have to remember that histograms use the area of the bar to represent the frequency, and not the height. So you want to show eight observations in an area four units wide – which means that it must be two units high, as shown in Figure 5.15(b). This gives the histogram an even more extended tail.

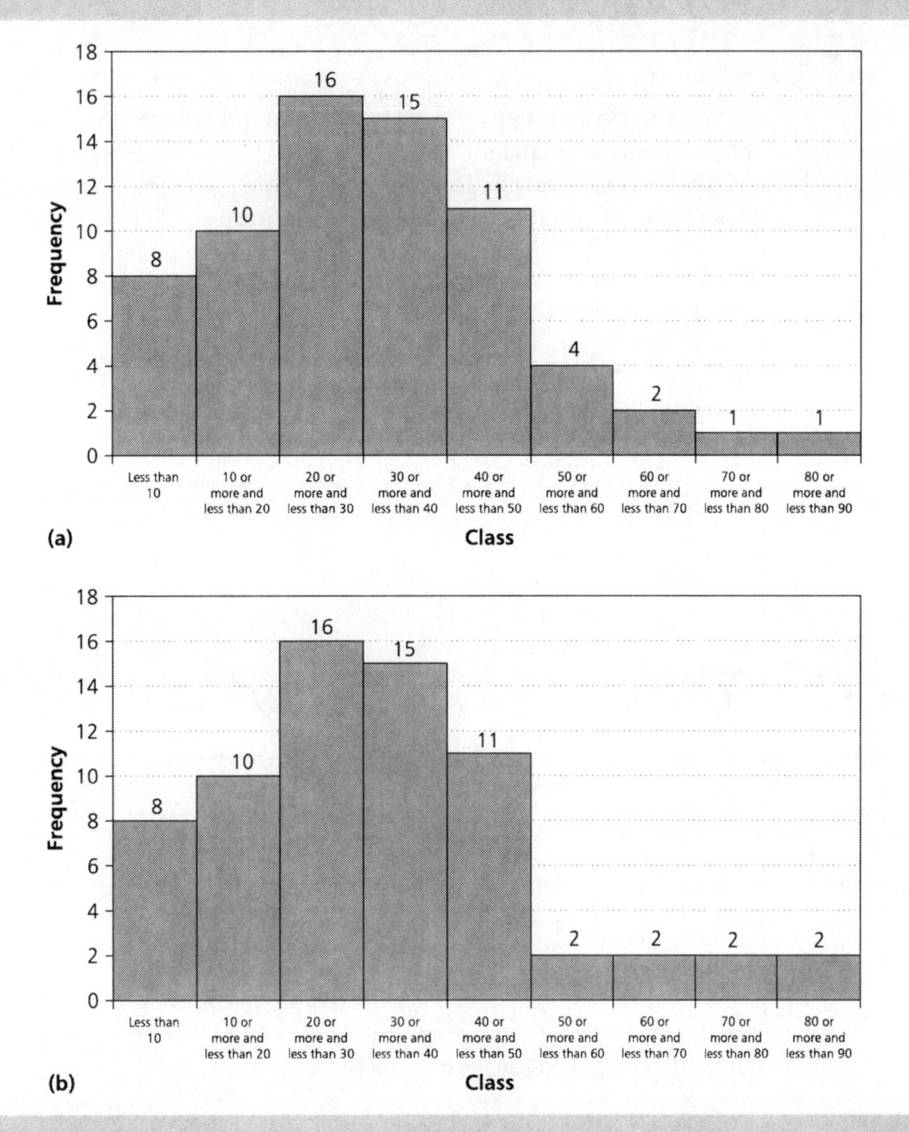

Figure 5.15 (a) Histogram for worked example 5.7 with nine classes, (b) the last four classes combined into one

You can see from the last example that you have to be careful when drawing histograms. A consistent problem is that the shape of a histogram depends on the way that you define classes. Another problem comes with open-ended classes, where there is no obvious way of dealing with a class like 'greater than 20'. One answer is to avoid such definitions wherever possible. Another is to make assumptions about limits, so that we might reasonably interpret 'greater than 20' as 'greater than 20 and less than 24'.

It can be difficult to draw histograms properly – and many people do not realise that they are different from bar charts. Although bar charts might be less precise, they often give better-looking results with less effort – so some people suggest sticking to bar charts.

Ogive

An ogive is a graph that shows the relationship between class (on the x-axis) and cumulative frequency (on the y-axis) for continuous data. With the cumulative frequency distribution in the following table, you can start drawing an ogive by plotting the point (100, 12) to show that 12 observations are in the class '100 or less'. Then you can plot the point (150, 38) which shows that 38 observations are 150 or less; then the point (200, 104) shows that 104 observations are 200 or less, then (250, 207), and so on. Plotting all of these points and joining them gives the result shown in Figure 5.16. Ogives are always drawn vertically, and they have this characteristic elongated 'S'-shape.

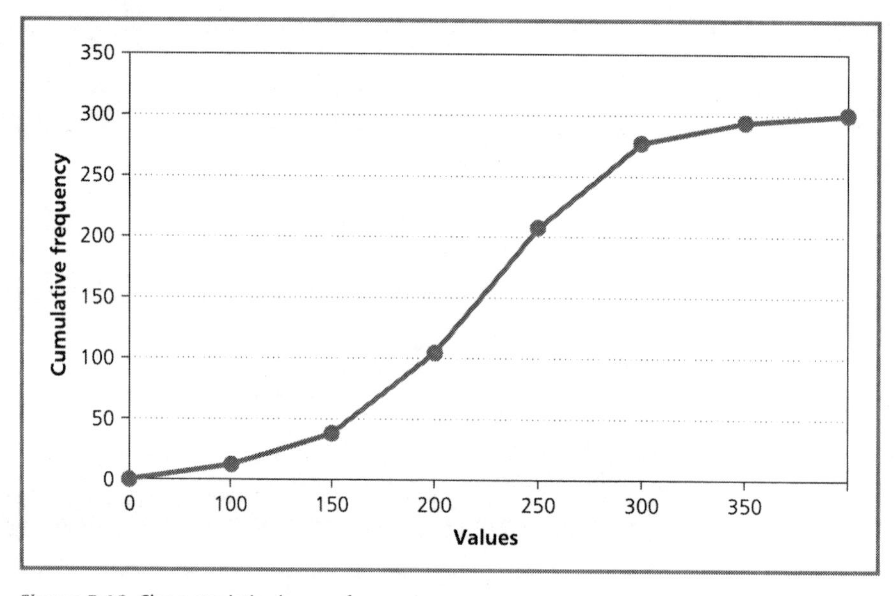

Figure 5.16 Characteristic shape of an ogive

Class	Frequency	Cumulative frequency
100 or less	12	12
More than 100 and less than or equal to 150	26	38
More than 150 and less than or equal to 200	66	104
More than 200 and less than or equal to 250	103	207
More than 250 and less than or equal to 300	70	277
More than 300 and less than or equal to 350	17	294
More than 350 and less than or equal to 400	6	300

A Lorenz curve is an extension of the ogive that is used in economics to show the distribution of income or wealth among a population. It is a graph of cumulative percentage wealth, income or some other measure of wealth, against cumulative percentage of the population. Because a few people have most of the wealth, this is not a standard 'S'-shape, as you can see in the following example.

WORKED EXAMPLE 5.8

Tax offices in Chu Nang County calculate the following percentages of total wealth – before and after tax – owned by various percentages of the population. Draw a Lorenz curve of this data.

Percentage of population	Percentage of wealth before tax	Percentage of wealth after tax
45	5	15
20	10	15
15	12	15
10	13	15
5	15	15
3	25	15
2	20	10

Solution

A Lorenz curve shows the cumulative percentage of wealth against the cumulative percentage of population. Figure 5.17 shows these calculations in a spreadsheet, followed by the Lorenz curves. Starting with a graph of the cumulative percentage of wealth before tax, the first point is (45, 5), followed by (65, 15), (80, 27), and so on. Similarly, with a graph of the cumulative percentage of wealth after tax, the first point is (45, 15), followed by (65, 30), (80, 45) and so on.

If the distribution of wealth is perfectly equitable, a Lorenz curve would be a straight line connecting the origin to the point (100, 100). If the graph is significantly below this, the distribution of wealth is unequal, and the further from the straight line the less equitable is the distribution. Here the Lorenz curve for after-tax wealth is considerably closer to the diagonal, and this shows that taxes have had an effect in redistributing wealth.

Worked example 5.8 continued

	A	B	C	D	E	F
1	Lorenz curves					
2						
3	Percentage of population	Cumulative percentage of populaton	Percentage of wealth before tax	Cumulative percentage of wealth before tax	Percentage of wealth after tax	Cumulative percentage of wealth after tax
4	0	0	0	0	0	0
5	45	45	5	5	15	15
6	20	65	10	15	15	30
7	15	80	12	27	15	45
8	10	90	13	40	15	60
9	5	95	15	55	15	75
10	3	98	25	80	15	90
11	2	100	20	100	10	100

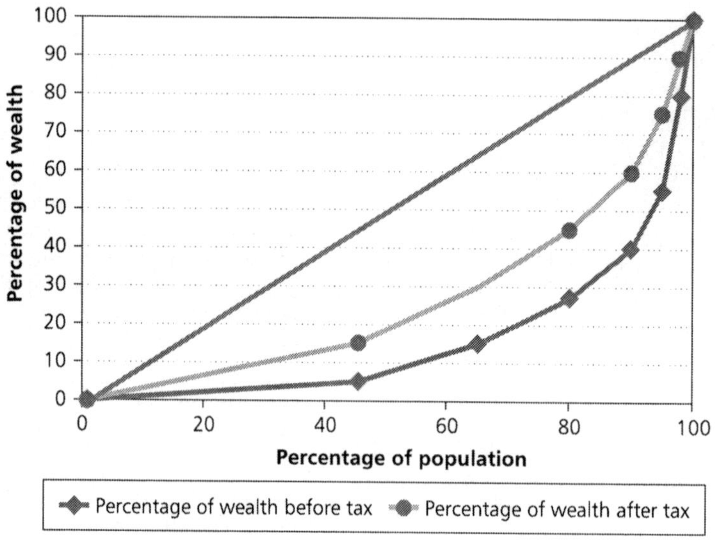

Figure 5.17 Lorenz curves before and after tax

Review questions

5.15 'In bar charts and histograms the height of the bar shows the number of observations in each class.' Is this true?

5.16 If two classes of equal width are combined into one for a histogram, how high is the resulting bar?

5.17 Why would you draw histograms when bar charts are easier and can have more impact?

5.18 What is the purpose of an ogive?

5.19 'A fair Lorenz curve should be a straight line connecting points (0, 0) and (100, 100).' Do you think this is true?

IDEAS IN PRACTICE Software for drawing diagrams

There is a lot of software for drawing diagrams, ranging from simple programs that come free with computer magazines to specialised graphics packages used by commercial artists. We mentioned some of these in Chapter 3, and can again mention ConceptDraw, CorelDraw, DrawPlus, Freelance Graphics, Harvard Graphics, PowerPoint, Sigmaplot, SmartDraw, Visio, and so on.

Other standard packages include drawing functions – particularly spreadsheets. Excel has a 'chart wizard' that easily turns spreadsheets into diagrams. Figure 5.18 shows some of the formats it offers.

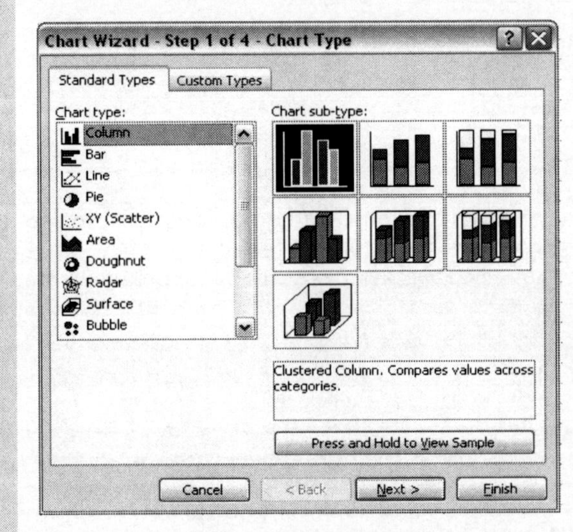

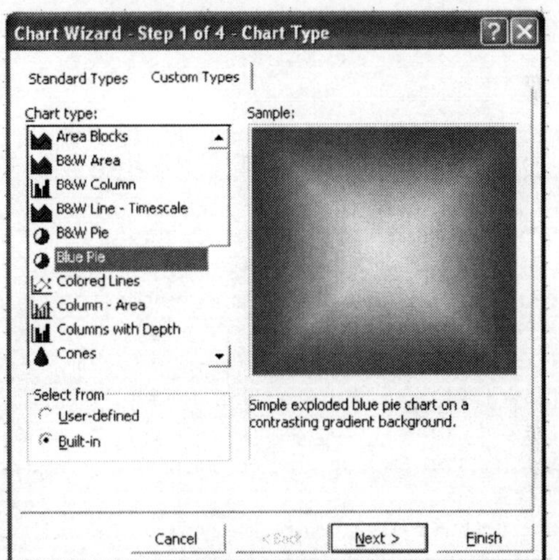

Figure 5.18 Some chart formats offered in Excel

CHAPTER REVIEW

This chapter showed how to summarise data in different types of diagrams.

- After collecting data, you have to process it into useful information. This starts with data reduction to remove the details and focus on the underlying patterns. Data presentation then shows the results in the best format. In practice, there is no clear distinction between these two.

- Diagrams can have a considerable impact, but you have to design them carefully to give an accurate and fair view. There are many types of diagram, and the choice is often a matter of personal preference.
- Tables are the most widely used method of summarising numerical data. They can show a lot of information and be tailored to specific needs. They are particularly useful for showing frequency distributions, which describe the number of observations in different classes. Associated calculations show percentage frequency distributions and cumulative distributions.
- Graphs show relationships between two variables, and highlight the underlying patterns.
- Pie charts describe categorical data, representing the relative frequency of observations by the sectors of a circle. Bar charts give more flexible presentations for categorical data, with the length of each bar proportional to the number of observations in the category. Bar charts can be drawn as pictograms, but you have to be careful not to divert attention away from, or obscure, the important figures.
- Histograms are often confused with bar charts, but they show frequency distributions for continuous data and represent the frequency by the area of a bar. These can be extended to show ogives and Lorenz curves.

CASE STUDY High Acclaim Trading

High Acclaim Trading is based in Delhi, from where it has rapidly increased international operations in recent years. A group of influential shareholders recently asked the finance director to review this international business. In turn, he asked Hari Chandrasan from the audit department to collect some data from company records for his presentation, stressing that he wanted to make an impact with his talk.

At first Hari was worried by the amount of detail available. The company seemed to keep enormous amounts of data on all aspects of its operations. This ranged from transaction records for the movement of virtually every product handled by the company, to subjective management views that nobody ever formally recorded. Often, there seemed no reason for keeping the data and it was rarely summarised or analysed.

Hari did a conscientious job of collecting and summarising data and felt that he had made considerable progress when he approached the finance director and handed over the results in the following table. He explained that 'This table shows some of our most important trading results. We trade in four main regions, and I have recorded eight key facts about the movements between them. Each element in the table shows the number of units shipped (in hundreds), the average income per unit (in dollars), the percentage gross profit, the percentage return on investment, a measure (between 1 and 5) of trading difficulty, potential for growth (again on a scale of 1 to 5), the number of finance administrators employed in each area, and the number of agents. I think this gives a good summary of our operations, and should give a useful focus for your presentation.'

Case study continued

		To			
		Africa	America	Asia	Europe
From	Africa	105, 45, 12, 4, 4, 1, 15, 4	85, 75, 14, 7, 3, 2, 20, 3	25, 60, 15, 8, 3, 2, 12, 2	160, 80, 13, 7, 2, 2, 25, 4
	America	45, 75, 12, 3, 4, 1, 15, 3	255, 120, 15, 9, 1, 3, 45, 5	60, 95, 8, 2, 2, 3, 35, 6	345, 115, 10, 7, 1, 4, 65, 5
	Asia	85, 70, 8, 4, 5, 2, 20, 4	334, 145, 10, 5, 2, 4, 55, 6	265, 85, 8, 3, 2, 4, 65, 7	405, 125, 8, 3, 2, 5, 70, 8
	Europe	100, 80, 10, 5, 4, 2, 30, 3	425, 120, 12, 8, 1, 4, 70, 7	380, 105, 9, 4, 2, 3, 45, 5	555, 140, 10, 6, 4, 1, 10, 8

The finance director looked at the figures for a few minutes and then asked for some details on how trade had changed over the past 10 years. Hari replied that in general terms the volume of trade had risen by 1.5, 3, 2.5, 2.5, 1, 1, 2.5, 3.5, 3 and 2.5% respectively in each of the last 10 years, while the average price had risen by 4, 4.5, 5.5, 7, 3.5, 4.5, 6, 5.5, 5 and 5% respectively.

The finance director looked up from the figures and said, 'To be honest I had hoped for something with a bit more impact. Could you work these into something more forceful within the next couple of days?'

Question

- **If you were Hari Chandrasan how would you put the figures into a suitable format for the presentation?**

PROBLEMS

5.1 Find some recent trade statistics published by the government and present these in different ways to emphasise different features. Discuss which formats are fairest and which are most misleading.

5.2 A question in a survey gets the answer 'Yes' from 47% of men and 38% of women, 'No' from 32% of men and 53% of women, and 'Do not know' from the remainder. How could you present this effectively?

5.3 The number of students taking a course in the past 10 years is summarised in the following table. Use a selection of graphical methods to summarise this data. Which do you think is the best?

Year	1	2	3	4	5	6	7	8	9	10
Male	21	22	20	18	28	26	29	30	32	29
Female	4	6	3	5	12	16	14	19	17	25

5.4 The following table shows the quarterly profit in millions of dollars reported by the Lebal Corporation, and the corresponding closing share quoted in cents on the Toronto Stock Exchange. Design suitable formats for presenting this data.

	Year 1				Year 2				Year 3			
Quarter	1	2	3	4	1	2	3	4	1	2	3	4
Profit	36	45	56	55	48	55	62	68	65	65	69	74
Share price	137	145	160	162	160	163	166	172	165	170	175	182

5.5 The following table shows the number of people employed by Testel Electronics over the past 10 years. How can you present this data?

Year	1	2	3	4	5	6	7	8	9	10
Number	24	27	29	34	38	42	46	51	60	67

5.6 Four regions of Yorkshire classify companies according to primary, manufacturing, transport, retail and service. The number of companies operating in each region in each category is shown in the following table. Show these figures in a number of different bar charts.

	Industry type				
	Primary	Manufacturing	Transport	Retail	Service
Daleside	143	38	10	87	46
Twendale	134	89	15	73	39
Underhill	72	67	11	165	55
Perithorp	54	41	23	287	89

5.7 Jefferson Chang recorded the average wages of 45 people as follows:

221 254 83 320 367 450 292 161 216 410
380 355 502 144 362 112 387 324 576 156
295 77 391 324 126 154 94 350 239 263
276 232 467 413 472 361 132 429 310 272
408 480 253 338 217

Draw a frequency table, histogram, percentage frequency and cumulative frequency table of this data.

5.8 Draw a histogram of the following data.

Class	Frequency
Less than 100	120
100 or more, and less than 200	185
200 or more, and less than 300	285
300 or more, and less than 400	260
400 or more, and less than 500	205
500 or more, and less than 600	150
600 or more, and less than 700	75
700 or more, and less than 800	35
800 or more, and less than 900	15

5.9 Draw an ogive of the data in Problem 5.8.

5.10 The wealth of a population is described in the following frequency distribution. Draw Lorenz curves and other diagrams to represent this data.

Percentage of people	5	10	15	20	20	15	10	5
Percentage of wealth before tax	1	3	6	15	20	20	15	20
Percentage of wealth after tax	3	6	10	16	20	20	10	15

5.11 The following table shows last year's total production and profits (in consistent units) from six factories. Use a graphics package to explore the ways that you can present this data.

Factory	A	B	C	D	E	F
Production	125	53	227	36	215	163
Profit	202	93	501	57	413	296

RESEARCH PROJECTS

5.1 Do a small survey of graphics packages and find one that you prefer. Why do you find this better than the others? Explore the different formats that it can produce for diagrams. Compare this with Excel, which has 30 chart types and many variations.

5.2 Jan Schwartzkopf has collected the following set of data. Explore ways of reducing, manipulating and presenting this data in diagrams.

245 487 123 012 159 751 222 035 487 655
197 655 458 766 123 453 493 444 123 537
254 514 324 215 367 557 330 204 506 804
941 354 226 870 652 458 425 248 560 510
234 542 671 874 710 702 701 540 360 654
323 410 405 531 489 695 409 375 521 624
357 678 809 901 567 481 246 027 310 679
548 227 150 600 845 521 777 304 286 220
667 111 485 266 472 700 705 466 591 398
367 331 458 466 571 489 257 100 874 577
037 682 395 421 233 577 802 190 721 320
444 690 511 103 242 386 400 532 621 144

5.3 Governments collect huge amounts of data and present it in long series of tables. Find some figures for transport over the past 20 years and present these in useful formats. Prepare a presentation of your findings suitable for transport managers, general business people and government transport planners.

Sources of information

References

1 Huff D., *How to Lie with Statistics*, Victor Gollancz, New York, 1954.

2 Kimble G.A., *How to Use (and Misuse) Statistics*, Prentice Hall, Englewood Cliffs, NJ, 1978.

3 Wainer H., How to display data badly, *The American Statistician*, volume 38, pages 137–147, May 1984.

4 Wainer H., *Visual Revelations*, Copernicus/Springer-Verlag, New York, 1997.

5 Cleveland W.S. and McGill R., Graphical perception; theory, experimentation and application to the development of graphical methods, *Journal of the American Statistical Association*, volume 79, pages 531–554, 1984.

6 Tufte E.R., *The Visual Display of Quantitative Information* (2nd edition), Graphics Press, Cheshire, CT, 2001.

Further reading

Most of the books on mathematics mentioned at the end of Chapter 2 also refer to graphs. Some other books include:

Chapman M. and Wykes C., *Plain Figures* (2nd edition), HMSO, London, 1996.

Few S., *Show Me the Numbers*, Analytics Press, Oakland, CA, 2004.

Harris R.L., *Information Graphics*, Oxford University Press, Oxford, 1999.

Hyggett R., *Graphs and Charts*, Palgrave Macmillan, Basingstoke, 1990.

Koomey J.G., *Turning Numbers into Knowledge*, Analytics Press, Oakland, CA, 2004.

Robbins N.B., *Creating More Effective Graphs*, John Wiley, Chichester, 2005.

Tufte E.R., *The Visual Display of Quantitative Information*, Graphics Press, Cheshire, CT, 1997.

CHAPTER 6

Using numbers to describe data

Contents

Chapter outline

The amount of detail in raw data obscures the underlying patterns. We use data reduction and presentation to clear away the detail and highlight the important features. There are two ways of doing this. The last chapter described diagrams for summarising data; in this chapter we continue the theme by looking at numerical descriptions. The most important of these describe the average and spread.

After finishing this chapter you should be able to:

- Appreciate the need for numerical measures of data
- Understand measures of location
- Find the arithmetic mean, median and mode of data
- Understand measures of data spread
- Find the range and quartile deviation of data
- Calculate mean absolute deviations, variances and standard deviations
- Use coefficients of variation and skewness.

Measuring data

We are usually more interested in the overall patterns in data rather than the minute detail, so we use data reduction and presentation to get summaries. The last chapter described some diagrams for this. They can have considerable impact, but they are better at giving overall impressions and a 'feel' for the data rather than objective measures. We really need some objective ways of describing and summarising data – and for this we need numerical measures.

Location and spread

Suppose that you have the following set of data, perhaps for weekly sales:

32 33 36 38 37 35 35 34 33 35 34 36 35 34 36 35 37 34 35 33

There are 20 values here, but what measures can you use to describe the data and differentiate it from the following set?

2 8 21 10 17 24 18 12 1 16 12 3 7 8 9 10 9 21 19 6

You could start by drawing frequency distributions, shown in Figure 6.1.

Each set of data has 20 values, but there are two clear differences:

- The second set is lower than the first set, with values centred around 12 rather than 35.
- The second set is more spread out than the first set, ranging from 1 to 24 rather than 32 to 38.

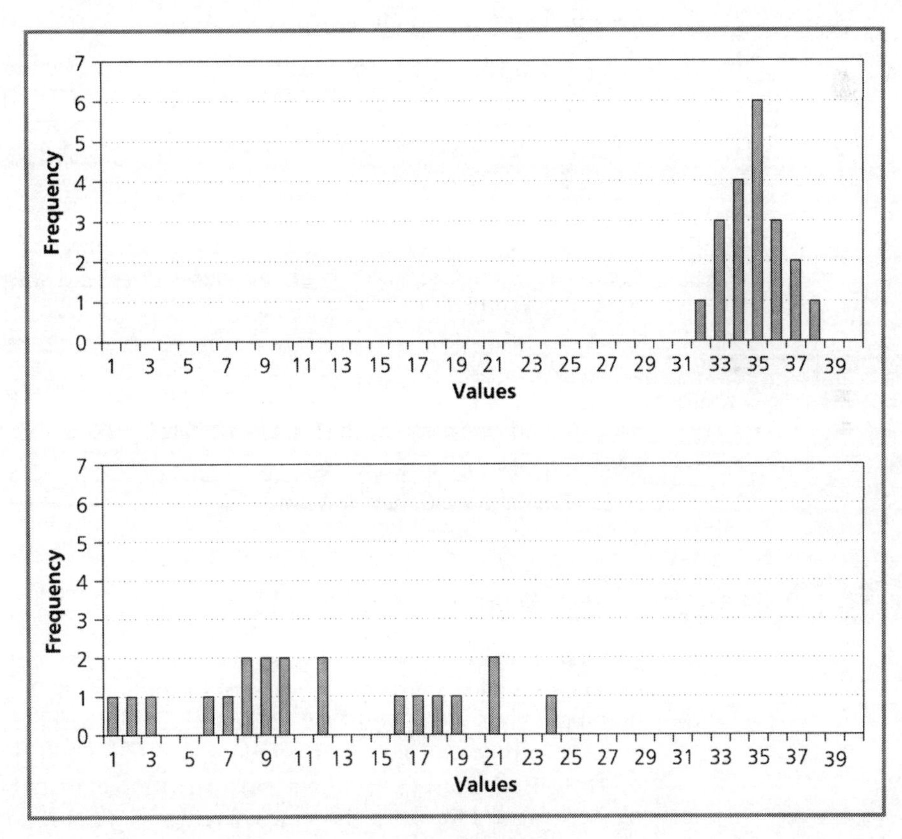

Figure 6.1 Frequency distributions for two sets of data

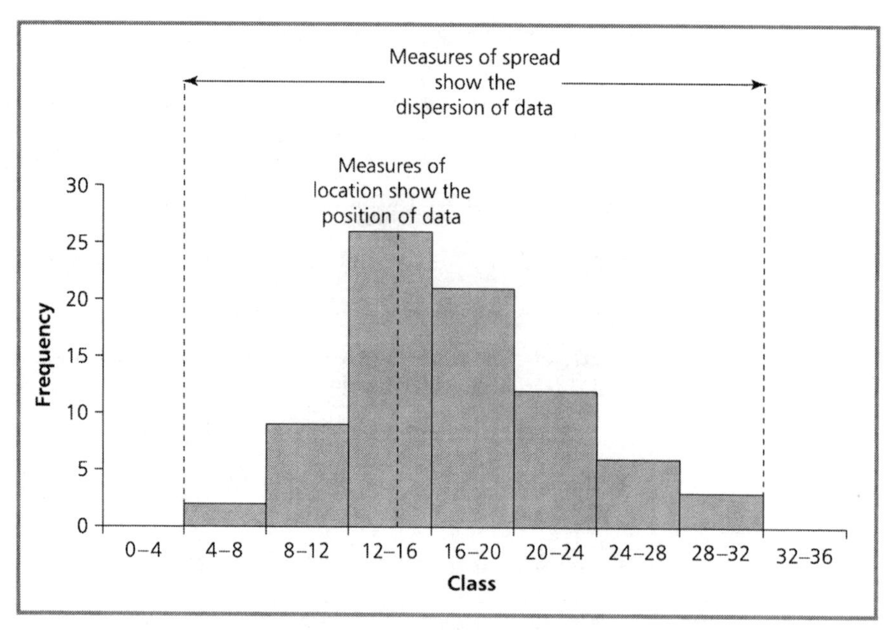

Figure 6.2 Describing the location and spread of data

This suggests two useful measures for data:

- a measure of location to show where the centre of the data is, giving some kind of typical or average value
- a measure of spread to show how spread out the data is around this centre, giving an idea of the range of values.

In a bar chart or histogram, like Figure 6.2, measures of location show where the data lies on the x-axis, while measures of spread show how dispersed the data is along the axis.

Review questions

6.1 What is the main weakness of using diagrams to describe data?

6.2 What do we mean by the location of data?

6.3 'You need to measure only location and spread to get a complete description of data.' Do you think this is true?

Measures of location

Most people are happy to use an average as a typical value – and this is certainly the most common measure of location. If the average age of students in a night class is 45, you have some feel for what the class looks like; if the average income of a group of people is £140,000 a year, you know they are prosperous; if houses in a village have an average of six bedrooms, you know they are large. However, the simple average can be misleading. For example, the group of people with an average income of £140,000 a year might consist of 10 people, nine of whom have an income of £20,000 a year and one of whom has an income of £1,220,000. The village where houses have an average of six bedrooms might have 99 houses with two bedrooms each, and a stately home with 402 bedrooms. In both of these examples the quoted average is accurate, but it does not represent a typical value or give any real feeling for the data. To get around this problem, we can define different types of average, the three most important alternatives being:

- arithmetic mean, or simple average
- median, which is the middle value
- mode, which is the most frequent value.

Arithmetic mean

If you ask a group of people to find the average of 2, 4 and 6, they will usually say 4. This average is the most widely used measure of location. It is technically called the arithmetic mean – usually abbreviated mean (there are other types of mean, but they are rarely used).

To find the mean of a set of values you:

- add all the values together to get the sum
- divide this sum by the number of values to get the mean.

To find the mean of 2, 4 and 6 you add them together to get 2 + 4 + 6 = 12, and then divide this sum by the number of values, 3, to calculate the mean as 12/3 = 4.

At this point we can introduce a notation that uses subscripts to describe these calculations much more efficiently. If we have a set of values, we can call the whole set x, and identify each individual value by a subscript. Then x_1 is the first value, x_2 is the second value, x_3 is the third value, and x_n is the nth value. The advantage of this notation is that we can refer to a general value as x_i. Then when $i = 5$, x_i is x_5. At first sight this might not seem very useful, but in practice it saves a lot of effort. For instance, suppose you have four values, x_1, x_2, x_3 and x_4, and want to add them together. You could write an expression for this:

$$y = x_1 + x_2 + x_3 + x_4$$

Alternatively, you could get the same result by writing:

y = sum of x_i when i = 1, 2, 3 and 4

A standard abbreviation replaces 'the sum of' by the Greek capital letter sigma, Σ. Then we get:

$y = \Sigma x_i$ when i = 1, 2, 3 and 4

And then we put the values of i around the Σ to give the standard form:

$$y = \sum_{i=1}^{4} x_i$$

The 'i = 1' below the Σ gives the name of the variable, i, and the initial value, 1. The '4' above the Σ gives the final value for i. The steps between the initial and final values are always assumed to be 1.

WORKED EXAMPLE 6.1

(a) If you have a set of values, x, how would you describe the sum of the first 10?
(b) How would you describe the sum of values numbered 18 to 35 in a set of data?
(c) If you have the following set of data, p, what is the value of $\sum_{i=4}^{8} p_i$?

5 14 13 6 8 10 3 0 5 1 15 8 0

Solution

(a) We want the sum of x_i when $i = 1$ to 10, which we can write as $\sum_{i=1}^{10} x_i$.
(b) Now we have a set of values, say a, and want the sum of a_i from $i = 18$ to 35. We can write this as $\sum_{i=18}^{35} a_i$.
(c) We want to calculate $p_4 + p_5 + p_6 + p_7 + p_8$. Reading the list of data, p_4 is the fourth number, 6, p_5 is the fifth number, 8, and so on. Then the calculation is $6 + 8 + 10 + 3 + 0 = 27$.

We can use this subscript notation to give a formal definition of the mean of a set of data. For some reason this mean is called $\bar{x}$, which is pronounced 'x bar', and is defined as:

$$\text{mean} = \bar{x} = \frac{x_1 + x_2 + x_3 + \ldots + x_n}{n} = \frac{\sum_{i=1}^{n} x_i}{n} = \frac{\sum x}{n}$$

Notice that we have also used the abbreviation $\sum x$ for the summation. When there can be no misunderstanding, we can replace the rather cumbersome $\sum_{i=1}^{n} x_i$ by the simpler $\sum x$, and assume that the sum includes all values of x_i from $i = 1$ to n. The fuller notation is more precise, but it makes even simple equations appear rather daunting.

WORKED EXAMPLE 6.2

James Wong found the times taken to answer six telephone enquiries as 3, 4, 1, 5, 7 and 1 minutes. What is the mean?

Solution

You find the mean by adding the values, x_i, and dividing by the number of values, n:

$$\text{mean} = \frac{\sum_{i=1}^{n} x_i}{n} = \frac{\sum x}{n}$$

$$= \frac{3 + 4 + 1 + 5 + 7 + 1}{6}$$

$$= \frac{21}{6} = 3.5 \text{ minutes}$$

This example shows that the mean of a set of integers is often not an integer itself – for example, an average family might have 1.7 children. So the mean gives an objective calculation for the location of data, but it obviously does not give a typical result. Another problem, which we saw in the examples at the beginning of the chapter, is that the mean is affected by a few extreme values and can be some distance away from most values. When you hear that the average mark of five students in an exam is 50% you would expect this to represent a typical value – but if the actual marks are 100%, 40%, 40%, 35% and 35%, four results are below the mean and only one is above.

The mean gives the same weight to every value, and although this seems reasonable, it can cause problems. When the three owner/directors of Henderson Associates had to decide how much of their annual profits to retain for future growth, each voted to retain 3%, 7% and 11% of the profits. Initially it seems that a reasonable compromise takes the mean of the three values, which is 7%. However, the three directors actually hold 10, 10 and 1,000 shares respectively, so this result no longer seems fair. The views of the third director should really be given more weight, and we can do this with a weighted mean.

$$\text{weighted mean} = \frac{\sum w_i x_i}{\sum w_i}$$

where: x_i = value i
w_i = weight given to value i.

With Henderson Associates it makes sense to assign weights in proportion to the number of shares each director holds, giving the following result:

$$\text{weighted mean} = \frac{\sum wx}{\sum w} = \frac{10 \times 3 + 10 \times 7 + 1{,}000 \times 11}{10 + 10 + 1{,}000} = 10.88$$

Usually the weights given to each value are not as clear as this, and they need some discussion and agreement. But this negotiation adds subjectivity to the calculations, and we no longer have a purely objective measure. Largely for this reason, the weighted mean is not widely used. However, we can extend its reasoning to estimate the mean of data that has already had some processing – typically with the raw data already summarised in a frequency distribution. Then we have grouped data where we do not know the actual values, but know the number of values in each class. Because we do not have the actual values we cannot find the true mean – but we can get a reasonable approximation by assuming that all values in a class lie at the midpoint of the class. If we have 10 values in a class 20 to 29, we assume that all 10 have the value (20 + 29)/2 = 24.5. Then we calculate the mean in the usual way.

When we have a frequency distribution of n values, there are:

- f_i values in class i, and
- x_i is the midpoint of class i.

Then the sum of all values is $\sum f_i x_i$ (usually abbreviated to $\sum fx$) and the number of values is $\sum f$. Then the mean of grouped data is:

$$\text{mean} = \bar{x} = \frac{\sum fx}{\sum f} = \frac{\sum fx}{n}$$

WORKED EXAMPLE 6.3

Estimate the mean of the data in the following discrete frequency distribution.

Class	1–3	4–6	7–9	10–12	13–15	16–18	19–21	22–24
Frequency	1	4	8	13	9	5	2	1

Solution

Remember that x_i is the midpoint of class i, so x_1 is the midpoint of the first class which is $(1 + 3)/2 = 2$, x_2 is the midpoint of the second class which is $(4 + 6)/2 = 5$, and so on. Figure 6.3 shows a spreadsheet with the calculations. As you can see, $\sum f = 43$ and $\sum fx = 503$. So the estimated mean is $503/43 = 11.7$.

	A	B	C	D	E
1	**Frequency distribution**				
2					
3	**Class**		**Midpoint**	**Frequency**	
4	**From**	**to**	***x***	***f***	***fx***
5	1	3	2	1	2
6	4	6	5	4	20
7	7	9	8	8	64
8	10	12	11	13	143
9	13	15	14	9	126
10	16	18	17	5	85
11	19	21	20	2	40
12	22	24	23	1	23
13	**Totals**			**43**	**503**
14	**Mean**				**11.70**

Figure 6.3 Calculating the arithmetic mean of grouped data

The arithmetic mean usually gives a reasonable measure for location and has the advantages of being:

- objective
- easy to calculate
- familiar and easy to understand
- calculated from all the data
- usually capable of giving a reasonable summary of the data
- useful in a number of other analyses.

However, we have seen that it has weaknesses, as it:

- works only with cardinal data
- is affected by outlying values
- can be some distance from most values
- gives fractional values, even for discrete data
- may not give an accurate view.

We really need some other measures to overcome these weaknesses, and the two most common are the median and mode.

Median

When a set of data is arranged in order of increasing size, the median is defined as the middle value. With five values – 10, 20, 30, 40 and 50 – the median is the middle or third value, which is 30. This does not really need any calculation, but we find it by:

- arranging the values in order of size
- finding the number of values
- identifying the middle value – which is the median.

With n values, the median is value number $(n + 1)/2$ when they are sorted into order. It follows that half the values are smaller than the median, and half are bigger.

WORKED EXAMPLE 6.4

The annualised returns from a set of low-risk bonds over the past four years have been

4.4 5.3 6.1 7.9 5.6 2.9 2.3 3.0 3.3 4.5 2.1 7.1 6.8 5.0 3.6 4.9 5.4

What is the median?

Solution

We start by sorting the data into ascending order:

Position	1	2	3	4	5	6	7	8	9	10	11	12	13	14	15	16	17
Value	2.1	2.3	2.9	3.0	3.3	3.6	4.4	4.5	4.9	5.0	5.3	5.4	5.6	6.1	6.8	7.1	7.9

There are 17 values, so the median is number $(17 + 1)/2 = 9$. This is 4.9, with eight values above it and eight below.

In this last example we deliberately chose an odd number of values, so that we could identify a middle one – but what happens when there is an even number? If the example had one more value of 8.1, then the middle point of the 18 values would be number $(18 + 1)/2 = 9.5$, which is midway between the ninth and tenth. The usual convention is to take the median as the average of these two. The ninth value is 4.9 and the tenth is 5.0, so we describe the median as $(4.9 + 5.0)/2 = 4.95$. Although this gives a value that did not actually occur, it is the best approximation we can get.

When data comes in a frequency distribution, finding the median is a bit more complicated. We start by seeing which class the median is in, and then finding how far up this class it is.

WORKED EXAMPLE 6.5

Find the median of the following continuous frequency distribution.

Class	0–0.99	1.00–1.99	2.00–2.99	3.00–3.99	4.00–4.99	5.00–5.99
Frequency	1	4	8	6	3	1

Solution

There are 23 values, so when they are sorted into order the median is number $(n + 1)/2 = (23 + 1)/2 = 12$. There is one value in the first class, four in the second class, and eight in the third class – so the median is the seventh value in the third class (2.00–2.99). As there are eight values in this class, it

Worked example 6.5 continued

is reasonable to assume that the median is seven-eighths of the way up the class. In other words:

median = lower limit of third class
+ 7/8 × class width
= 2.00 + 7/8 × (2.99 − 2.00) = 2.87

This calculation is equivalent to drawing an ogive (remember from the last chapter that this plots the cumulative number of values against value) and finding the point on the *x*-axis that corresponds to the 12th value (as shown in Figure 6.4).

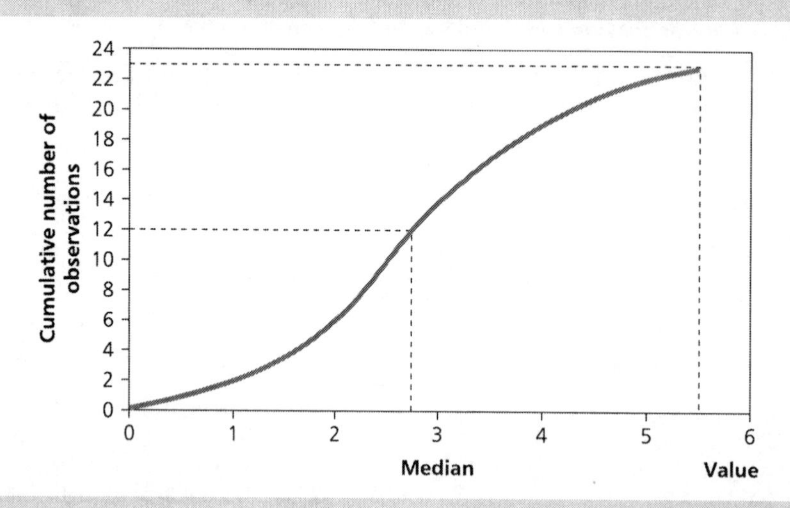

Figure 6.4 Identifying the median from an ogive

The median has the advantages of:

- being easy to understand
- giving a value that actually occurred (except with grouped data)
- sometimes giving a more reliable measure than the mean
- not being affected by outlying values
- needing no calculation (except for grouped data).

On the other hand it has weaknesses, in that it:

- can be used only with cardinal data
- does not really consider data that is not at the median
- can give values for grouped data that have not actually occurred
- is not so easy to use in other analyses.

Mode

The mode is the value that occurs most often. If we have four values, 5, 7, 7 and 9, the value that occurs most often is 7, so this is the mode. Like the median, the mode relies more on observation than calculation, and we find it by:

- drawing a frequency distribution of the data
- identifying the most frequent value – which is the mode.

WORKED EXAMPLE 6.6

Maria Panelli recorded the number of goals that her local football team scored in the last 12 matches as 3, 4, 3, 1, 5, 2, 3, 3, 2, 4, 3 and 2. What is the mode of the goals?

Solution

The following table shows the frequency distribution for these 12 values. As you can see, the most frequent value is 3, so this is the mode. This is shown in Figure 6.5(a). This compares with a mean of 2.9 and a median of 3.

Class	Frequency
1	1
2	3
3	**5**
4	2
5	1

Unfortunately, data is often not as convenient as in the last example. If the numbers that Maria Panelli recorded were:

3, 5, 3, 7, 6, 7, 4, 3, 7, 6, 7, 3, 2, 3, 2, 4, 6, 7, 8

you can see that the most common values are 3 and 7, which both appear five times. Then the data has two modes – or it is bimodal – at 3 and 7, as shown in Figure 6.5(b). Data commonly has several modes, making it multimodal. On the other hand, if you draw a frequency distribution of:

3, 5, 4, 3, 5, 2, 2, 1, 2, 5, 4, 1, 4, 1, 3

you see that each value occurs three times, so there is no mode, as shown in Figure 6.5(c).

It is a bit more difficult to find the mode of data that is grouped in a frequency distribution. We start by identifying the modal class, which is the class with most values. This gives the range within which the mode lies, but we still have to identify an actual value. The easiest way of doing this is to draw two crossing lines, shown in the histogram in Figure 6.6. The point where these two lines cross is the mode. In practice, it is debatable whether this adds much to our understanding of the data, so it is rarely used.

The mode has the advantages of:

- being an actual value (except for grouped data)
- showing the most frequent value, and arguably the most typical
- needing no calculation (except for grouped data)
- not being affected by outlying values.

On the other hand its weaknesses include:

- there can be several modes, or none
- it ignores all data that is not at the mode
- it cannot be used in further analyses.

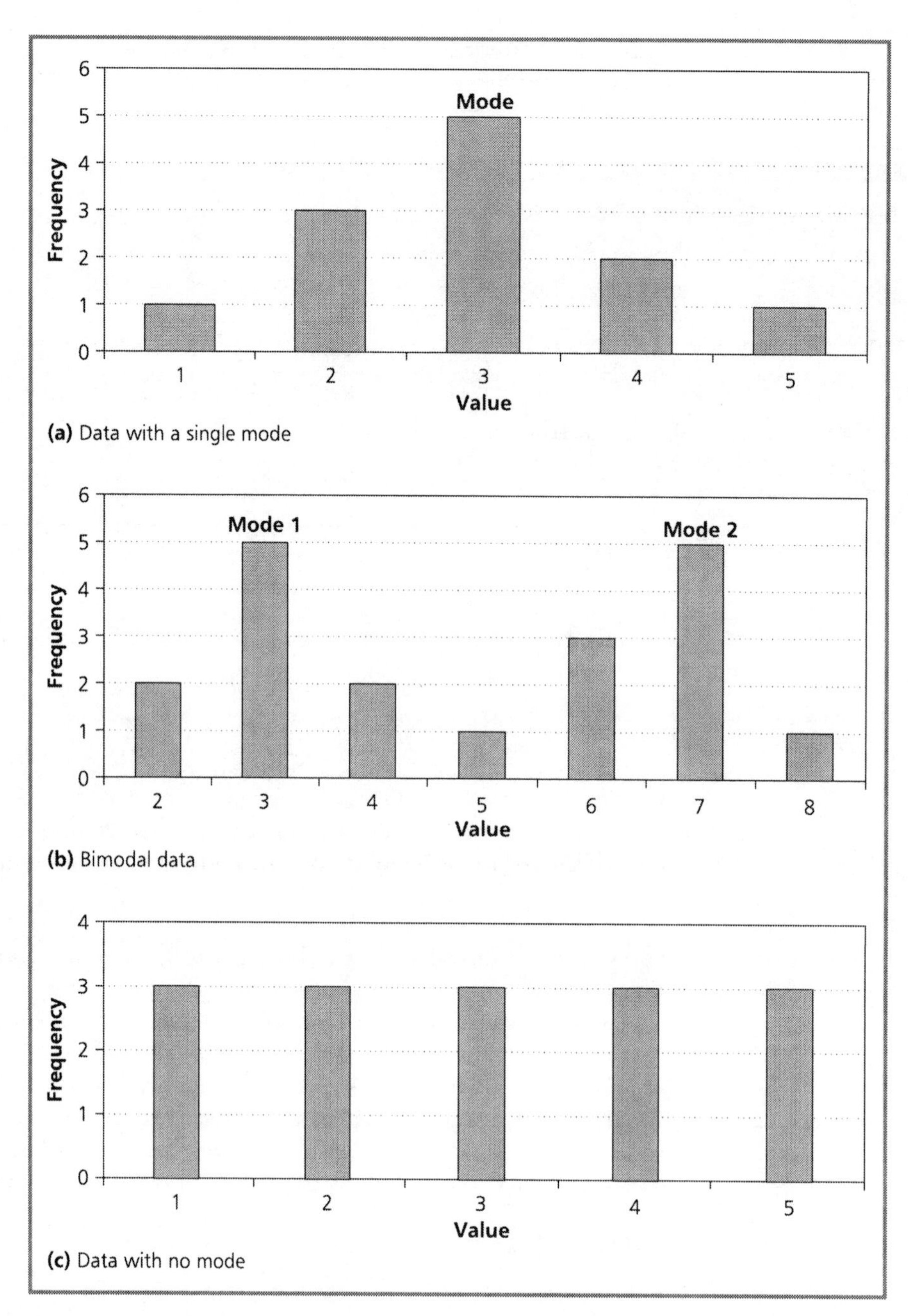

Figure 6.5 Different patterns for the mode

Choice of measure

Each of these three measures for location gives a different view:

- The mean is the simple average
- The median is the middle value
- The mode is the most frequent value.

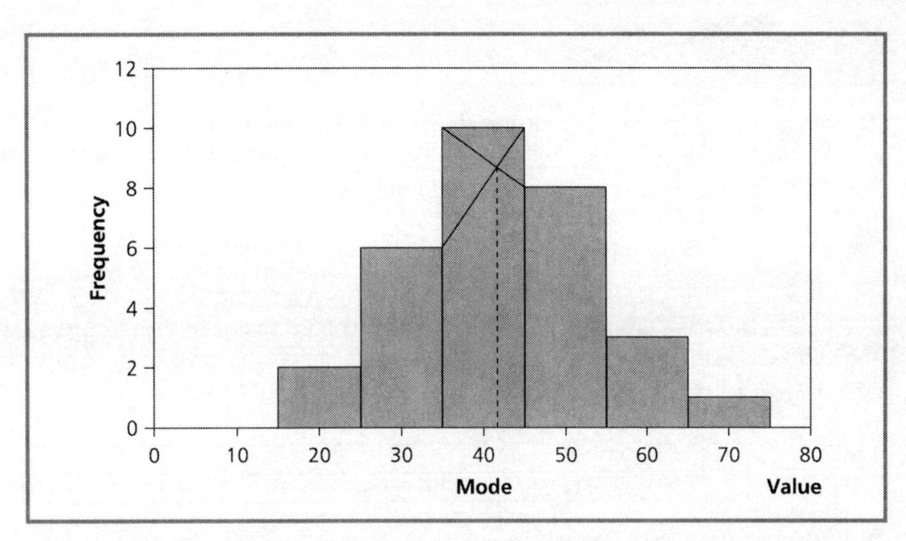

Figure 6.6 Identifying the mode of grouped data

Figure 6.7 shows the typical relationship between these in a histogram. Usually the measures are quite close to each other – and when the histogram is symmetrical they coincide. Sometimes, though, the histogram is very asymmetrical and the measures are some distance apart. The mean is certainly the most widely used, but the median often gives a fairer picture. As with diagrams, the choice of best is often a matter of opinion.

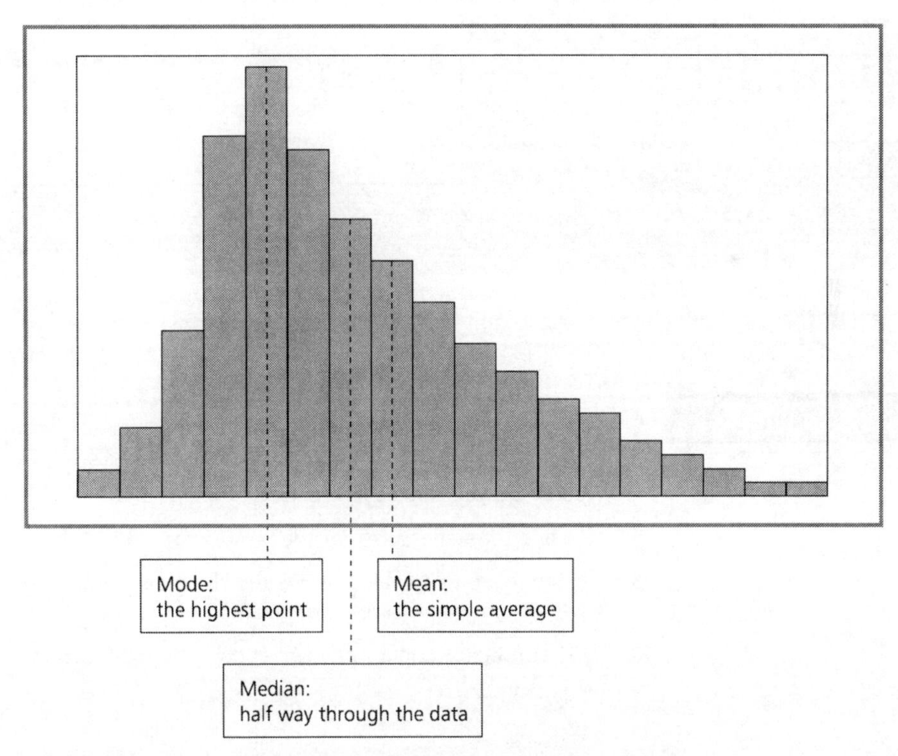

Figure 6.7 Relationship between mean, median and mode

WORKED EXAMPLE 6.7

Taranangama Village Health Centre employs two doctors, one clinical technician, three nurses and four receptionists. Last year the centre published their rates of pay, shown in Figure 6.8. What do these show?

Solution

The figures show the gross pay for each person in the centre, a bar chart of the distribution, and summaries of the mean, median and mode. The calculations were done using the spreadsheet's standard functions AVERAGE, MEDIAN and MODE. The mean is $58,800 – but only two people earn more than this, while eight earn less. Only the technician is within $13,800 of the mean. The median is $42,000, which gives a better view of typical pay at the centre. The mode is $16,000 – but, again, this is not a typical value and simply shows that two receptionists are the only people paid the same amount.

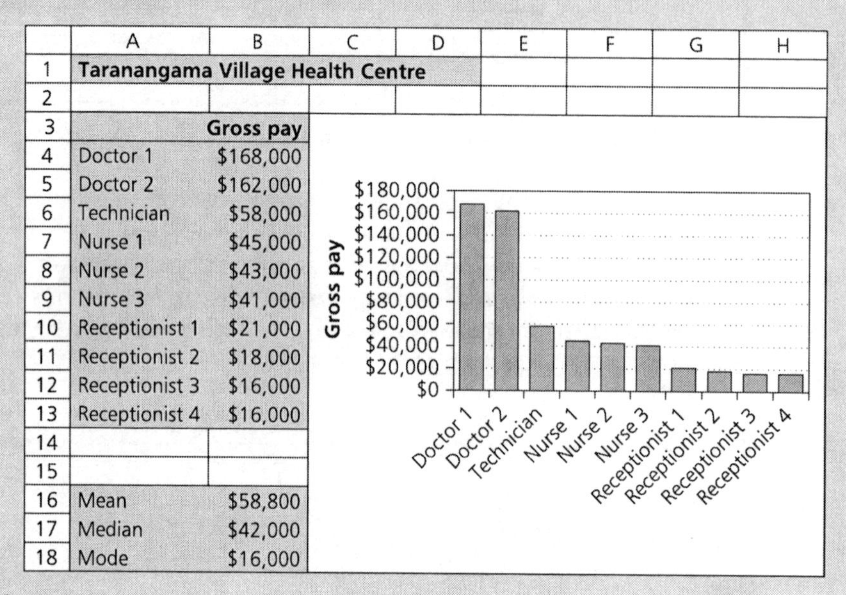

	A	B
1	**Taranangama Village Health Centre**	
2		
3		**Gross pay**
4	Doctor 1	$168,000
5	Doctor 2	$162,000
6	Technician	$58,000
7	Nurse 1	$45,000
8	Nurse 2	$43,000
9	Nurse 3	$41,000
10	Receptionist 1	$21,000
11	Receptionist 2	$18,000
12	Receptionist 3	$16,000
13	Receptionist 4	$16,000
14		
15		
16	Mean	$58,800
17	Median	$42,000
18	Mode	$16,000

Figure 6.8 Gross pay at Taranangama Village Health Centre

Review questions

6.4 What is a 'measure of location'?

6.5 'The average of a set of data has a clear meaning that accurately describes the data.' Do you think this is true?

6.6 Define three measures for the location of a set of data.

6.7 If the mean of 10 values is 34, and the mean of an additional five values is 37, what is the mean of all 15 values?

6.8 What functions on a spreadsheet describe the location of data?

IDEAS IN PRACTICE Tax on house purchase

The UK government wants more people to own their own houses. In the past, they encouraged this by giving tax relief on mortgage interest, and in the mid-1990s returned almost £3 billion to people who were buying their own homes. However, government policies change. They abolished tax relief on mortgages, and the Council for Mortgage Lenders argued that the increasing effects of inheritance tax (paid on inherited property) and stamp duty (paid when buying property) significantly increased the tax burden on homeowners.[1] By 2005, payments in inheritance tax had reached £3 billion (largely because of rising property values) and payments in stamp duty rose to £5 billion.[2,3]

The overall effect was an average increase in tax of £550 a year for each homeowner.[4] However, this average came from dividing the total increase in tax collected by the number of houses. In reality, three groups of people were affected: people with mortgages no longer had tax relief on the interest and paid extra tax of about 1.5% of their mortgage value per year; people who bought houses costing more than £120,000 paid 1% of the value in stamp duty; and inheritance tax started on estates valued at more than £275,000 and rose to 40% of the value. The real picture is more complicated than the headline suggests – with many people not affected at all, and a few paying a lot.

Measures of spread

The mean, median and mode are measures for the location of a set of data, but they give no idea of its spread or dispersion. The mean age of students in a night class might be 45 – but this does not say whether they are all around the same age, or whether their ages range from 5 to 95. The amount of dispersion is often important. A library might have an average of 300 visitors a day, but it is much easier for staff to deal with small variations (from say 290 on quiet days to 310 on busy ones) than large variations (between 0 and 1,000).

Range and quartiles

The simplest measure of spread is the range, which is the difference between the largest and smallest values in a set of data. Clearly, the broader the range the more spread out the data.

range = largest value – smallest value

This is usually an easy calculation, but there is a warning for grouped data. If you simply take the range as the difference between the top of the largest class and the bottom of the smallest one, the result depends on the definition of classes rather than on actual values.

Another problem is that one or two extreme values can affect the range, making it artificially wide. An obvious way of avoiding this is to ignore extreme values that are a long way from the centre. We can do this using quartiles. When data is sorted into ascending size, quartiles are defined as the values that divide the values into quarters. In particular:

- The first quartile, Q_1, is the value a quarter of the way through the data with 25% of values smaller and 75% bigger. It is value number $(n + 1)/4$.

- The second quartile, Q_2, is the value halfway through the data with 50% of values smaller and 50% bigger. This is the median, which is value number $(n + 1)/2$.
- The third quartile, Q_3, is the value three-quarters of the way through the data with 75% of values smaller and 25% bigger. It is value number $3(n + 1)/4$.

With 11 ordered values:

12, 14, 17, 21, 24, 30, 39, 43, 45, 56, 58

the first quartile is value number $(11 + 1)/4 = 3$, which is 17. The second quartile, or median, is value number $(11 + 1)/2 = 6$, which is 30. The third quartile is value number $3 \times (11 + 1)/4 = 9$, which is 45. Figure 6.9 shows these results in a 'box plot' or 'box-and-whisker diagram'. This shows the range between the first and third quartiles by a box, with two whiskers showing the extreme values.

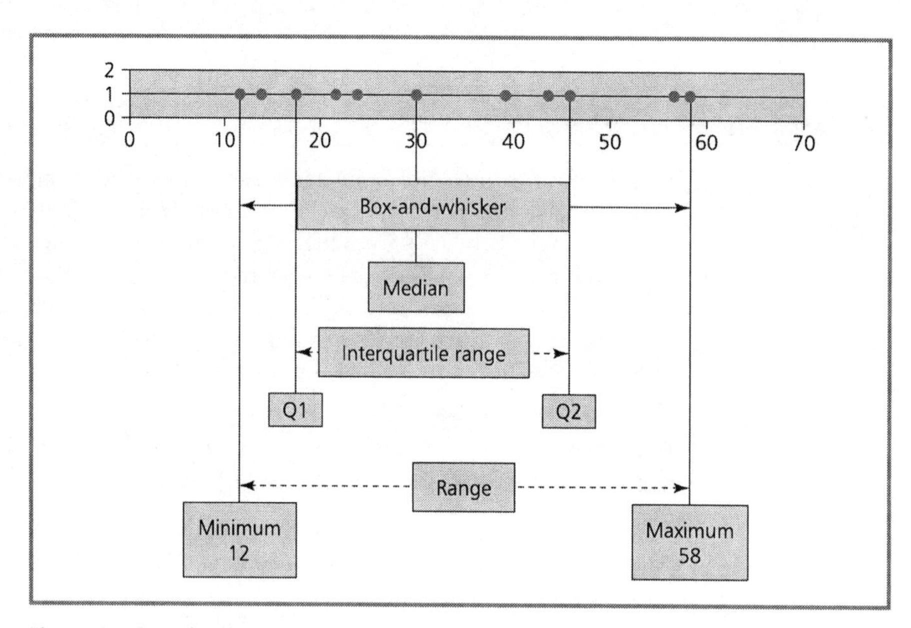

Figure 6.9 Box plot diagram showing the spread of data

Obviously, we chose 11 values so that the quartiles were easy to find. But what happens if there are, say, 200 values, where the first quartile is value number $(200 + 1)/4 = 50.25$? When there are many values, the usual convention is simply to round to the nearest integer. If you want the 50.25th value, you simply round down and approximate it by the 50th; if you want the 50.75th value, you round this up and approximate it by the 51st. And if you want the 50.5th value you might take the average of the 50th and 51st values. In practice, the difference should be small with a reasonable number of values.

You can use the quartiles to define a narrower range $Q_3 - Q_1$ that contains 50% of values – giving the interquartile range. Then the quartile deviation or semi-interquartile range is defined as:

$$\text{interquartile range} = Q_3 - Q_1$$

$$\text{quartile deviation} = \frac{\text{interquartile range}}{2} = \frac{Q_3 - Q_1}{2}$$

WORKED EXAMPLE 6.8

Find the quartile deviation of the following continuous frequency distribution.

Class	0–9.9	10–19.9	20–29.9	30–39.9	40–49.9	50–59.9	60–69.9
Values	5	19	38	43	34	17	4

Solution

There are 160 values, or 40 in each quarter. As this number is fairly large, we can approximate the first quartile by the 40th value, the median by the 80th, and the third quartile by the 120th.

- There are 24 values in the first two classes, so the first quartile, Q_1, is the 16th value out of 38 in the class 20–29.9. A reasonable estimate has the quartile 16/38 of the way through this class, so:

$$Q_1 = 20 + (16/38) \times (29.9 - 20) = 24.2$$

- There are 62 values in the first three classes so the median, Q_2, is the 18th value out of 43 in the class 30–39.9. A reasonable estimate puts this 18/43 of the way through this class, so:

$$Q_2 = 30 + (18/43) \times (39.9 - 30) = 34.1$$

- There are 105 values in the first four classes, so the third quartile, Q_3, is the 15th value out of 34 in the class of 40–49.9. A reasonable estimate for this is:

$$Q_3 = 40 + (15/34) \times (49.9 - 40) = 44.4$$

Then the quartile deviation is:

$$(Q_3 - Q_1)/2 = (44.4 - 24.2)/2 = 10.1$$

Several variations on the quartile deviation are based on percentiles. For example, the 5th percentile is defined as the value with 5% of values below it, and the 95th percentile is defined as the value with 95% of values below it. A common measure finds the range between the 5th and 95th percentiles, as this still includes most of the values but ignores any outlying ones.

Mean absolute deviation

The range and quartile deviation focus on a few values and are clearly related to the median. Other measures of spread include more values, and are related to the mean. In particular, they consider the distance that each value is away from the mean, which is called the deviation.

$$\text{deviation} = \text{value} - \text{mean value} = x_i - \bar{x}$$

Each value has a deviation, so the mean of these deviations gives a measure of spread. Unfortunately, the mean deviation has the major disadvantage of allowing positive and negative deviations to cancel. If we have the three values 3, 4 and 8, the mean is 5 and the mean deviation is:

$$\text{mean deviation} = \frac{\Sigma(x - \bar{x})}{n} = \frac{(3-5) + (4-5) + (8-5)}{3} = 0$$

Even dispersed data has a mean deviation of zero, which is why this measure is never used. A more useful alternative is the mean absolute deviation (MAD), which simply takes the absolute values of deviations. In other words, it ignores negative signs and adds all deviations as if they are positive. The result is a measure of the mean distance of values from the mean – so the larger the mean absolute deviation, the more dispersed the data.

$$\text{mean absolute deviation} = \frac{\sum \text{ABS}(x - \bar{x})}{n}$$

$$\text{MAD} = \frac{\sum |x - \bar{x}|}{n}$$

where: x = the values
$\bar{x}$ = mean value
n = number of values
$\text{ABS}(x - \bar{x})$ = the absolute value of $x - \bar{x}$ (that is, ignoring the sign) which is also written as $|x - \bar{x}|$.

WORKED EXAMPLE 6.9

What is the mean absolute deviation of 4, 7, 6, 10 and 8?

Solution

The calculation for the mean absolute deviation starts by finding the mean of the numbers, which is:

$$\bar{x} = \frac{4 + 7 + 6 + 10 + 8}{5} = 7$$

Then the mean absolute deviation is:

$$\text{MAD} = \frac{\sum |x - \bar{x}|}{n}$$

$$= \frac{|4 - 7| + |7 - 7| + |6 - 7| + |10 - 7| + |8 - 7|}{5}$$

$$= \frac{|-3| + |0| + |-1| + |3| + |1|}{5} = \frac{3 + 0 + 1 + 3 + 1}{5}$$

$$= 1.6$$

This shows that on average the values are 1.6 units away from the mean. In practice you will normally use a standard function like AVEDEV in Excel for this calculation.

Calculating the MAD for grouped data is a bit more awkward. To find the mean of grouped data, we took the midpoint of each class and multiplied this by the number of values in the class. Using the same approach to calculate a mean absolute deviation, we approximate the absolute deviation of each class by the difference between its midpoint and the mean of the data. Then the calculation for the mean absolute deviation for grouped data is:

$$\text{mean absolute deviation} = \frac{\sum |x - \bar{x}| f}{\sum f} = \frac{\sum |x - \bar{x}| f}{n}$$

where: x = midpoint of a class
f = number of values in the class
$\bar{x}$ = mean value
n = total number of values.

WORKED EXAMPLE 6.10

Find the mean absolute deviation of the following data.

Class	0–4.9	5–9.9	10–14.9	15–19.9
Frequency	3	5	9	7
Class	20–24.9	25–29.9	30–34.9	35–39.9
Frequency	4	2	1	1

Solution

Figure 6.10 shows the calculations in a spreadsheet (the details are given in full, but obviously you never really have to be this explicit).

There are 32 values with a mean of 15.4. The deviation of each class is the distance its midpoint is away from this mean. Then we find the mean absolute deviation by taking the absolute deviations, multiplying by the frequency, adding the results, and dividing by the number of values. The result is 6.6, which shows that values are, on average, 6.6 away from the mean.

	A	B	C	D	E	F	G	H
1	**Mean absolute deviation**							
2								
3	**Class**		**Midpoint**	**Frequency**	**Product**	**Deviation**	**Absolute deviation**	**Product**
4	**From**	**To**	x	f	fx	$(x - \text{mean})$	$\lvert x - \text{mean}\rvert$	$f\lvert x - \text{mean}\rvert$
5	0	4.9	2.5	3	7.4	−13.0	13.0	38.9
6	5	9.9	7.5	5	37.3	−8.0	8.0	39.8
7	10	14.9	12.5	9	112.1	−3.0	3.0	26.7
8	15	19.9	17.5	7	122.2	2.0	2.0	14.2
9	20	24.9	22.5	4	89.8	7.0	7.0	28.1
10	25	29.9	27.5	2	54.9	12.0	12.0	24.1
11	30	34.9	32.5	1	32.5	17.0	17.0	17.0
12	35	39.9	37.5	1	37.5	22.0	22.0	22.0
13	**Sums**			**32**	**493.4**			**210.9**
14	**Means**				**15.4**			**6.6**
15								
16	**Mean absolute deviation =**				**6.6**			

Figure 6.10 Calculation of the mean absolute deviation

The MAD is easy to calculate, uses all the data, and has a clear meaning. However, it also has weaknesses. For instance, it gives equal weight to all values, and can be affected by a few outlying numbers. Perhaps a more fundamental problem is the difficulty of using it in other analyses. This limits its use, and a more widely used alternative is the variance.

Variance and standard deviation

The mean absolute deviation stops positive and negative deviations from cancelling by taking their absolute values. An alternative is to square the deviations and calculate a mean squared deviation – which is always referred to as the variance.

$$\text{variance} = \frac{\Sigma(x - \bar{x})^2}{n}$$

This has all the benefits of MAD, but overcomes some of its limitations – but with one obvious problem, that the units are the square of the units of the original values. If the values are measured in tonnes, the variance has the meaningless units of tonnes squared; if the values are in dollars, the variance is in dollars squared. To return units to normal, we simply take the square root of the variance. This gives the most widely used measure of spread, which is the standard deviation.

$$\text{standard deviation} = \sqrt{\frac{\Sigma(x - \bar{x})^2}{n}} = \sqrt{\text{variance}}$$

WORKED EXAMPLE 6.11

What are the variance and standard deviation of 2, 3, 7, 8 and 10?

Solution

Again, the calculation starts by finding the mean of the numbers, $\bar{x}$, which is (2 + 3 + 7 + 8 + 10)/5 = 6. The variance is the mean squared deviation, which is:

$$\text{variance} = \frac{\Sigma(x - \bar{x})^2}{n}$$

$$= \frac{(2-6)^2 + (3-6)^2 + (7-6)^2 + (8-6)^2 + (10-6)^2}{5}$$

$$= \frac{(-4)^2 + (-3)^2 + 1^2 + 2^2 + 4^2}{5}$$

$$= \frac{16 + 9 + 1 + 4 + 16}{5} = \frac{46}{5} = 9.2$$

The standard deviation is the square root of the variance:

$$\text{standard deviation} = \sqrt{9.2} = 3.03$$

Again, in practice you are more likely to use a standard spreadsheet function for these calculations, such as VARP and STDEVP.

Again, we can extend the calculations for variance and standard deviation to grouped data, using the same approach as for the MAD, approximating values by the midpoints of classes. Then:

$$\text{variance} = \frac{\Sigma(x - \bar{x})^2 f}{\Sigma f} = \frac{\Sigma(x - \bar{x})^2 f}{n}$$

$$\text{standard deviation} = \sqrt{\text{variance}} = \sqrt{\frac{\Sigma(x - \bar{x})^2 f}{\Sigma f}} = \sqrt{\frac{\Sigma(x - \bar{x})^2 f}{n}}$$

where: x = midpoint of a class
f = number of values in the class
$\bar{x}$ = mean value
n = total number of values.

WORKED EXAMPLE 6.12

Find the variance and standard deviation of the following data.

Class	0–9.9	10–19.9	20–29.9	30–39.9
Frequency	1	4	8	13
Class	40–49.9	50–59.9	60–69.9	70–79.9
Frequency	11	9	5	2

Solution

Figure 6.11 shows the calculations in the same spreadsheet format as Figure 6.10. As you can see, there are 53 values with a mean of 41.2. The deviation of each class is the distance its midpoint is away from the mean. Then we find the variance by taking the square of the deviations, multiplying by the frequency, adding the results, and dividing by the number of values. This gives a value for the variance of 257.5. Taking the square root of this gives the standard deviation of 16.0.

	A	B	C	D	E	F	G	H
1								
2								
3								
4	**Class**		**Midpoint**	**Frequency**	**Product**	**Deviation**	**Squared deviation**	**Product**
5	**From**	**To**	***x***	***f***	***fx***	**(*x* – mean)**	**(*x* – mean) ^ 2**	***f*(*x* – mean) ^ 2**
6	0	9.9	5.0	1	5.0	–36.2	1312.4	1312.4
7	10	19.9	15.0	4	59.8	–26.2	687.8	2751.3
8	20	29.9	25.0	8	199.6	–16.2	263.3	2106.4
9	30	39.9	35.0	13	454.4	–6.2	38.8	504.0
10	40	49.9	45.0	11	494.5	3.8	14.2	156.6
11	50	59.9	55.0	9	494.6	13.8	189.7	1707.4
12	60	69.9	65.0	5	324.8	23.8	565.2	2825.9
13	70	79.9	75.0	2	149.9	33.8	1140.7	2281.3
14	**Sums**			**53**	**2182.4**			**13645.3**
15	**Means**				**41.2**			**257.5**
16								
17	**Variance =**			**257.5**				
18	**Standard deviation =**			**6.0**				

Figure 6.11 Calculation of variance and standard deviation for grouped data

Unfortunately, the variance and standard deviation do not have such a clear meaning as the mean absolute deviation. A large variance shows more spread than a smaller one, so data with a variance of 42.5 is less spread out than equivalent data with a variance of 22.5, but we cannot say much more than this. However, they are useful in a variety of other analyses, and this makes them the most widely used measures of dispersion. For instance, a crucial observation is that a known proportion of values is within a specified number of standard deviations from the mean. Chebyshev first did this analysis, and found that for any data with a standard deviation of s:

- It is possible that no values will fall within one standard deviation of the mean – which is within the range $(\bar{x} + s)$ to $(\bar{x} - s)$.
- At least three-quarters of values will fall within two standard deviations of the mean – which is within the range $(\bar{x} + 2s)$ to $(\bar{x} - 2s)$.
- At least eight-ninths of values will fall within three standard deviations of the mean – which is within the range $(\bar{x} + 3s)$ to $(\bar{x} - 3s)$.
- In general, at least $(1 - 1/k^2)$ values will fall within k standard deviations of the mean – which is within the range $(\bar{x} + ks)$ to $(\bar{x} - ks)$.

This rule is actually quite conservative, and empirical evidence suggests that for a frequency distribution with a single mode, 68% of values usually fall within one standard deviation of the mean, 95% of values within two standard deviations and almost all values within three standard deviations.

Another important point is that you can sometimes add variances. Provided two sets of values are completely unrelated (which is technically described as their covariance being zero), the variance of the sum of data is equal to the sum of the variances of each set. For example, if the daily demand for an item has a variance of 4, while the daily demand for a second item has a variance of 5, the variance of total demand for both items is 4 + 5 = 9. You can never add standard deviations in this way.

WORKED EXAMPLE 6.13

The mean weight and standard deviation of airline passengers are 72 kg and 6 kg respectively. What is the mean weight and standard deviation of total passenger weight in a 200-seat aeroplane?

Solution

You find the total mean weight of passengers by multiplying the mean weight of each passenger by the number of passengers:

$$\text{mean} = 200 \times 72 = 14{,}400 \text{ kg}$$

You cannot add the standard deviations like this, but you can add the variances. So the variance in weight of 200 passengers is the variance in weight of each passenger multiplied by the number of passengers:

$$\text{variance} = 200 \times 6^2 = 7{,}200 \text{ kg}^2$$

The standard deviation in total weight is $\sqrt{7{,}200} =$ 84.85 kg.

Review questions

6.9 List four measures for data spread. Are there any other measures?

6.10 Why is the mean deviation not used to measure data dispersion?

6.11 If the mean of a set of values is 10.37 metres, what are the units of the variance and standard deviation?

6.12 Why is the standard deviation so widely used, when its practical meaning is unclear?

6.13 The number of cars entering a shopping mall car park per hour has a mean of 120 and standard deviation of 10. In one hour an observer reports 210 cars entering. What can you say about this?

6.14 What functions in a spreadsheet find the dispersion of data?

Other measures of data

One reason why the standard deviation is important is that it is used in other analyses, including the coefficient of variation and the coefficient of skewness.

Coefficient of variation

The measures of spread that we have described give absolute values – so they describe a particular set of data, but it is difficult to use them for comparisons. It would be useful to have a measure of relative spread that considers both the amount of spread and its location. The usual measure for this is the coefficient of variation, which is defined as the ratio of standard deviation over the mean.

$$\text{coefficient of variation} = \frac{\text{standard deviation}}{\text{mean}}$$

The higher the coefficient of variation, the more dispersed the data. If the cost of operating various facilities in one year has a coefficient of variation of 0.8 and this rises to 0.9 in the following year, it means that the variation in cost has increased, regardless of how the cost has changed in absolute terms.

WORKED EXAMPLE 6.14

Ambrose Financial classify shares in the energy sector as low, medium or high risk. In recent years, these have had mean annual returns of 9.2%, 17.0% and 14.8% respectively. The standard deviations have been 3.9%, 9.8% and 13.6% respectively. What does this tell you?

Solution

The coefficients of variation for share returns are:

- low risk:

  mean = 9.2%, standard deviation = 3.9%
  coefficient of variation = 3.9/9.2 = 0.42

- medium risk:

  mean = 17.0%, standard deviation = 9.8%
  coefficient of variation = 9.8/17.0 = 0.58

- high risk:

  mean = 14.8%, standard deviation = 13.6%
  coefficient of variation = 13.6/14.8 = 0.92

The returns from high-risk shares are more spread out than from lower-risk ones – which is almost a definition of risk. Medium-risk shares had the highest returns, and the relatively low coefficient of variation suggests a comparatively stable performance.

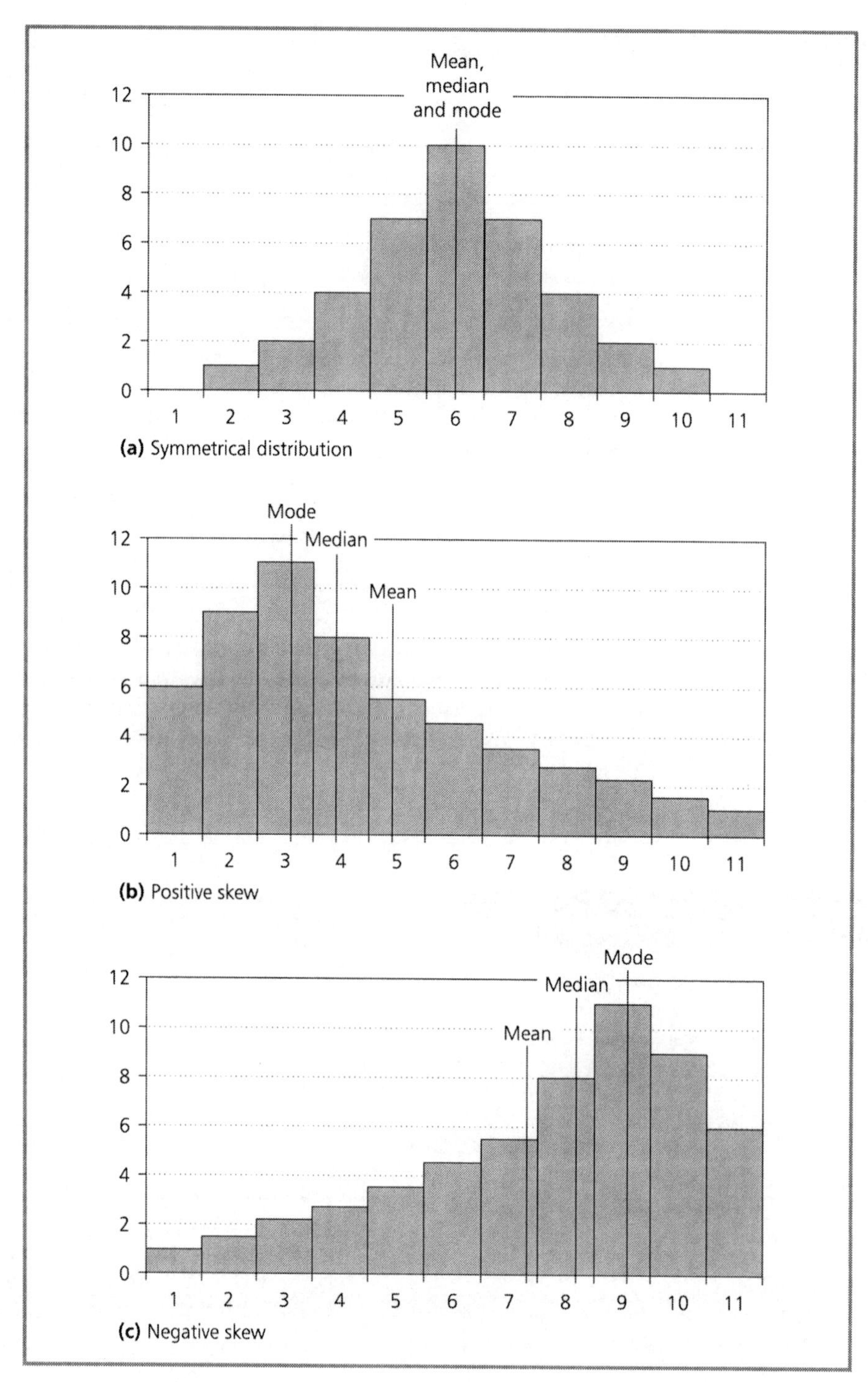

Figure 6.12 Skewness in frequency distributions

Coefficient of skewness

The coefficient of skewness describes the 'shape' of a set of data. A frequency distribution may be symmetrical about its mean, or it may be skewed. A negative or left-skewed distribution has a longer tail to the left (as shown in Figure 6.12(c)); a positive or right-skewed distribution has a longer tail to the right (as shown in Figure 6.12(b)).

In a symmetrical distribution the mean, median and mode all have the same value (Figure 6.12(a)). A positive skew means that the mean is bigger than the median, while a negative skew means that the median is bigger than the mean. A formal measure for the amount of skewness comes from Pearson's coefficient of skewness. This has the rather unusual definition of:

$$\text{coefficient of skewness} = \frac{3 \times (\text{mean} - \text{median})}{\text{standard deviation}}$$

This automatically gives the correct sign of the skew, but its precise interpretation is rather difficult. Values around +1 or −1 are generally considered highly skewed.

Review questions

6.15 Why would you use the coefficient of variation?

6.16 What does the coefficient of skewness measure?

6.17 Two sets of data have means 10.2 and 33.4 and variances 4.3 and 18.2. What does this tell you?

IDEAS IN PRACTICE Prinseptia

Prinseptia is a diversified international company operating largely in southern Europe. In 2005 they bought an art auction house in Tuscany. A year later they reviewed operations to see how their investment was developing. At this point they had 44 weeks of contract information and produced their first progress report and planning document.

One part of this document included the figures shown in Figure 6.13 with the aim of giving – when viewed with other information – a review of weekly contract value.

Ideas in practice continued

	A	B	C	D	E	F	G	H
1	**Prinseptia contract value**							
2								
3	**Weekly contract values**					**Data description**		
4	42	18	33	31		Count	44	
5	51	24	17	42		Sum	1487	
6	47	31	22	71				
7	30	56	18	35		Mean	33.80	
8	22	27	24	17		Median	30	
9	39	54	30	34		Mode	18	
10	48	62	41	29				
11	63	30	26	19		Minimum	12	
12	58	33	20	17		Maximum	71	
13	71	26	18	12		Range	59	
14	24	26	28	21		Variance	235.12	
15						Stan dev	15.33	
16						Coef of variation	0.45	
17								
18						Quartile 1	22	
19						Quartile 2	30	
20						Quartile 3	42	
21								
22						Coef of skewness	0.93	
23								

	Class	Frequency
35	**Class**	**Frequency**
36	0–9	0
37	10–19	8
38	20–29	13
39	30–39	10
40	40–49	5
41	50–59	4
42	60–69	2
43	70–79	2

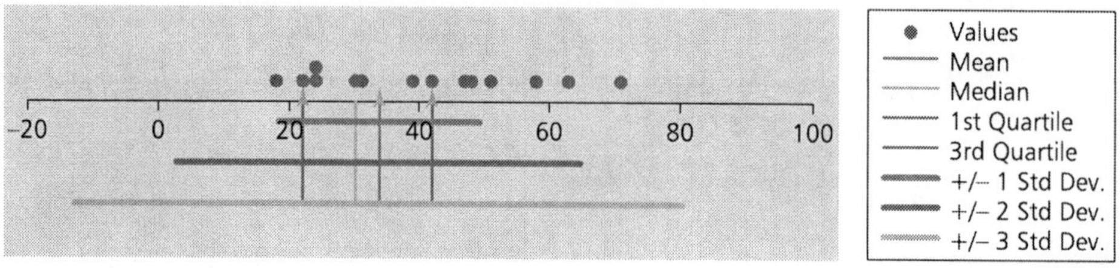

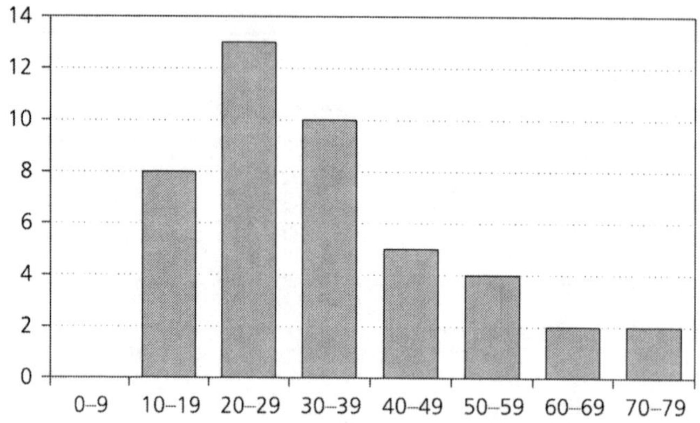

Figure 6.13 Summary of contract value in Prinseptia

CHAPTER REVIEW

This chapter described a number of numerical measures of data.

- The last chapter described some diagrams for summarising data, and this chapter showed how numerical measures give more objective and accurate descriptions. Two key measures describe the location and spread of data.
- Measures of location find the centre of data or a typical value. The (arithmetic) mean is the most widely used measure, giving an average value. Alternatives are the median (which is the middle value, when they are ranked in order of size) and the mode (which is the most frequently occurring value).
- Other measures are needed for the spread of data. The obvious measure is range, but this can be affected by a few outlying results. More reliable values come from the interquartile range or quartile deviation.
- The deviation is the difference between a value and the mean. A basic measure gives the mean absolute deviation. Alternatively, we can square the deviations and calculate the mean squared deviation – or the variance.
- The square root of the variance is the standard deviation, which is the most widely used measure of spread. It is used for other analyses, such as the coefficient of variation (which gives a relative view of spread) and the coefficient of skewness (which describes the shape of a distribution).

CASE STUDY Consumer Advice Office

When people buy things, they have a number of statutory rights. A basic right is that the product should be of adequate quality and fit for the purpose intended. When customers think these rights have been infringed, they might contact their local government's trading standards service.

Mary Lomamanu has been working in Auckland as a consumer advice officer for the past 14 months, where her job is to advise people who have complaints against traders. She listens to the complaints, assesses the problem and then takes the follow-up action she thinks is needed. Often she can deal with a client's problem quite quickly – when she thinks the trader has done nothing wrong, or when she advises customers to go back to the place they bought a product and complain to the manager. But some cases are more difficult and need a lot of follow-up, including legal work and appearances in court.

The local government is always looking for ways to reduce costs and improve their service, so it is important for Mary to show that she is doing a good job. She is particularly keen to show that her increasing experience and response to pressures means that she is more efficient and deals with more clients. To help with this, she has kept records of the number of clients she dealt with during her first eight weeks at work, and during the same eight weeks this year.

- Number of customers dealt with each working day in the first eight weeks:

  6 18 22 9 10 14 22 15 28 9 30 26 17 9 11 25 31 17 25 30 32 17 27 34 15 9 7 10 28 10 31 12 16 26 21 37 25 7 36 29

- Number of customers dealt with each working day in the last eight weeks:

  30 26 40 19 26 31 28 41 18 27 29 30 33 43 19 20 44 37 29 22 41 39 15 9 22 26 30 35 38 26 19 25 33 39 31 30 20 34 43 45

During the past year she estimates that her working hours have increased by an average of two hours a week, which is unpaid overtime. Her wages increased by 3% after allowing for inflation.

Question

- **Mary needs a way of presenting these figures to her employers in a form that they will understand. How do you think she should set about this?**

PROBLEMS

6.1 When Winnie Mbecu was in hospital for two weeks, the number of visitors she received on consecutive days were 4, 2, 1, 5, 1, 3, 3, 5, 2, 1, 6, 4, 1 and 4. How would you describe this data?

6.2 Find the mean, median and mode of the following numbers. What other measures can you use?

24 26 23 24 23 24 27 26 28 25 21 22 25 23 26 29 27 24 25 24 24 25

6.3 What measures can you use for the following discrete frequency distribution?

Class	0–5	6–10	11–15	16–20
Frequency	1	5	8	11
Class	21–25	26–30	31–35	36–40
Frequency	7	4	2	1

6.4 What measures can you use for the following continuous frequency distribution?

Class	1.00–2.99	3.00–4.99	5.00–6.99	7.00–8.99
Frequency	2	6	15	22
Class	9.00–10.99	11.00–12.99	13.00–14.99	15.00–16.99
Frequency	13	9	5	2

6.5 How would you describe the following data?

3 45 28 83 62 44 60 18 73 44 59 67 78 32
74 28 67 97 34 44 23 66 25 12 58 9 34 58
29 45 37 91 73 50 10 71 72 19 18 27 41 91
90 23 23 33

6.6 The Langborne Hotel is concerned about the number of people who book rooms by telephone but do not actually turn up. The following table shows the numbers of people who have done this over the past few weeks. How can they summarise this data?

Day	1	2	3	4	5	6	7	8	9	10	11	12	13	14	15
No-shows	4	5	2	3	3	2	1	4	7	2	0	3	1	4	5

Day	16	17	18	19	20	21	22	23	24	25	26
No-shows	2	6	2	3	3	4	2	5	5	2	4

Day	27	28	29	30	31	32	33	34	35	36	37
No-shows	3	3	1	4	5	3	6	4	3	1	4

Day	38	39	40	41	42	43	44	45
No-shows	5	6	3	3	2	4	3	4

6.7 In the last chapter (research project 5.2) we described a set of data that had been collected by Jan Schwartzkopf. What numerical summaries can you use for this data?

6.8 Describe the distributions of incomes in a number of different countries.

RESEARCH PROJECTS

6.1 Spreadsheets have procedures for automatically describing data, such as the 'Data Analysis' tool in Excel (if this is missing you have to load the Analysis ToolPac as an add-in). An option in this is 'Descriptive Statistics' which automatically finds 13 measures for a set of data (illustrated in Figure 6.14). Explore the analyses done by these procedures.

6.2 Spreadsheets are not really designed for statistical analysis, but there are many specialised packages. Perhaps the best known is Minitab, with others including SPSS, S-plus, Systat and JMP. Do a small survey of packages that include statistical measures. Compare their features and say which package you think is most useful.

6.3 Find a set of data about the performance of sports teams, such as last year's results from a football league. Describe the performance of the teams, both numerically and graphically.

	A	B	C	D
1	**Data description**			
2				
3	**Data**		***Data Description***	
4	45			
5	35		Mean	45.41
6	63		Standard Error	3.92
7	21		Median	45.00
8	34		Mode	45.00
9	45		Standard Deviation	16.15
10	60		Sample Variance	260.76
11	19		Kurtosis	–0.75
12	72		Skewness	–0.21
13	54		Range	53.00
14	42		Minimum	19.00
15	67		Maximum	72.00
16	20		Sum	772
17	48		Count	17
18	51			
19	39			
20	57			

Figure 6.14 Data description with Excel

Include these in a report to the directors of the league to review the year's performance.

6.4 Most organisations try to present data fairly, but some presentations are criticised as giving the wrong impression. Perhaps the data is skewed and the median would give a fairer view than the mean; perhaps there are outlying values and the quartile deviation would be fairer than the range. People presenting the data usually argue that they have used objective measures and readers have interpreted these in the wrong ways. Have a look for summaries of data that you feel are misleading. Say why they are misleading and how you would improve them.

Sources of information

References

1 HM Revenue and Customs, *Income Tax Statistics and Distributions*, HMSO, London, 2006.

2 Websites at www.hmrc.gov.uk and www.statistics.gov.uk.

3 Council for Mortgage Lenders, Inheritance tax and home ownership, *CML News and Views*, London, 24th January 2006.

4 Murray-West R., Home-owners are £550 a year poorer under Labour, *The Daily Telegraph*, 25th January 2006.

Further reading

Most statistics books cover the material in this chapter, and you might start looking through the following (some more general statistics books are given in Chapter 14):

Clarke G.M. and Cooke D., *A Basic Course in Statistics* (5th edition), Hodder Arnold, London, 2004.

Levine D.M., Stephan D., Krehbiel T.C. and Berenson M.L., *Statistics for Managers* (3rd edition), Prentice Hall, Upper Saddle River, NJ, 2001.

Wonnacott R.J. and Wonnacott T.H., *Business Statistics* (5th edition), John Wiley, Chichester, 1999.

Section 2
Modelling in Business

14 Solving equations

Objectives: This chapter:

- explains what is meant by an equation and its solution
- shows how to solve linear, simultaneous and quadratic equations

An **equation** states that two quantities are equal, and will always contain an **unknown quantity** that we wish to find. For example, in the equation $5x + 10 = 20$ the unknown quantity is x. To **solve** an equation means to find all values of the unknown quantity that can be substituted into the equation so that the left side equals the right side. Each such value is called a **solution** or alternatively a **root** of the equation. In the example above the solution is $x = 2$ because when $x = 2$ is substituted both the left side and the right side equal 20. The value $x = 2$ is said to **satisfy** the equation.

14.1 Solving linear equations

A **linear** equation is one of the form $ax + b = 0$ where a and b are numbers and the unknown quantity is x. The number a is called the **coefficient** of x. The number b is called the **constant term**. For example, $3x + 7 = 0$ is a linear equation. The coefficient of x is 3 and the constant term is 7. Similarly, $-2x + 17.5 = 0$ is a linear equation. The coefficient of x is -2 and the constant term is 17.5. Note that the unknown quantity occurs only to the first power, that is, as x, and not as x^2, x^3, $x^{1/2}$ etc. Linear equations may appear in other forms that may seem to be different but are nevertheless equivalent. Thus

$$4x + 13 = -7, \qquad 3 - 14x = 0 \qquad \text{and} \qquad 3x + 7 = 2x - 4$$

are all linear equations that could be written in the form $ax + b = 0$ if necessary.

An equation such as $3x^2 + 2 = 0$ is not linear because the unknown quantity occurs to the power 2. Linear equations are solved by trying to obtain the unknown quantity on its own on the left-hand side, that is, by making the unknown quantity the subject of the equation. This is done using the rules given for transposing formulae in Chapter 13. Consider the following examples.

WORKED EXAMPLE

14.1 Solve the equation $x + 10 = 0$.

Solution We make x the subject by subtracting 10 from both sides to give $x = -10$. Therefore $x = -10$ is the solution. It can be easily checked by substituting into the original equation:

$$(-10) + 10 = 0 \qquad \text{as required}$$

Note from the last worked example that the solution should be checked by substitution to ensure it satisfies the given equation. If it does not then a mistake has been made.

WORKED EXAMPLES

14.2 Solve the equation $4x + 8 = 0$.

Solution In order to find the unknown quantity x we attempt to make it the subject of the equation. Subtracting 8 from both sides we find

$$4x + 8 - 8 = 0 - 8 = -8$$

That is,

$$4x = -8$$

Then dividing both sides by 4 gives

$$\frac{4x}{4} = \frac{-8}{4}$$

so that $x = -2$. The solution of the equation $4x + 8 = 0$ is $x = -2$.

14.3 Solve the equation $5x + 17 = 4x - 3$.

Solution First we collect all terms involving x together. This is done by subtracting $4x$ from both sides to remove this term from the right. This gives

$$5x - 4x + 17 = -3$$

That is, $x + 17 = -3$. To make x the subject of this equation we now subtract 17 from both sides to give $x = -3 - 17 = -20$. The solution of the equation $5x + 17 = 4x - 3$ is $x = -20$. Note that the answer can be easily checked by substituting $x = -20$ into the original equation and verifying that the left side equals the right side.

14.4 Solve the equation $\dfrac{x - 3}{4} = 1$.

Solution We attempt to obtain x on its own. First note that if we multiply both sides of the equation by 4 this will remove the 4 in the denominator. That is,

$$4 \times \left(\frac{x - 3}{4}\right) = 4 \times 1$$

so that

$$x - 3 = 4$$

Finally adding 3 to both sides gives $x = 7$.

Self-assessment questions 14.1

1. Explain what is meant by a root of an equation.
2. Explain what is meant by a linear equation.
3. State the rules that can be used to solve a linear equation.
4. You may think that a formula and an equation look very similar. Try to explain the distinction between a formula and an equation.

Exercise 14.1

1. Verify that the given values of x satisfy the given equations:
   (a) $x = 7$ satisfies $3x + 4 = 25$
   (b) $x = -5$ satisfies $2x - 11 = -21$
   (c) $x = -4$ satisfies $-x - 8 = -4$
   (d) $x = \frac{1}{2}$ satisfies $8x + 4 = 8$
   (e) $x = -\frac{1}{3}$ satisfies $27x + 8 = -1$
   (f) $x = 4$ satisfies $3x + 2 = 7x - 14$
2. Solve the following linear equations:
   (a) $3x = 9$ (b) $\dfrac{x}{3} = 9$ (c) $3t + 6 = 0$
   (d) $3x - 13 = 2x + 9$ (e) $3x + 17 = 21$
   (f) $4x - 20 = 3x + 16$
   (g) $5 - 2x = 2 + 3x$
   (h) $\dfrac{x + 3}{2} = 3$ (i) $\dfrac{3x + 2}{2} + 3x = 1$
3. Solve the following equations:
   (a) $5(x + 2) = 13$
   (b) $3(x - 7) = 2(x + 1)$
   (c) $5(1 - 2x) = 2(4 - 2x)$
4. Solve the following equations:
   (a) $3t + 7 = 4t - 2$
   (b) $3v = 17 - 4v$
   (c) $3s + 2 = 14(s - 1)$

5. Solve the following linear equations:
(a) $5t + 7 = 22$ (b) $7 - 4t = -13$
(c) $7 - 4t = 27$ (d) $5 = 14 - 3t$
(e) $4x + 13 = -x + 25$
(f) $\frac{x+3}{2} = \frac{x-3}{4}$ (g) $\frac{1}{3}x + 6 = \frac{1}{2}x + 2$
(h) $\frac{1}{5}x + 7 = \frac{1}{3}x + 5$
(i) $\frac{2x+4}{5} = \frac{x-3}{2}$ (j) $\frac{x-7}{8} = \frac{3x+1}{5}$

6. The following equations may not appear to be linear at first sight but they can all be rewritten in the standard form of a linear equation. Find the solution of each equation.
(a) $\frac{1}{x} = 5$ (b) $\frac{1}{x} = \frac{5}{2}$ (c) $\frac{1}{x+1} = \frac{5}{2}$
(d) $\frac{1}{x-1} = \frac{5}{2}$ (e) $\frac{1}{x} = \frac{1}{2x+1}$
(f) $\frac{3}{x} = \frac{1}{2x+1}$ (g) $\frac{1}{x+1} = \frac{1}{3x+2}$
(h) $\frac{3}{x+1} = \frac{2}{4x+1}$

14.2 Solving simultaneous equations

Sometimes equations contain more than one unknown quantity. When this happens there are usually two or more equations. For example in the two equations

$$x + 2y = 14 \qquad 3x + y = 17$$

the unknowns are x and y. Such equations are called **simultaneous equations** and to solve them we must find values of x and y that satisfy both equations at the same time. If we substitute $x = 4$ and $y = 5$ into either of the two equations above we see that the equation is satisfied. We shall demonstrate how simultaneous equations can be solved by removing, or **eliminating**, one of the unknowns.

WORKED EXAMPLES

14.5 Solve the simultaneous equations

$$x + 3y = 14 \qquad (14.1)$$

$$2x - 3y = -8 \qquad (14.2)$$

Solution Note that if these two equations are added the unknown y is removed or eliminated:

$$\begin{array}{rl} x + 3y = 14 & \\ 2x - 3y = -8 & + \\ \hline 3x \quad = 6 & \\ \hline \end{array}$$

so that $x = 2$. To find y we substitute $x = 2$ into either equation. Substituting into Equation 14.1 gives

$$2 + 3y = 14$$

Solving this linear equation will give y. We have

$$2 + 3y = 14$$
$$3y = 14 - 2 = 12$$
$$y = \frac{12}{3} = 4$$

Therefore the solution of the simultaneous equations is $x = 2$ and $y = 4$. Note that these solutions should be checked by substituting back into both given equations to check that the left-hand side equals the right-hand side.

14.6 Solve the simultaneous equations

$$5x + 4y = 7 \qquad (14.3)$$
$$3x - y = 11 \qquad (14.4)$$

Solution Note that, in this example, if we multiply the first equation by 3 and the second by 5 we shall have the same coefficient of x in both equations. This gives

$$15x + 12y = 21 \qquad (14.5)$$
$$15x - 5y = 55 \qquad (14.6)$$

We can now eliminate x by subtracting Equation 14.6 from Equation 14.5, giving

$$\begin{array}{r} 15x + 12y = \ 21 \\ 15x - 5y = \ 55 \\ \hline 17y = -34 \\ \hline \end{array} \quad -$$

from which $y = -2$. In order to find x we substitute our solution for y into either of the given equations. Substituting into Equation 14.3 gives

$$5x + 4(-2) = 7 \quad \text{so that} \quad 5x = 15 \quad \text{or} \quad x = 3$$

The solution of the simultaneous equations is therefore $x = 3$, $y = -2$.

Exercise 14.2

1. Verify that the given values of x and y satisfy the given simultaneous equations.
   (a) $x = 7$, $y = 1$ satisfy $2x - 3y = 11$, $3x + y = 22$
   (b) $x = -7$, $y = 2$ satisfy $2x + y = -12$, $x - 5y = -17$
   (c) $x = -1$, $y = -1$ satisfy $7x - y = -6$, $x - y = 0$

2. Solve the following pairs of simultaneous equations:
   (a) $3x + y = 1, \quad 2x - y = 2$
   (b) $4x + 5y = 21, \quad 3x + 5y = 17$
   (c) $2x - y = 17, \quad x + 3y = 12$
   (d) $-2x + y = -21, \quad x + 3y = -14$
   (e) $-x + y = -10, \quad 3x + 7y = 20$
   (f) $4x - 2y = 2, \quad 3x - y = 4$
3. Solve the following simultaneous equations:
   (a) $5x + y = 36$, $3x - y = 20$
   (b) $x - 3y = -13$, $4x + 2y = -24$
   (c) $3x + y = 30$, $-5x + 3y = -50$
   (d) $3x - y = -5$, $-7x + 3y = 15$
   (e) $11x + 13y = -24$, $x + y = -2$

14.3 Solving quadratic equations

A **quadratic equation** is an equation of the form $ax^2 + bx + c = 0$ where a, b and c are numbers and x is the unknown quantity we wish to find. The number a is the **coefficient** of x^2, b is the coefficient of x, and c is the **constant term**. Sometimes b or c may be zero, although a can never be zero. For example

$$x^2 + 7x + 2 = 0 \qquad 3x^2 - 2 = 0 \qquad -2x^2 + 3x = 0 \qquad 8x^2 = 0$$

are all quadratic equations.

Key point

A quadratic equation has the form $ax^2 + bx + c = 0$ where a, b and c are numbers, and x represents the unknown we wish to find.

WORKED EXAMPLES

14.7 State the coefficient of x^2 and the coefficient of x in the following quadratic equations:

(a) $4x^2 + 3x - 2 = 0$ (b) $x^2 - 23x + 17 = 0$ (c) $-x^2 + 19 = 0$

Solution

(a) In the equation $4x^2 + 3x - 2 = 0$ the coefficient of x^2 is 4 and the coefficient of x is 3.

(b) In the equation $x^2 - 23x + 17 = 0$ the coefficient of x^2 is 1 and the coefficient of x is -23.

(c) In the equation $-x^2 + 19 = 0$ the coefficient of x^2 is -1 and the coefficient of x is zero, since there is no term involving just x.

14.8 Verify that both $x = -7$ and $x = 5$ satisfy the quadratic equation $x^2 + 2x - 35 = 0$.

Solution We substitute $x = -7$ into the left-hand side of the equation. This yields

$$(-7)^2 + 2(-7) - 35$$

That is,

$$49 - 14 - 35$$

This simplifies to zero, and so the left-hand side equals the right-hand side of the given equation. Therefore $x = -7$ is a solution.

Similarly, if $x = 5$ we find

$$(5^2) + 2(5) - 35 = 25 + 10 - 35$$

which also simplifies to zero. We conclude that $x = 5$ is also a solution.

Solution by factorisation

If the quadratic expression on the left-hand side of the equation can be factorised solutions can be found using the method in the following examples.

WORKED EXAMPLES

14.9 Solve the quadratic equation $x^2 + 3x - 10 = 0$.

Solution The left-hand side of the equation can be factorised to give

$$x^2 + 3x - 10 = (x + 5)(x - 2) = 0$$

Whenever the product of two quantities equals zero, then one or both of these quantities must be zero. It follows that either $x + 5 = 0$ or $x - 2 = 0$ from which $x = -5$ and $x = 2$ are the required solutions.

14.10 Solve the quadratic equation $6x^2 + 5x - 4 = 0$.

Solution The left-hand side of the equation can be factorised to give

$$6x^2 + 5x - 4 = (2x - 1)(3x + 4) = 0$$

It follows that either $2x - 1 = 0$ or $3x + 4 = 0$ from which $x = \frac{1}{2}$ and $x = -\frac{4}{3}$ are the required solutions.

14.11 Solve the quadratic equation $x^2 - 8x = 0$.

Solution Factorising the left-hand side gives

$$x^2 - 8x = x(x - 8) = 0$$

from which either $x = 0$ or $x - 8 = 0$. The solutions are therefore $x = 0$ and $x = 8$.

14.12 Solve the quadratic equation $x^2 - 36 = 0$.

Solution The left-hand side factorises to give

$$x^2 - 36 = (x + 6)(x - 6) = 0$$

so that $x + 6 = 0$ or $x - 6 = 0$. The solutions are therefore $x = -6$ and $x = 6$.

14.13 Solve the equation $x^2 = 81$.

Solution Writing this in the standard form of a quadratic equation we obtain $x^2 - 81 = 0$. The left-hand side can be factorised to give

$$x^2 - 81 = (x - 9)(x + 9) = 0$$

from which $x - 9 = 0$ or $x + 9 = 0$. The solutions are then $x = 9$ and $x = -9$.

Solution of quadratic equations using the formula

When it is difficult or impossible to factorise the quadratic expression $ax^2 + bx + c$, solutions of a quadratic equation can be sought using the following formula:

Key point

If $ax^2 + bx + c = 0$, then $x = \dfrac{-b \pm \sqrt{b^2 - 4ac}}{2a}$

This formula gives possibly two solutions: one solution is obtained by taking the positive square root and the second solution by taking the negative square root.

WORKED EXAMPLES

14.14 Solve the equation $x^2 + 9x + 20 = 0$ using the formula.

Solution Comparing the given equation with the standard form $ax^2 + bx + c = 0$ we see that $a = 1$, $b = 9$ and $c = 20$. These values are substituted into the formula:

$$x = \frac{-b \pm \sqrt{b^2 - 4ac}}{2a}$$

$$= \frac{-9 \pm \sqrt{81 - 4(1)(20)}}{(2)(1)}$$

$$= \frac{-9 \pm \sqrt{81 - 80}}{2}$$

$$= \frac{-9 \pm \sqrt{1}}{2}$$

$$= \frac{-9 \pm 1}{2}$$

$$= \begin{cases} -4 & \text{by taking the positive square root} \\ -5 & \text{by taking the negative square root} \end{cases}$$

The two solutions are therefore $x = -4$ and $x = -5$.

14.15 Solve the equation $2x^2 - 3x - 7 = 0$ using the formula.

Solution In this example $a = 2$, $b = -3$ and $c = -7$. Care should be taken with the negative signs. Substituting these into the formula we find

$$x = \frac{-(-3) \pm \sqrt{(-3)^2 - 4(2)(-7)}}{2(2)}$$

$$= \frac{3 \pm \sqrt{9 + 56}}{4}$$

$$= \frac{3 \pm \sqrt{65}}{4}$$

$$= \frac{3 \pm 8.062}{4}$$

$$= \begin{cases} 2.766 & \text{by taking the positive square root} \\ -1.266 & \text{by taking the negative square root} \end{cases}$$

The two solutions are therefore $x = 2.766$ and $x = -1.266$.

If the values of a, b and c are such that $b^2 - 4ac$ is positive the formula will produce two solutions known as **distinct real roots** of the equation. If $b^2 - 4ac = 0$ there will be a single root known as a **repeated root**. Some books refer to the equation having **equal roots**. If the equation is such that $b^2 - 4ac$ is negative the formula requires us to find the square root of a negative number. In ordinary arithmetic this is impossible and we say that in such a case the quadratic equation does not possess any real roots.

The quantity $b^2 - 4ac$ is called the **discriminant**, because it allows us to distinguish between the three possible cases. In summary:

Key point

Given

$$ax^2 + bx + c = 0$$

then

$b^2 - 4ac > 0$ two distinct real roots

$b^2 - 4ac = 0$ repeated (equal) root

$b^2 - 4ac < 0$ no real roots

WORKED EXAMPLES

14.16 Can the equation $x^2 + 49 = 0$ be solved using the formula?

Solution In this example $a = 1$, $b = 0$ and $c = 49$. Therefore $b^2 - 4ac = 0 - 4(1)(49)$, which is negative. Therefore this equation does not possess any real roots.

14.17 Use the formula to solve the equation $4x^2 + 4x + 1 = 0$.

Solution In this example $a = 4$, $b = 4$ and $c = 1$. Applying the formula gives

$$x = \frac{-4 \pm \sqrt{4^2 - 4(4)(1)}}{(2)(4)}$$

$$= \frac{-4 \pm \sqrt{16 - 16}}{8}$$

$$= \frac{-4 \pm 0}{8} = -\frac{1}{2}$$

There is a single, repeated root $x = -\frac{1}{2}$. Note that $b^2 - 4ac = 0$.

Self-assessment questions 14.3

1. Under what conditions will a quadratic equation possess distinct real roots?
2. Under what conditions will a quadratic equation possess a repeated root?

Exercise 14.3

1. Solve the following quadratic equations by factorisation:
   (a) $x^2 + x - 2 = 0$ (b) $x^2 - 8x + 15 = 0$ (c) $4x^2 + 6x + 2 = 0$
   (d) $x^2 - 6x + 9 = 0$ (e) $x^2 - 81 = 0$ (f) $x^2 + 4x + 3 = 0$
   (g) $x^2 + 2x - 3 = 0$ (h) $x^2 + 3x - 4 = 0$ (i) $x^2 + 6x + 5 = 0$
   (j) $x^2 - 12x + 35 = 0$ (k) $x^2 + 12x + 35 = 0$ (l) $2x^2 + x - 3 = 0$
   (m) $2x^2 - x - 6 = 0$ (n) $2x^2 - 7x - 15 = 0$ (o) $3x^2 - 2x - 1 = 0$
   (p) $9x^2 - 12x - 5 = 0$ (q) $7x^2 + x = 0$ (r) $4x^2 + 12x + 9 = 0$

2. Solve the following quadratic equations using the formula:
   (a) $3x^2 - 6x - 5 = 0$ (b) $x^2 + 3x - 77 = 0$ (c) $2x^2 - 9x + 2 = 0$
   (d) $x^2 + 3x - 4 = 0$ (e) $3x^2 - 3x - 4 = 0$ (f) $4x^2 + x - 1 = 0$
   (g) $x^2 - 7x - 3 = 0$ (h) $x^2 + 7x - 3 = 0$ (i) $11x^2 + x + 1 = 0$
   (j) $2x^2 - 3x - 7 = 0$

3. Solve the following quadratic equations:
   (a) $6x^2 + 13x + 6 = 0$ (b) $3t^2 + 13t + 12 = 0$ (c) $t^2 - 7t + 3 = 0$

Test and assignment exercises 14

1. Solve the following equations:
   (a) $13t - 7 = 2t + 5$ (b) $-3t + 9 = 13 - 7t$ (c) $-5t = 0$

2. Solve the following equations:
   (a) $4x = 16$ (b) $\frac{x}{12} = 9$ (c) $4x - 13 = 3$ (d) $4x - 14 = 2x + 8$
   (e) $3x - 17 = 4$ (f) $7 - x = 9 + 3x$ (g) $4(2 - x) = 8$

3. Solve the following equations:
   (a) $2y = 8$ (b) $5u = 14u + 3$ (c) $5 = 4I$ (d) $13i + 7 = 2i - 9$
   (e) $\frac{1}{4}x + 9 = 3 - \frac{1}{2}x$ (f) $\frac{4x + 2}{2} + 8x = 0$

4. Solve the following equations:
   (a) $3x^2 - 27 = 0$ (b) $2x^2 + 18x + 14 = 0$ (c) $x^2 = 16$
   (d) $x^2 - x - 72 = 0$ (e) $2x^2 - 3x - 44 = 0$ (f) $x^2 - 4x - 21 = 0$

5. The solutions of the equation $x^2 + 4x = 0$ are identical to the solutions of $3x^2 + 12x = 0$. True or false?

6. Solve the following simultaneous equations:
   (a) $x - 2y = -11,\quad 7x + y = -32$ (b) $2x - y = 2,\quad x + 3y = 29$
   (c) $x + y = 19,\quad -x + y = 1$

CHAPTER 3

Drawing graphs

Contents

Chapter outline

Graphs give a lot of information in a simple and effective format. This chapter shows how to draw line graphs on Cartesian co-ordinates. We start with simple linear graphs, and then build up to more complicated functions, including quadratic equations, higher polynomials and exponential curves. We return to this theme in Chapter 5, when we discuss other types of diagram for presenting information.

After finishing this chapter you should be able to:

- Appreciate the benefits of graphs
- Use Cartesian co-ordinates to draw graphs
- Draw straight line graphs and interpret the results
- Draw graphs of quadratic equations and calculate the roots
- Draw graphs of more complicated curves, including polynomials and exponential curves.

Graphs on Cartesian co-ordinates

The last chapter showed how to build an algebraic model of a situation – but most people find it difficult to understand what is happening, or to follow the logic of a set of equations. Diagrams are much better at presenting information, and you can look at a well-drawn diagram and quickly see its main features. We develop this theme in Chapter 5, but here we introduce the line graph or graph to show the relationship between two variables.

Cartesian axes

The most common type of graph has two rectangular (or Cartesian) axes. The horizontal axis is traditionally labelled x and the vertical axis is labelled y (as shown in Figure 3.1). The x is the independent variable, which is the one that we can set or control, and y is the dependent variable, whose value is set by x. Then x might be the amount we spend on advertising, and y is the resulting sales; x might be the interest rate we charge for lending money, and y is the corresponding amount borrowed; x might be the price we charge for a service, and y is the resulting demand.

When we talk about dependent and independent variables, we do not assume any cause and effect. There might be a clear relationship between two variables, but this does not necessarily mean that a change in one actually causes a change in the other. For example, a department store might find that when it reduces the price of overcoats the sales of ice cream rise. There might be a clear relationship between these two, but one does not cause the other – and both are likely to be a result of hot weather. Unfortunately, people do not always recognise this, and they imagine ridiculous causes-and-effects (which we discuss in Chapter 9).

The point where the two axes cross is the origin. This is the point where both x and y have the value zero. At any point above the origin, y is positive, and at any point below it, y is negative; at any point to the right of the origin,

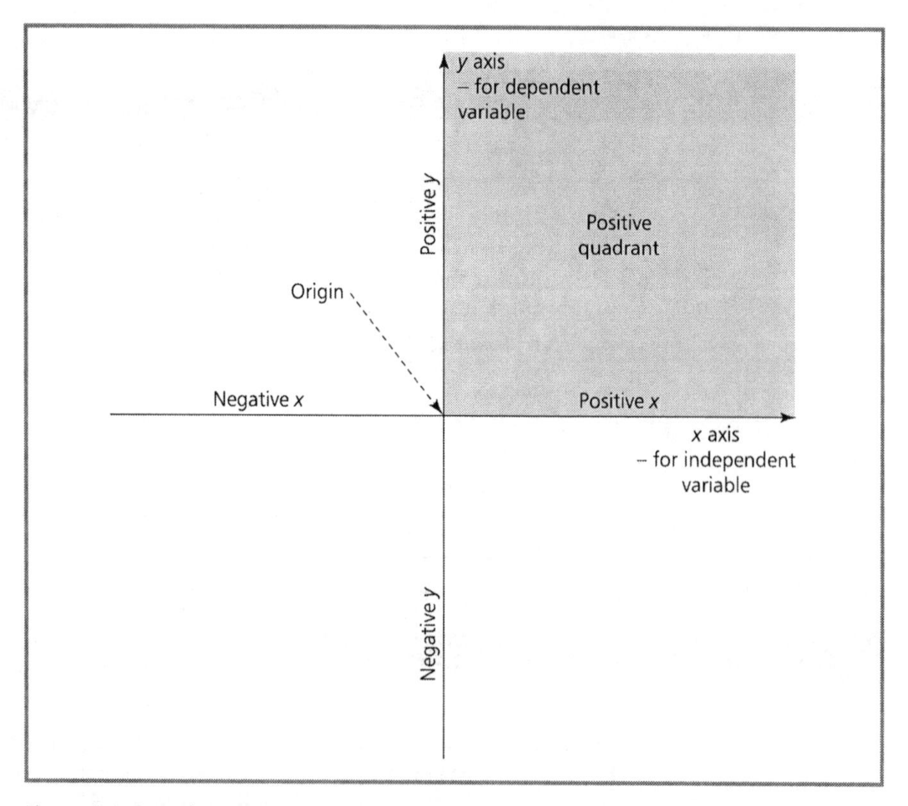

Figure 3.1 Cartesian axes

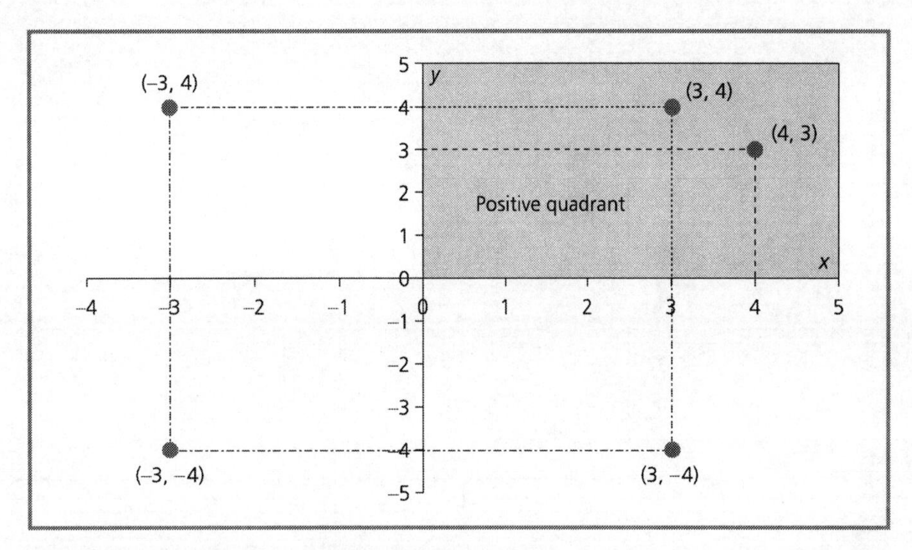

Figure 3.2 Locating points with Cartesian co-ordinates

x is positive, and at any point to the left of it, x is negative. Often, we are only interested in positive values of x and y – perhaps with a graph of income against sales. Then we show only the top right-hand corner of the graph, which is the **positive quadrant**.

We can describe any point on a graph by two numbers called **co-ordinates**. The first number gives the distance along the x axis from the origin, and the second number gives the distance up the y axis. For example, the point $x = 3$, $y = 4$ is situated three units along the x axis and four units up the y axis. A standard notation describes co-ordinates as (x, y), so this is point (3, 4). The only thing you have to be careful about is that (3, 4) is not the same as (4, 3), as you can see in Figure 3.2. And these points are some way from (−3, 4), (3, −4) and (−3, −4).

Points on the x axis have co-ordinates $(x, 0)$ and points on the y axis have co-ordinates $(0, y)$. The origin is the point where the axes cross; it has co-ordinates (0, 0).

WORKED EXAMPLE 3.1

Plot the following points on a graph.

x	2	5	7	10	12	15
y	7	20	22	28	41	48

Solution

As all the numbers are positive, we need draw only the positive quadrant. Then the first point, (2, 7), is two units along the x axis and seven units up the y axis, and is shown as point A in Figure 3.3.

The second point, (5, 20), is five units along the x axis and 20 units up the y axis, and is shown by point B. Adding the other points in the same way gives the result shown in Figure 3.3.

There is a clear relationship between x and y, and we can emphasise this by joining the points. For this either we can draw a line connecting all the points to show the details, or we can ignore the details and draw a line of the general trend (shown in Figure 3.4).

Worked example 3.1 continued

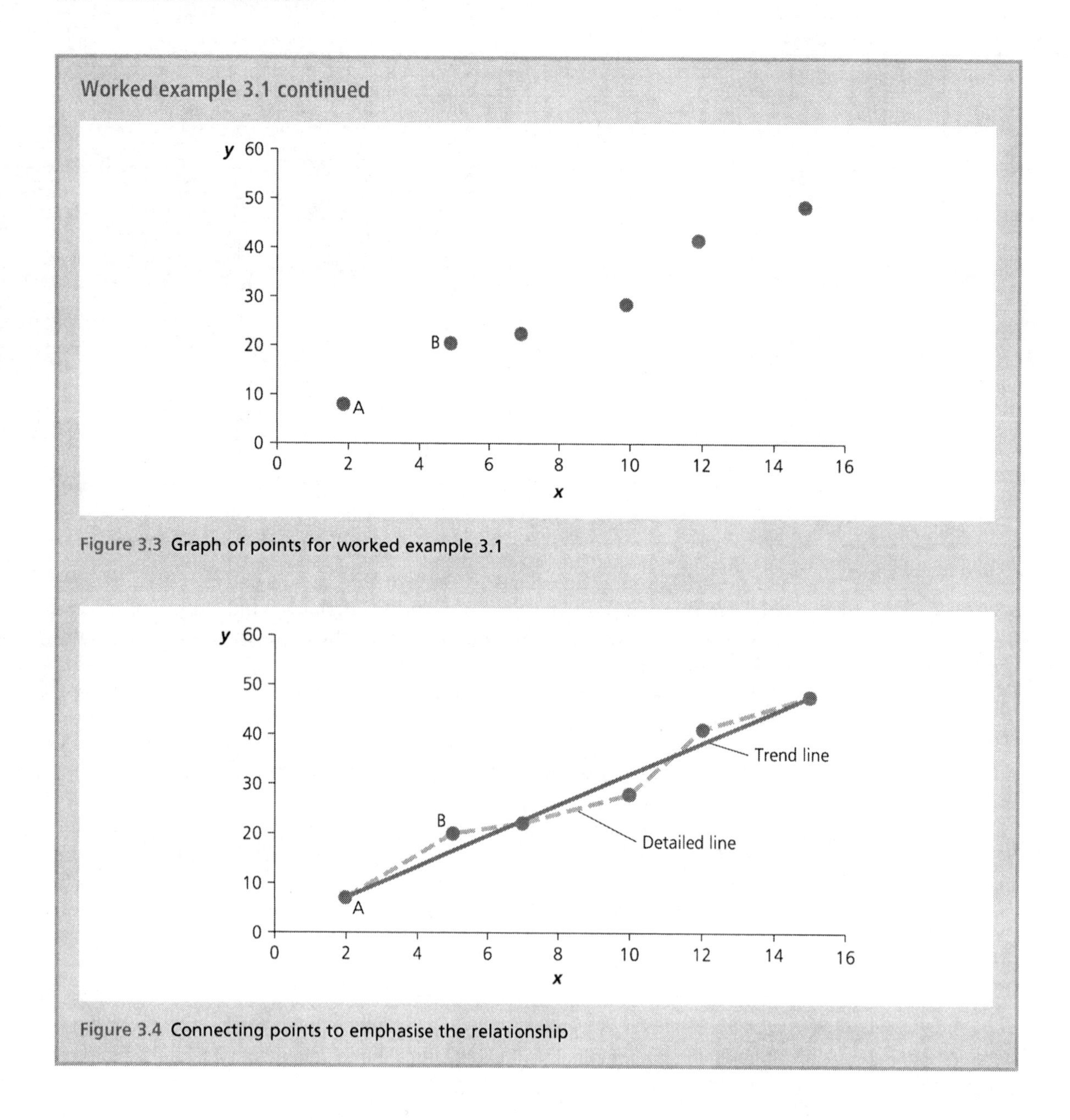

Figure 3.3 Graph of points for worked example 3.1

Figure 3.4 Connecting points to emphasise the relationship

Of course, you can draw graphs in the traditional way, by hand on graph paper, but the easiest and most reliable way uses specialised graphics packages. Many of these are available, such as ConceptDraw, CorelDraw, DrawPlus, Freelance Graphics, Harvard Graphics, Sigmaplot, SmartDraw and Visio. Many other packages also have graphics functions, such as presentation packages, desktop publishing, design packages and picture editors. Excel has a graphics function, and Figure 3.5 shows an example of the results when you press the 'chart wizard' button.

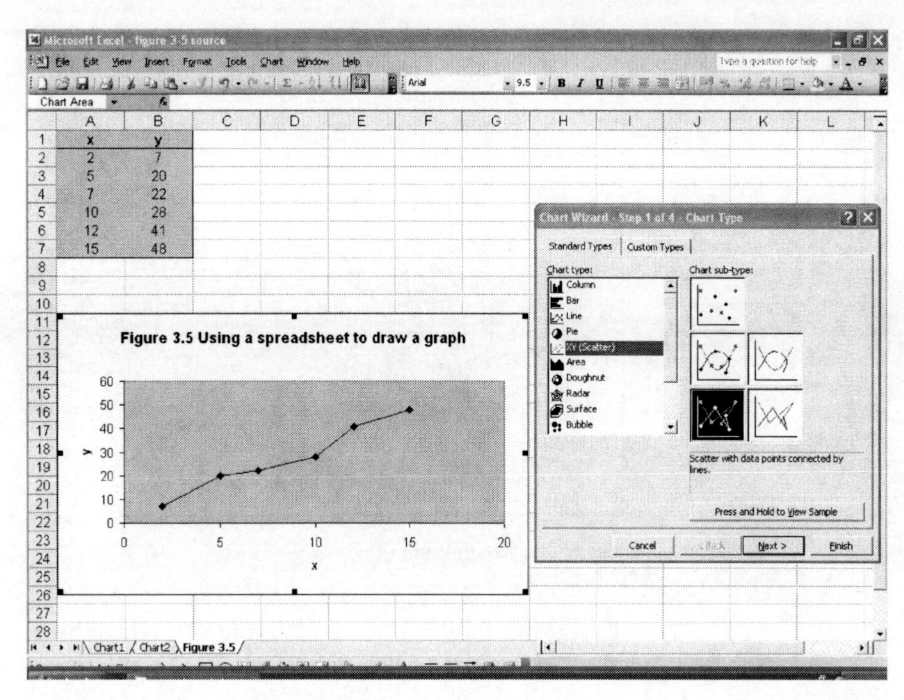

Figure 3.5 Using a spreadsheet to draw a graph

Drawing straight line graphs

The usual way of drawing a graph is to plot a series of points (x, y) and then draw a line through them. For complicated graphs we need a lot of points to get the right shape, but for straightforward graphs we need only a few points – and in the simplest case we can draw a straight line graph through only two points. You can see this in a simple case, where y always has a constant value whatever the value of x. For example, if $y = 10$ for all values of x, then we can take two arbitrary values of x, say 2 and 14, and get two points (2, 10) and (14, 10). Then we can draw a straight line through these that is 10 units above the y axis and parallel to it (as shown in Figure 3.6).

In general, a graph of $y = c$, where c is any constant, is a straight line that is parallel to the x axis and c units above it. This line divides the area of the graph into three zones:

- At any point *on* the line, y is equal to the constant, so $y = c$.
- At any point *above* the line, y is greater than c, so $y > c$.
- At any point *below* the line, y is less than c, so $y < c$.

We could equally say:

- At any point *on or above* the line, y is greater than or equal to c, so $y \geq c$.
- At any point *on or below* the line, y is less than or equal to c, so $y \leq c$.

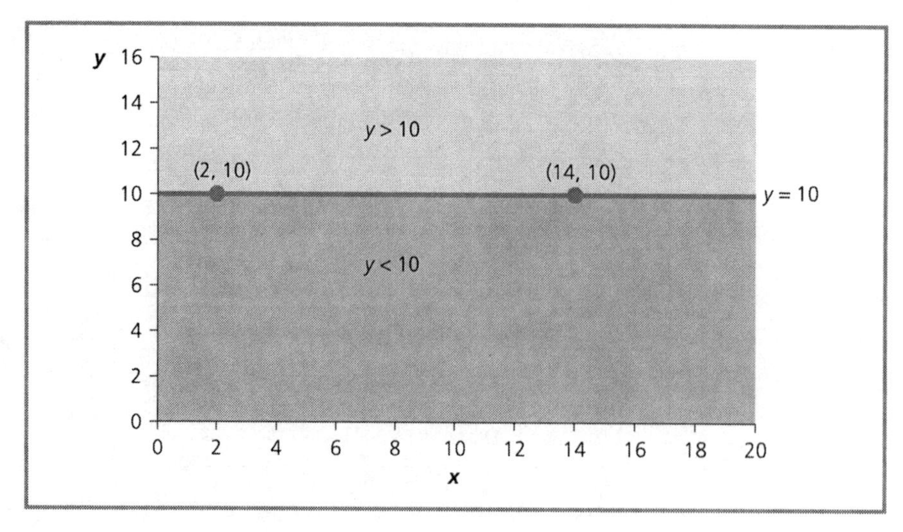

Figure 3.6 Straight line graph of $y = 10$

The graph of $y = c$ is an example of a straight line graph. Not surprisingly, any relationship that gives a straight line graph is called a linear relationship.

> Linear relationships have the general form:
>
> $$y = ax + b$$
>
> where:
>
> x and y are the independent and dependent variables
>
> a and b are constants.

WORKED EXAMPLE 3.2

Draw a graph of $y = 10x + 50$.

Solution

This is a straight line graph of the standard form $y = ax + b$, with $a = 10$ and $b = 50$. We need only two points to draw the line and can take any convenient ones. Here we will arbitrarily take the points where $x = 0$ and $x = 20$.

- When $x = 0$, $y = 10x + 50 = 10 \times 0 + 50 = 50$, which defines the point (0, 50).
- When $x = 20$, $y = 10x + 50 = 10 \times 20 + 50 = 250$, which defines the point (20, 250).

Plotting these points and drawing a line through them gives the graph shown in Figure 3.7.

Worked example 3.2 continued

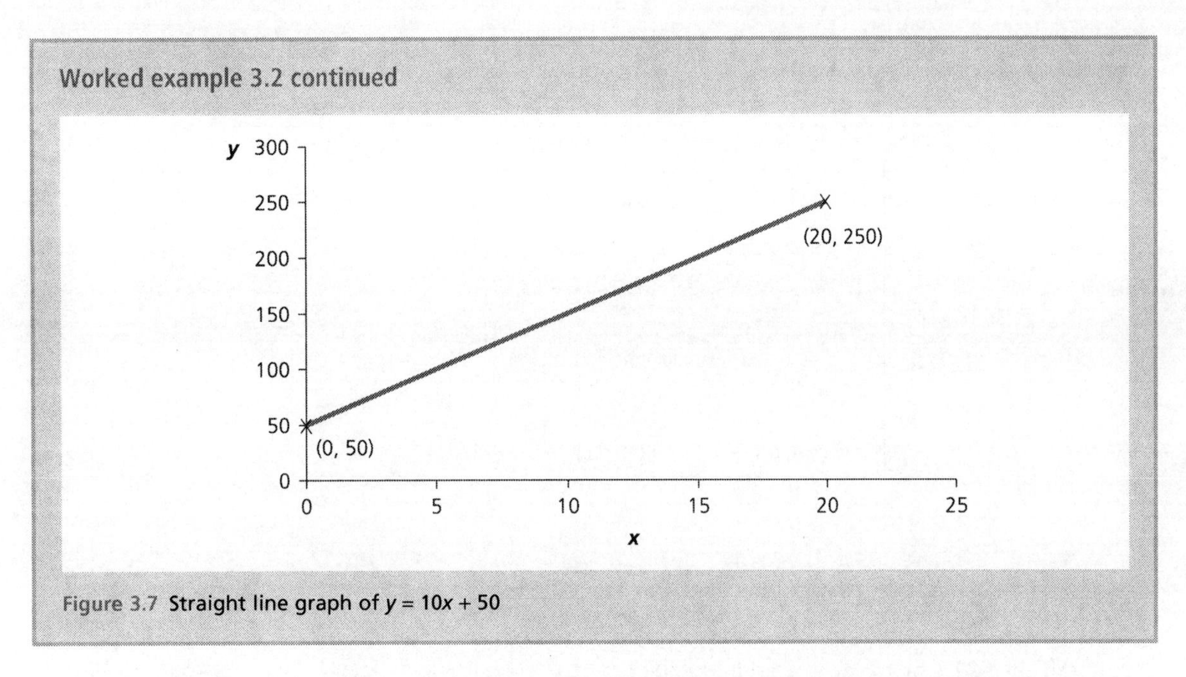

Figure 3.7 Straight line graph of $y = 10x + 50$

When you look at a straight line graph, there are two obvious features:

- the intercept, which shows where the line crosses the y axis;
- the gradient, which shows how steep the line is.

When the line crosses the y axis, x has the value 0. And if we substitute $x = 0$ into the equation $y = ax + b$, you see that $ax = 0$, so $y = b$. In other words, the constant b is the intercept of the line.

The gradient of a line shows how quickly it is rising, and is defined as the increase in y for a unit increase in x. The gradient is clearly the same at every point on a straight line, so we can find the increase in y when x increases from, say, n to $n + 1$:

- When $x = n$, $y = ax + b = an + b$.
- When $x = n + 1$, $y = ax + b = a(n + 1) + b = an + a + b$.

As you can see, the difference between these two is a, and this shows that an increase of 1 in x always gives an increase of a in y. So the constant a is the gradient, meaning that the general equation for a straight line is:

$y = \text{gradient} \times x + \text{intercept}$

WORKED EXAMPLE 3.3

Describe the graph of the equation $y = 4x + 20$.

Solution

This is a straight line graph with intercept of 20 and gradient of 4, as shown in Figure 3.8.

You can also see the following:

- For any point actually on the line, $y = 4x + 20$.
- For any point above the line, $y > 4x + 20$.
- For any point below the line, $y < 4x + 20$.

Worked example 3.3 continued

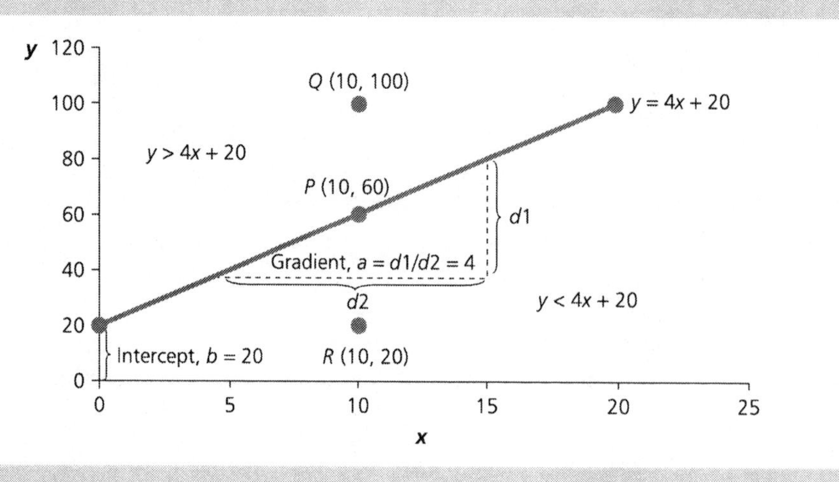

Figure 3.8 Straight line graph of $y = 4x + 20$

You can check this by taking any arbitrary points. For example, when $x = 10$ the corresponding value of y on the line is $y = 4 \times 10 + 20 = 60$, giving the point P at (10, 60). The point Q has co-ordinates (10, 100), is above the line, and y is clearly greater than $4x + 20$; the point R has co-ordinates (10, 20), is below the line, and y is clearly less than $4x + 20$.

WORKED EXAMPLE 3.4

Anita notices that the sales of a product vary with its price, so that:

sales = 100 − 5 × price

What are her sales when the price is 6?

Solution

Substituting the price, 6, into the equation gives sales of $100 - 5 \times 6 = 70$. But we can find more information from a graph. The relationship is a straight line with the equation $y = ax + b$, where y is the sales, x is the price, a is the gradient of −5, and b is the intercept of 100. The negative gradient shows that y decreases as x increases – and with every unit increase in price, sales fall by 5. To draw the graph (shown in Figure 3.9) we take two arbitrary points, say $x = 0$ and $x = 10$:

- When $x = 0$, $y = 100 - 5x = 100 - 5 \times 0 = 100$, giving the point (0, 100).
- When $x = 10$, $y = 100 - 5x = 100 - 5 \times 10 = 50$, giving the point (10, 50).

There is an upper limit on sales, given by the intercept – and even when the price is reduced to zero the expected sales are 100. Any point above the line shows that sales are higher than expected, while any point below shows that they are lower.

Worked example 3.4 continued

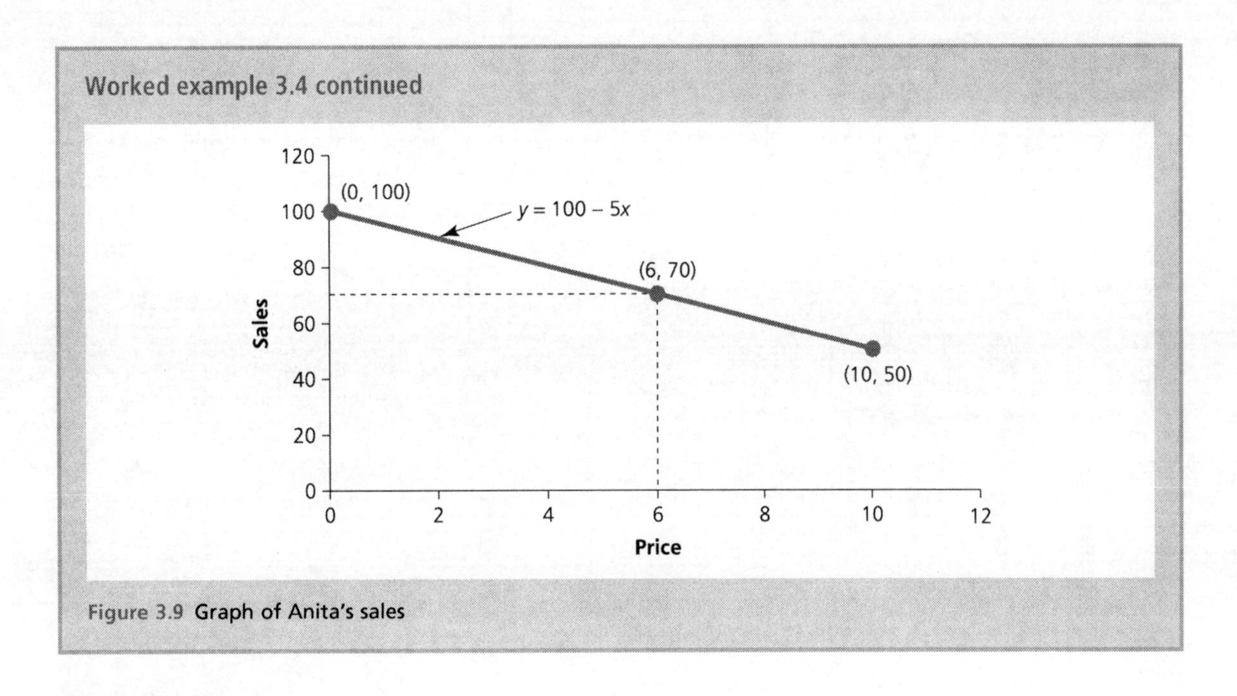

Figure 3.9 Graph of Anita's sales

Review questions

3.1 What is meant by a dependent variable?

3.2 Graphs show the changes in y caused by changes in x. Is this true?

3.3 With Cartesian co-ordinates, what are the co-ordinates of the origin?

3.4 Is there a difference between the points (3, –4) and (–3, 4)?

3.5 Describe the graph of the equation $y = -2x - 4$.

3.6 What are the gradients of the lines (a) $y = 10$, (b) $y = x$, (c) $y = 10 - 6x$?

3.7 If $y = 3x + 5$, what can you say about all the points above the graph of this line?

Quadratic equations

Any relationship between variables that is not linear is – not surprisingly – called a non-linear relationship. These have more complicated graphs, but we can draw them using the same principles as straight lines. The only concern is that we need more points to show the exact shape of the curve. The easiest way of getting these is to take a series of convenient values for x, and substitute them into the equation to find corresponding values for y. Then plot the resulting points (x, y) and draw a line through them.

WORKED EXAMPLE 3.5

Draw a graph of the equation $y = 2x^2 + 3x - 3$, between $x = -6$ and $x = 5$.

Solution

We are interested in values of x between −6 and +5, so take a series of points within this range and substitute them to find corresponding values for y. We can start with:

- $x = -6$, and substitution gives $y = 2x^2 + 3x - 3 = 2 \times (-6)^2 + 3 \times (-6) - 3 = 51$
- $x = -5$, and substitution gives $y = 2x^2 + 3x - 3 = 2 \times (-5)^2 + 3 \times (-5) - 3 = 32$

and so on, to give the following table.

x	−6	−5	−4	−3	−2	−1	0	1	2	3	4	5
y	51	32	17	6	−1	−4	−3	2	11	24	41	62

Plotting these points on Cartesian axes and drawing a curved line through them gives the graph in Figure 3.10.

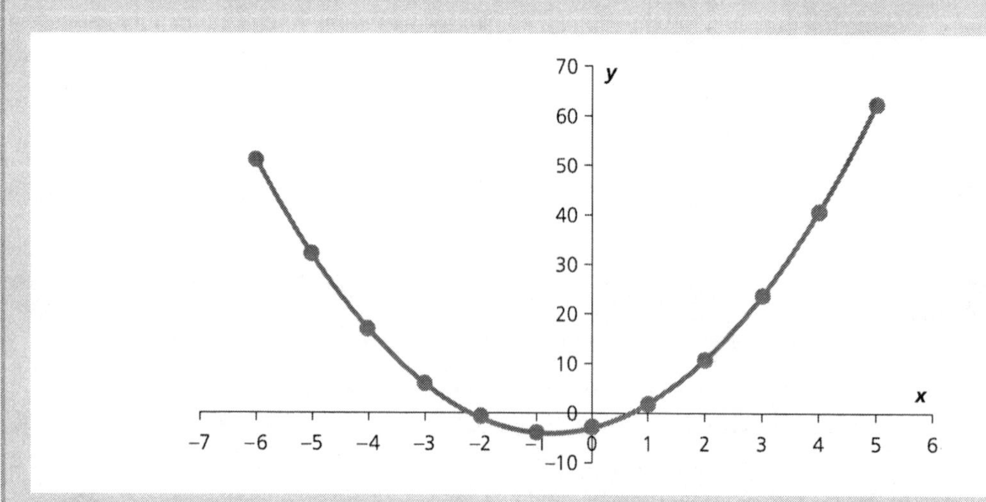

Figure 3.10 Graph of $y = 2x^2 + 3x - 3$

The last example showed a quadratic equation. These have the general form $y = ax^2 + bx + c$ where a, b and c are constants. Their graphs are always U-shaped – but when a is negative the graph is inverted and it looks like a hill rather than a valley. The top of the hill, or bottom of the valley, is called a turning point, where the graph changes direction and the gradient changes sign.

Quadratic equations are quite common, as we can show from an example of production costs. Suppose economies of scale and other effects mean that the average cost of making a product changes with the number of units made. The basic cost of making one unit might be €200, and this falls by €5 for every unit of weekly production. Then the unit cost is $200 - 5x$, where x is the weekly production. If there are fixed overheads of €2,000 a week:

$$\begin{aligned}\text{total weekly cost} &= \text{overheads} + \text{number of units made in the week} \\ &\quad \times \text{unit cost} \\ &= 2{,}000 + x \times (200 - 5x) \\ &= 2{,}000 + 200x - 5x^2\end{aligned}$$

WORKED EXAMPLE 3.6

Sonja Thorsen bought shares worth €10,000 in her employer's profit-sharing scheme. When the share price rose by €10, she kept 1,000 shares and sold the rest for €11,000. How can you describe her share purchases?

Solution

If Sonja originally bought x shares, the price of each was €10,000/x. When this rose to (10,000/x + 10) she sold (x – 1,000) shares for €11,000. So:

$$11{,}000 = \text{number of shares sold} \times \text{selling price}$$
$$= (x - 1{,}000) \times (10{,}000/x + 10)$$

Rearranging this equation gives:

$$11{,}000 = (x - 1{,}000) \times \left(\frac{10{,}000}{x} + 10\right)$$
$$= 10{,}000 + 10x - \frac{10{,}000{,}000}{x} - 10{,}000$$

or

$$11{,}000x = 10{,}000x + 10x^2 - 10{,}000{,}000 - 10{,}000x$$

i.e.

$$10x^2 - 11{,}000x - 10{,}000{,}000 = 0$$

In the next section we show how to solve this equation, and find that Sonja originally bought 1,691 shares. You can check this by seeing that she bought 1,691 shares at 10,000/1,691 = €5.91 each. When the shares rose to €15.91, she sold 691 of them for 691 × 15.91 = €11,000, and kept the remainder with a value of 1,000 × 15.91 = €15,910.

WORKED EXAMPLE 3.7

Draw a graph of $y = 15 + 12x - 3x^2$ for values of x between –2 and 6. Where does this curve cross the x axis?

Solution

We can take a range of values for x and substitute these to get corresponding values for y, as follows.

x	–2	–1	0	1	2	3	4	5	6
y	–21	0	15	24	27	24	15	0	–21

Plotting these points and joining them together gives the results in Figure 3.11. As a has a negative value of –3, the graph is an inverted U, and you can see that it crosses the x axis at x = –1 and x = 5.

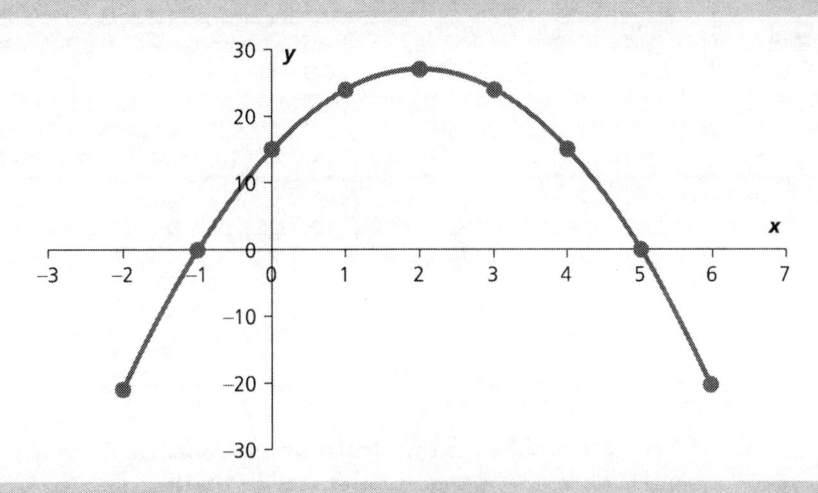

Figure 3.11 Graph of $y = 15 + 12x - 3x^2$

In the last example, we found the points where the curve crossed the x axis. By definition, these are the two points where $ax^2 + bx + c = 0$, and they are called the roots of the quadratic. You can estimate these from a graph, but there is a standard calculation for finding them (whose derivation you can find in the Companion Website **www.pearsoned.co.uk/waters**). This shows that the two points where $y = 0$ correspond to the values of x where:

$$x = \frac{-b + \sqrt{b^2 - 4ac}}{2a} \quad \text{and} \quad x = \frac{-b - \sqrt{b^2 - 4ac}}{2a}$$

In the worked example above, $a = -3$, $b = 12$ and $c = 15$, and we can substitute these values to get:

$$x = \frac{-12 + \sqrt{12^2 - 4 \times (-3) \times 15}}{2 \times (-3)} \quad \text{and} \quad x = \frac{-12 - \sqrt{12^2 - 4 \times (-3) \times 15}}{2 \times (-3)}$$

$$= \frac{-12 + \sqrt{(144 + 180)}}{-6} \qquad = \frac{-12 - \sqrt{(144 + 180)}}{-6}$$

$$= (-12 + 18) / (-6) \qquad = (-12 - 18) / (-6)$$

$$= -1 \qquad = 5$$

This confirms our findings from the graph, that the curve crosses the x axis at the points $(-1, 0)$ and $(5, 0)$.

WORKED EXAMPLE 3.8

Find the roots of the equation $2x^2 + 3x - 2 = 0$.

Solution

This is a quadratic with $a = 2$, $b = 3$ and $c = -2$. Substituting these values into the standard equations gives the two roots:

$$x = \frac{-b + \sqrt{b^2 - 4ac}}{2a}$$

$$= \frac{-3 + \sqrt{3^2 - 4 \times 2 \times (-2)}}{2 \times 2}$$

$$= (-3 + \sqrt{25}) / 4$$

$$= 0.5$$

and

$$x = \frac{-b - \sqrt{b^2 - 4ac}}{2a}$$

$$= \frac{-3 - \sqrt{3^2 - 4 \times 2 \times (-2)}}{2 \times 2}$$

$$= (-3 - \sqrt{25}) / 4$$

$$= -2$$

You can check these values by substituting them in the original equation:

$$2 \times 0.5^2 + 3 \times 0.5 - 2 = 0$$

and

$$2 \times (-2)^2 + 3 \times (-2) - 2 = 0$$

The only problem with calculating the roots comes when $4ac$ is greater than b^2. Then $b^2 - 4ac$ is negative, and we have to find the square root of a negative number. This is not defined in real arithmetic, so we conclude that there are no real roots and they are both imaginary.

Review questions

3.8 Are the graphs of all quadratic equations exactly the same shape?

3.9 What are the roots of a quadratic equation?

3.10 What can you say about the roots of $y = x^2 + 2x + 3$?

3.11 Why is it better to calculate the roots of a quadratic equation than to read them from a graph?

IDEAS IN PRACTICE **Emjit Chandrasaika**

In his spare time, Emjit Chandrasaika sells computer software through his website. Because he does this from home, and considers it a mixture of business and pleasure, he does not keep a tight check on his accounts. He thinks that he gets a basic income of £12 for every unit he sells, but economies of scale mean that this increases by £2 for every unit. He estimates the fixed costs of his website, advertising and time is £1,000 a month.

Emjit's income per unit is $12 + 2x$, where x is the number of units that he sells per month. Then:

$$\begin{aligned}\text{profit} &= \text{number of units sold per month} \times \text{unit income} - \text{overheads}\\ &= x(12 + 2x) - 1{,}000\\ &= 2x^2 + 12x - 1{,}000\end{aligned}$$

When this equals zero his income just covers his costs, and this happens when:

$$x = \frac{-b + \sqrt{b^2 - 4ac}}{2a} = \frac{-12 + \sqrt{12^2 - 4 \times 2 \times (-1{,}000)}}{2 \times 2} = 19.6$$

or

$$x = \frac{-b - \sqrt{b^2 - 4ac}}{2a} = \frac{-12 - \sqrt{12^2 - 4 \times 2 \times (-1{,}000)}}{2 \times 2} = -25.6$$

Obviously, he cannot sell a negative number of units, so he must sell 20 units a month to make a profit. His actual sales are much more than this, and rising by 50% a year. This analysis is encouraging Emjit to consider a move into full-time web sales.

Drawing other graphs

When we can express one variable, y, in terms of another, x, we say that 'y is a function of x', and write this as $y = f(x)$. With a straight line, y is a linear function of x, which means that $y = f(x)$ and $f(x) = ax + b$; with a quadratic $y = f(x)$, and $f(x) = ax^2 + bx + c$. This is just a convenient shorthand that can save time explaining relationships. You can draw a graph of any relationship where y is a function of x, with $y = f(x)$.

Polynomials

We have drawn graphs of straight lines (where $y = ax + b$) and quadratic equations (where $y = ax^2 + bx + c$). These are two examples of polynomials – which is the general term for equations that contain a variable, x, raised to some power. For straight lines we raised x to the power 1, for quadratics we raised x to the power 2 – and for more complicated polynomials we raise x

to higher powers. Cubic equations contain x raised to the power 3, with the form $y = ax^3 + bx^2 + cx + d$. The constants a, b, c, d are called coefficients of the polynomial. Higher polynomials have more complex curves, and when drawing graphs you have to plot enough points to show the details.

WORKED EXAMPLE 3.9

Draw a graph of the function $y = x^3 - 1.5x^2 - 18x$ between $x = -5$ and $x = +6$.

Solution

Figure 3.12 shows a spreadsheet of the results. The top part shows a series of values of y calculated for x between −5 and 6; then the Chart Wizard actually draws the graph. This has a trough around $x = 3$ and a peak around $x = -2$. Cubic equations always have this general shape, with two turning points, but they vary in detail; some are the other way around, some have the two turning points merged into one, and so on.

	A	B	C	D	E	F	G	H	I	J	K	L	M
1	**Graph of cubic equation**												
2													
3	***x***	−5	−4	−3	−2	−1	0	1	2	3	4	5	6
4	***y***	−72.5	−16	13.5	22	15.5	0	−18.5	−34	−40.5	−32	−2.5	54

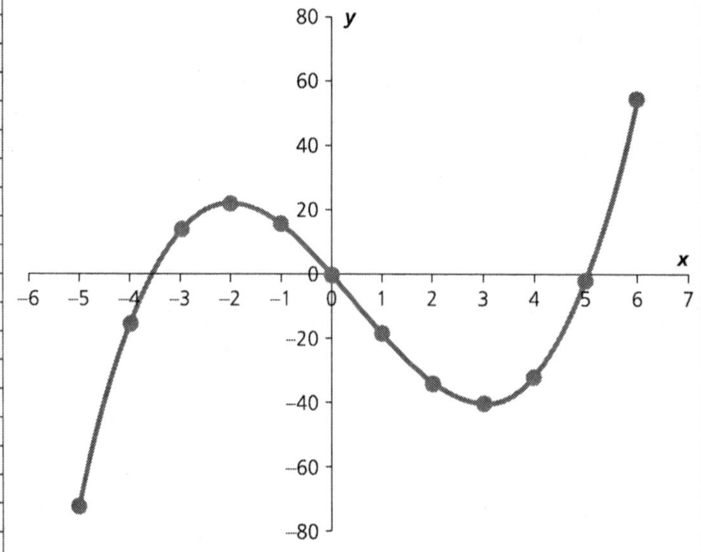

Figure 3.12 Graph of $y = x^3 - 1.5x^2 - 18x$

Exponential curves

We mentioned earlier the exponential constant, e, which is defined as e = 2.7182818. . . . This strange number is useful for describing functions that rise or fall at an accelerating rate. Exponential curves have the general form $y = ne^{mx}$, where n and m are constants. The exact shape depends on the values of n and m, but when m is positive there is an accelerating rise – described as exponential growth – and when m is negative there is a decreasing fall – described as exponential decline.

WORKED EXAMPLE 3.10

Draw graphs of $y = e^x$ and $y = e^{0.9x}$ for values of x between 0 and 10.

Solution

Figure 3.13 shows these results in a spreadsheet. When e is raised to a positive power, the characteristic exponential curves rise very quickly with x.

	A	B	C	D	E	F	G	H	I	J	K	L
1	**Graphs of exponential growth**											
2												
3	***x***	**0**	**1**	**2**	**3**	**4**	**5**	**6**	**7**	**8**	**9**	**10**
4	**$e^{0.9x}$**	1	2	6	15	37	90	221	545	1339	3294	8103
5	**e^x**	1	3	7	20	55	148	403	1097	2981	8103	22026

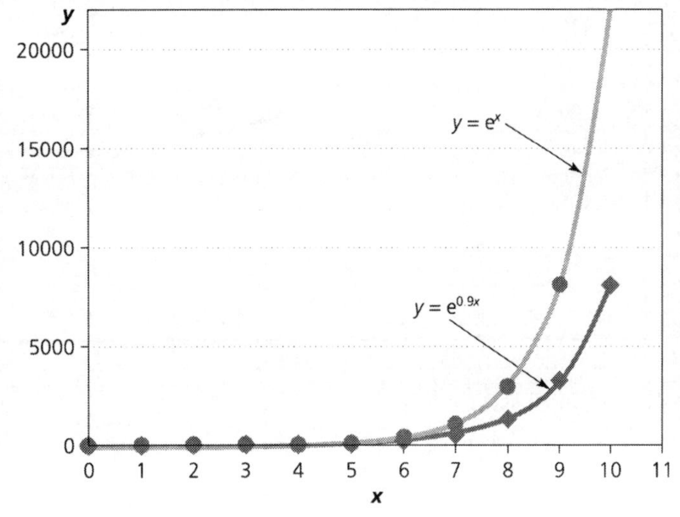

Figure 3.13 Graphs of exponential growth

WORKED EXAMPLE 3.11

Draw the graph of $y = 1000e^{-0.5x}$ between $x = 0$ and $x = 10$.

Solution

Figure 3.14 shows the calculations and graph on a spreadsheet. When e is raised to a negative power, the exponential curve falls quickly towards zero and then flattens out with increasing x.

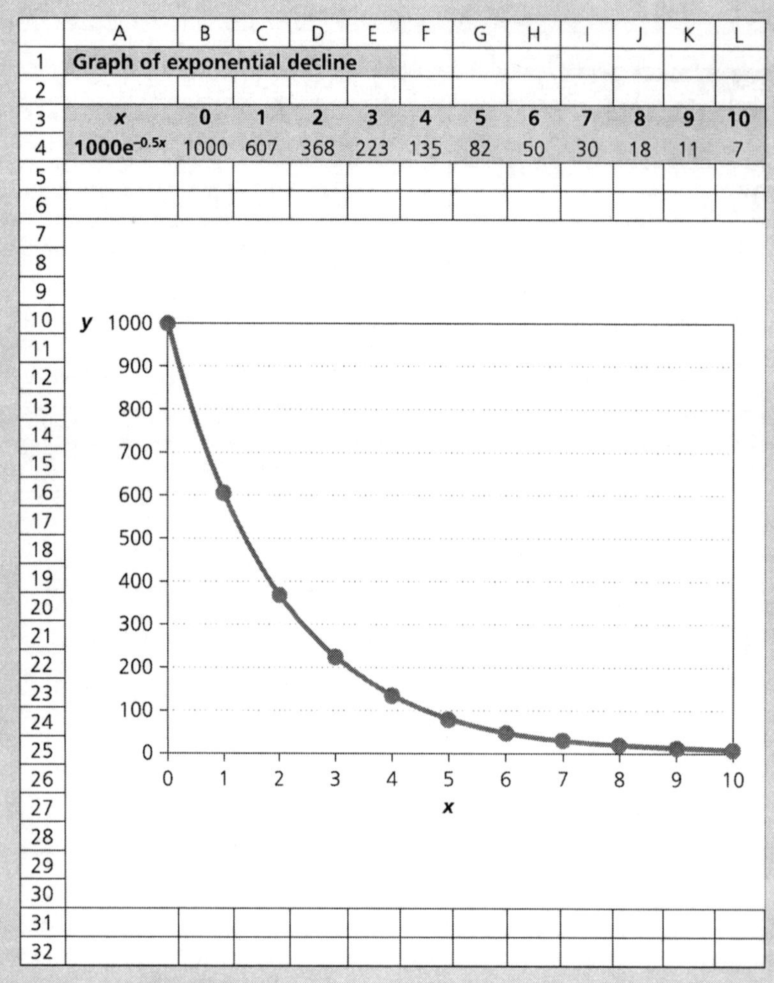

	A	B	C	D	E	F	G	H	I	J	K	L
1	**Graph of exponential decline**											
2												
3	***x***	**0**	**1**	**2**	**3**	**4**	**5**	**6**	**7**	**8**	**9**	**10**
4	**$1000e^{-0.5x}$**	1000	607	368	223	135	82	50	30	18	11	7

Figure 3.14 Graph of exponential decline

Review questions

3.12 What is a polynomial?

3.13 What is a turning point in a graph?

3.14 How can you draw a graph of exponential growth?

3.15 Can you draw a graph of $y = 12x + 7z$, where both x and z are variables?

IDEAS IN PRACTICE Konrad Schimmer

You can find examples of graphs in almost any newspaper or magazine. Many of these are time series, which show a series of observations taken at regular intervals of time – such as monthly unemployment figures, daily rainfall, weekly demand for a product, and annual profit. Financial analysts use many types of graph, as they are the best way of showing trends and underlying patterns.

Konrad Schimmer is a financial analyst of the Frankfurt Stock Exchange, and he plots graphs for every aspect of companies' performance. Typically he plots the quarterly profit for the past six years, monthly sales for the past three years, or closing share price over the past year. Figure 3.15 shows one of his graphs for comparing two companies, with the closing share prices at the end of each week for the past year. Konrad studies the details of such graphs, looking for trends, unusual patterns, possible causes, and how the company is likely to perform in the future. He has used this approach to amass considerable wealth.

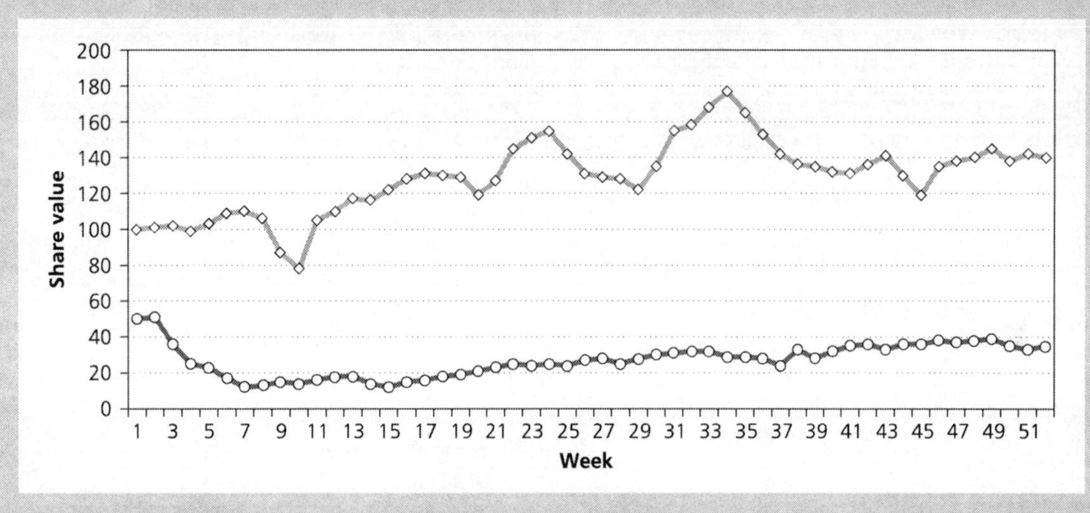

Figure 3.15 Comparison of closing weekly share prices

CHAPTER REVIEW

This chapter showed how to draw different types of graph.

- Diagrams give an easy and efficient way of presenting information. People can look at a well-drawn diagram and quickly see the main features and patterns.
- Graphs are one of the most useful types of diagram, and usually use Cartesian co-ordinates to show a relationship between two variables.
- Straight line graphs have the form $y = ax + b$, where a is the gradient and b is the intercept. You can draw straight line graphs by plotting two points and drawing the line through them.
- You can extend this method to more complicated curves, such as quadratic equations. These have the general form $y = ax^2 + bx + c$, and are U-shaped – or inverted when a is negative.

- The roots of a quadratic equation are the points where the curve crosses the x axis, and there is a standard calculation to identify these points.
- You can use the standard method for drawing graphs for any relationship where y is a function of x, meaning that $y = f(x)$, including polynomials and exponential curves.

CASE STUDY McFarlane & Sons

John McFarlane works for his family company, which has sold traditional clothing from four shops in the east of Scotland since 1886. He wants to compare the performance of each shop, and has collected some detailed information for the past year. Now he wants a convenient format to present this to the company Board of Directors.

John's problem is that he has a huge amount of data. The following table shows the number of units of five products sold each month in each of the shops. John has this kind of information for several hundred products, along with costs, profit margins, advertising expenditure – and many other figures.

Month	Shop	Product A	Product B	Product C	Product D	Product E
January						
	1	15	87	2	21	65
	2	12	42	0	15	32
	3	8	21	3	33	40
	4	7	9	3	10	22
February						
	1	16	80	1	22	67
	2	16	43	2	12	34
	3	8	24	5	31	41
	4	8	8	2	9	21
March						
	1	18	78	6	15	70
	2	16	45	6	8	30
	3	8	21	8	23	44
	4	10	7	2	8	19
April						
	1	21	83	11	16	71
	2	17	46	13	7	30
	3	11	19	9	25	47
	4	9	8	4	9	21
May						
	1	24	86	2	25	66
	2	20	49	7	16	32
	3	14	23	3	37	46
	4	10	6	3	13	22
June						
	1	27	91	3	33	65
	2	23	52	1	17	33
	3	15	20	0	51	47
	4	12	9	2	17	10
July						
	1	27	88	2	38	65
	2	22	55	0	20	38
	3	16	20	2	58	46
	4	9	8	1	19	20

Case study continued

Month	Shop	Product A	Product B	Product C	Product D	Product E
August						
	1	20	90	1	37	68
	2	21	57	0	24	35
	3	11	23	1	60	40
	4	10	8	0	20	18
September						
	1	17	84	7	26	65
	2	17	63	8	17	31
	3	10	21	4	39	46
	4	6	7	9	12	19
October						
	1	17	85	24	19	70
	2	14	61	23	13	33
	3	11	21	21	30	39
	4	9	7	19	11	21
November						
	1	15	85	37	11	69
	2	13	55	36	10	33
	3	9	22	28	15	44
	4	9	9	19	5	21
December						
	1	15	88	81	17	68
	2	12	54	65	14	34
	3	7	18	67	24	40
	4	8	7	53	8	22

Question

- **How could John McFarlane use graphs to present information to the company Board of Directors?**

PROBLEMS

3.1 Draw a graph of the points (2, 12), (4, 16), (7, 22), (10, 28) and (15, 38). How would you describe this graph?

3.2 Draw a graph of the following points. What can you say about the results?

x	1	3	6	8	9	10	13	14	17	18	21	25	26	29
y	22	24	31	38	41	44	52	55	61	64	69	76	81	83

3.3 The number of people employed in a chain of workshops is related to the size (in consistent units) by the equation:

$$\text{employees} = \text{size} / 1{,}000 + 3$$

Draw a graph of this equation and use it to find the number of employees in a workshop of size 50,000 units.

3.4 Draw graphs of (a) $y = 10$, (b) $y = x + 10$, (c) $y = x^2 + x + 10$, and (d) $y = x^3 + x^2 + x + 10$.

3.5 What are the roots of (a) $x^2 - 6x + 8$, (b) $3x^2 - 2x - 5$, and (c) $x^2 + x + 1$?

3.6 Deng Chow Chan found that the basic income generated by his main product is £10 a unit, but this increases by £1 for every unit he makes. If he has to cover fixed costs of £100, how many units must he sell to cover all his costs?

3.7 The output, y, from an assembly line is related to one of the settings, x, by the equation

$$y = -5x^2 + 2{,}500x - 12{,}500$$

What is the maximum output from the line, and the corresponding value for x?

3.8 Martha Berryman finds that the unit cost of using production equipment is:

$$\text{cost} = 1.5x^2 - 120x + 4{,}000$$

where x is the number of units produced. Draw a graph to find the lowest unit cost. What production level does this correspond to?

3.9 Compare the graphs of $y = 2^x$ and $y = 3^x$.

3.10 Draw a graph of $y = 1/x$ for x between -5 and $+5$.

3.11 If you leave £100 in the bank earning 6% interest, at the end of n years you will have 100×1.06^n. Draw a graph of this amount over the next 20 years.

RESEARCH PROJECTS

3.1 Spreadsheets are a convenient way of drawing graphs, but there are more specialised graphics packages. What additional features do these specialised packages have? Do a small survey of packages, comparing their graphics features. What other features would you like?

3.2 Find some examples of graphs presented in newspapers and magazines. Describe some that are particularly good, and others that are particularly bad. What can the bad ones learn from the good ones?

3.3 You can monitor the trends in share prices using various indices, such as the London Stock Exchange FTSE 100 or FTSE 250 indices. Similar indices are calculated for other stock exchanges, such as the Nikkei in Tokyo, Dow-Jones in New York, Hang Seng in Hong Kong, Dax in Frankfurt, and CAC in Paris. Collect some figures for a specific company over some period and draw graphs to compare its performance with the broader stock market. Can you find any obvious trends? What do you expect to happen in the future?

Sources of information

Further reading

Most of the books on mathematics mentioned in Chapter 2 include sections on graphs. Some other useful books on graphs include:

Few S., *Show Me the Numbers*, Analytics Press, 2004.

Hyggett R., *Graphs and Charts*, Palgrave Macmillan, Basingstoke, 1990.

Robbins N.B., *Creating More Effective Graphs*, John Wiley, Chichester, 2005.

Walkenbach J., *Excel Charts*, Hungry Minds, Inc., New York, 2002.

Zelazny G., *Say it with Charts* (4th edition), McGraw-Hill, New York, 2001.

CHAPTER 4

Correlation and regression

LEARNING OBJECTIVES

- **To identify, by diagram, whether a possible relationship exists between two variables;**
- **To quantify the strength of association between variables using the correlation coefficient;**
- **To show how a relationship can be expressed as an equation;**
- **To identify linear equations when written and when graphed;**
- **To examine regression, a widely used linear model, and to consider its uses and limitations.**

Introduction

In many business situations, it is reasonable to suggest that relationships exist between variables. For example, it would be logical to assume that the sales of a mass-produced good are related to its price and advertising expenditure.

For decision making purposes it is useful to identify whether a linear relationship exists between two variables and, if appropriate, quantify its strength. A relationship can be identified using a graph called a **scatter diagram**, and its strength can be quantified using a statistical measure called the **correlation coefficient**.

Once such an association has been found, it can often be very useful to produce a forecasting **model** which can be used to predict one variable if the other is known (e.g., it may be possible to predict sales if advertising expenditure is known).

In this chapter, two methods of quantifying the strength of the relationship (the correlation) between two variables will be presented. This will be followed by a section discussing how a linear model for forecasting can be constructed and used once a relationship has been discovered.

Before proceeding with the theory relating to the development of a forecasting model it is worth considering what is actually meant by the use of the word 'model' in this context.

A model may be used in several different ways: the idea of scale models as used by engineers or architects, a kit used to make an aeroplane or car or even someone who shows off clothes on a catwalk may come to mind. In each of these situations the model is used to demonstrate or show people how something will look or behave. In the context of this unit, a model may mean an equation or specially prepared spreadsheet but it is still meant to be some sort of representation of the real world which helps the user to experiment – seeing the effect of changes, making forecasts or making decisions.

4.1 The scatter diagram

A scatter diagram is simply a plot of data points on an *X–Y* graph.

The *y*-axis is used to represent the dependent variable of interest to the decision maker, whilst the *x*-axis is used to represent a variable which can be controlled or measured by the decision maker (often called the independent variable). Each pair of values is subsequently represented on the graph by a point or cross.

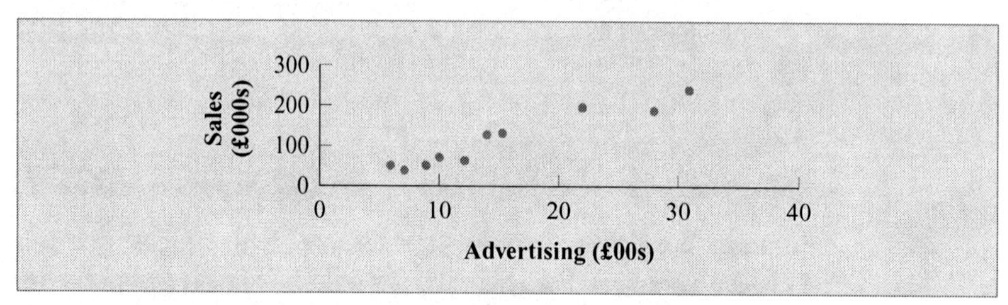

Figure 4.1 **Scatter diagram of sales and advertising expenditure**

In the scatter diagram shown in Figure 4.1, the *y* variable is the value of sales, whilst the *x* variable is advertising expenditure for a certain mass-produced good. This is because sales would be the variable that a decision maker may be interested in predicting (i.e., *y*), whilst advertising expenditure may be changed to suit the decision maker (i.e., *x*). Weekly sales and advertising expenditure are recorded and each pair is represented on the graph by a point (•). The overall pattern of the points on this graph suggests that a relationship may exist between sales and advertising costs. In particular, the scatter diagram suggests the more money spent on advertising, the greater the value of sales. The pattern of the points roughly form a straight line suggesting that there is possibly a linear association between the two variables.

Depending upon the variables being considered, the relationship suggested by the scatter diagram may be strongly linear, non-linear or even non-existent. Therefore, a scatter diagram is a useful first indication of whether an association exists between two variables.

Causal relationships

Before performing further analysis, it is important to be able to hypothesize on whether a cause and effect relationship might exist between the variables concerned, and to clearly identify which is the dependent variable.

A scatter diagram of pairs of data, showing business failures against graduating students, might suggest a strong positive relationship, since both groups have increased over the past years. But clearly there is nothing to suggest a direct relationship between the two; it is mere coincidence that both have increased.

Hence it is very important to be able to justify in advance that variable y is the *effect* resulting from changes in x, the *cause* variable.

In the case above, it seems sensible to say that changes in sales are *caused* by changes in advertising expenditure so it is safe to proceed with the next stage – quantifying the strength of the relationship through correlation analysis.

4.2 Correlation coefficients

Correlation analysis is a mathematical technique which is used to measure the *strength* of association between two variables. This measurement takes into account the 'degree of scatter' between the data values. Obviously, the less scattered the data, the stronger the relationship (correlation) is between the two variables.

The correlation coefficient is denoted by the symbol r and can *only* take a value between -1 and $+1$ inclusive.

Before looking at the details of how r is calculated, its meaning in relation to various scatter diagrams will be discussed.

In Figure 4.2, r equals $+1$ which indicates that there is perfect positive correlation between the two variables. This means all of the data lies on a straight line sloping upwards, showing that as the value of x increases so does the value of y (which is why correlation can be said to be positive) and for every known value of x, the value of y can be predicted exactly.

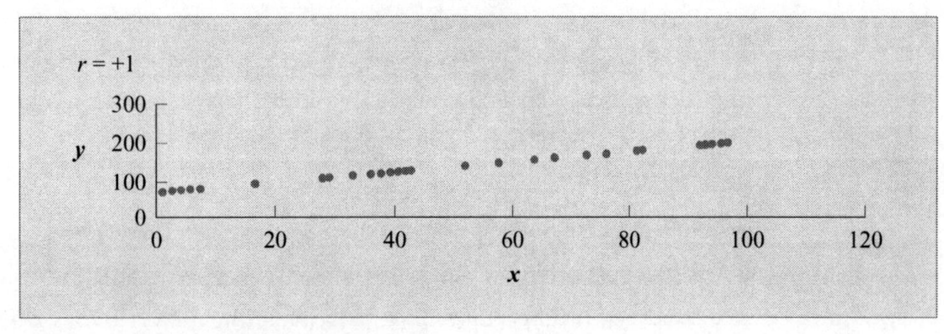

Figure 4.2 **Scatter diagram where $r = 1$**

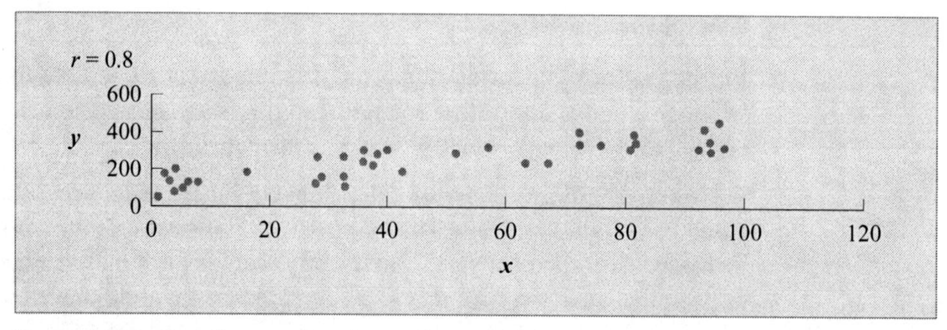

Figure 4.3 **Scatter diagram showing *r* of around 0.8**

In Figure 4.3, it can be seen that as x increases y still increases, and that the data are quite closely grouped together. In this case it can be said that there is evidence of strong positive correlation between the two variables and this would yield a value of r around 0.8.

Now consider the further scatter diagrams shown in Figure 4.4. In the diagram on the left it can be seen that the value of x is not influencing the value of y in any way (y is constant), in this case the value of $r = 0$ shows there is no correlation (association) between the two variables. In the diagram on the right there is some scatter but there is no particular association between the value of x and the value of y. Therefore it can be said there is very little correlation between the two variables. Here the value of r would be somewhere between –0.3 and +0.3.

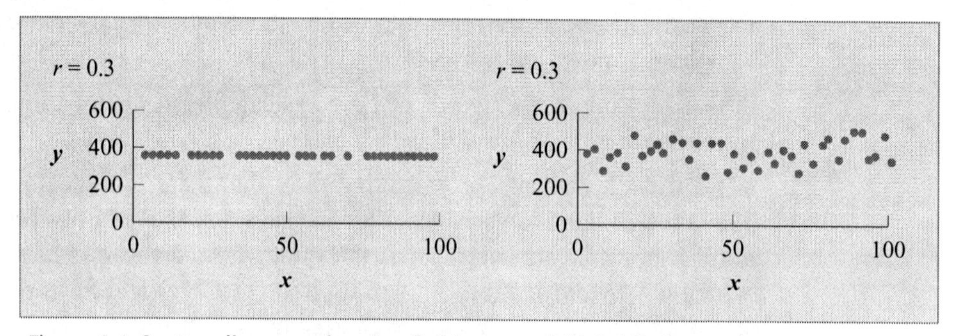

Figure 4.4 **Scatter diagrams showing (left) zero and (right) little correlation**

Negative values of r can be interpreted in the same way as positive values – the only difference is that the diagram would show that as the value of x increases the value of y decreases. Figure 4.5 illustrates this.

In summary:

- values approaching +1 suggest a strong positive association;
- values approaching –1 suggest a strong negative association;
- values near 0 suggest possibly no association at all.

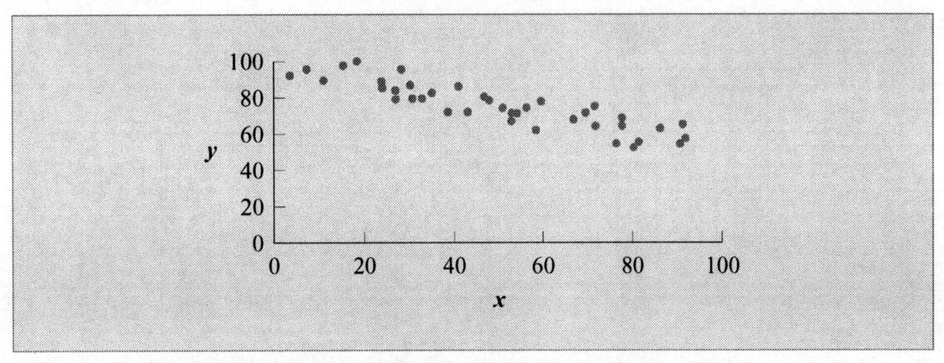

Figure 4.5 **Scatter diagram showing strong negative correlation**

The next point to consider is the calculation of r.

4.3 Calculating the correlation coefficient

Pearson's product moment correlation coefficient measures the strength of a possible linear relationship between the variables. The formula for its calculation is:

$$r = \frac{n\sum xy - \sum x \sum y}{\sqrt{\left[n\sum x^2 - (\sum x)^2\right]\left[n\sum y^2 - (\sum y)^2\right]}}$$

This formula looks complicated and tends to cause difficulties with many statistics students (luckily many scientific calculators and spreadsheets have automatic built-in functions for its calculation). However, in an attempt to overcome this, Example 4.1 will illustrate the method of calculation step by step.

EXAMPLE 4.1

The table overleaf shows advertising expenditure and associated sales of a particular product. By examining a scatter diagram and calculating Pearson's product moment correlation coefficient, comment on the association between the two variables.

Step 1: Establish the independent (x) and dependent (y) variables and graph them

It is very likely that expenditure would affect sales. Therefore expenditure is defined as the independent variable and is plotted on the x-axis with sales as the dependent variable plotted on the y-axis. This produces the scatter diagram shown in Figure 4.6.

Example 4.1 *continued*

Sales (£000s)	Expenditure (£00s)
25	8
35	12
29	11
24	5
38	14
12	3
18	6
27	8
17	4
30	9

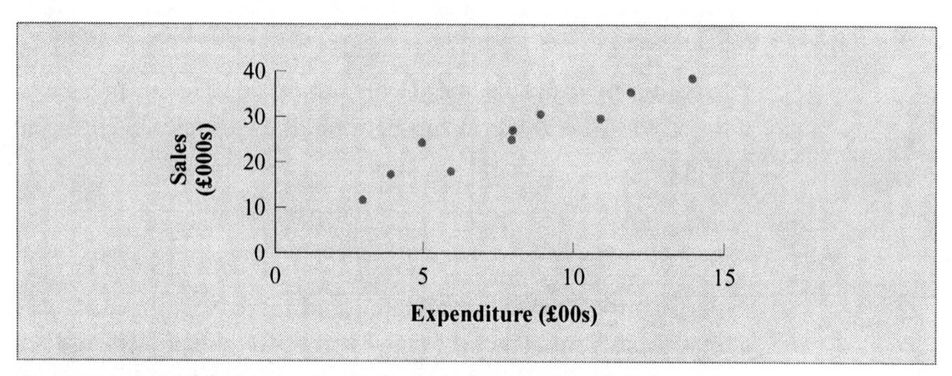

Figure 4.6 **Scatter diagram, showing expenditure versus sales**

Step 2: Examine the graph

The graph indicates that as expenditure increases sales increase, it also appears that the data are quite closely grouped together. This would suggest there is strong positive correlation between the two variables. To back up these observations the value of r can be calculated.

Step 3: Calculate the correlation coefficient

Looking at the formula more closely, the individual elements required are:

$\sum x$ – the sum of all the x values;

$\sum y$ – the sum of all the y values;

$\sum x^2$ – the x values squared then added together;

$\sum y^2$ – the y values squared then added together;

$\sum xy$ – the sum of the x values multiplied by the y values;

n – the number of (expenditure, sales) pairs.

In order to calculate these a table is needed:

Sales (y)	**Expenditure** (x)	x^2	y^2	xy
25	8	8 * 8 = 64	25 * 25 = 625	8 * 25 = 200
35	12	12 * 12 = 144	1225	420
29	11	11 * 11 = 121	841	319
24	5	25	576	120
38	14	196	1444	532
12	3	9	144	36
18	6	36	324	108
27	8	64	729	216
17	4	16	289	68
30	9	81	900	270
$\Sigma y = 255$	$\Sigma x = 80$	$\Sigma x^2 = 756$	$\Sigma y^2 = 7097$	$\Sigma xy = 2289$

and $n = 10$.

The summary values are substituted into the correlation coefficient formula and worked through:

$$r = \frac{n\Sigma xy - \Sigma x \Sigma y}{\sqrt{[n\Sigma x^2 - (\Sigma x)^2][n\Sigma y^2 - (\Sigma y)^2]}}$$

$$r = \frac{(10 * 2289) - (80 * 255)}{\sqrt{[(10 * (756) - 80^2][(10 * 7097) - 255^2]}}$$

$$r = \frac{(22890 - 20400)}{\sqrt{(7560 - 6400)(70970 - 65025)}}$$

$$r = \frac{2490}{\sqrt{6896200}} = \frac{2490}{2626.0617}$$

So $r = 0.948$ (to 3 d.p.)

The value of r is close to +1, so this suggests that a very strong positive relationship exists between the two variables.

Since it is such a widely used statistic, most spreadsheet packages and many scientific calculators have in-built functions which can be used to find the value of r once the two sets of data have been entered. This is the way in which the correlation coefficient is usually calculated in practice.

4.4 The rank correlation coefficient

With Pearson's product moment correlation coefficient the two sets of data need to be numeric. It is also possible to measure the association between numeric and non-numeric variables if the non-numeric data have been given in the form of **ranks** (for example, product names ranked in order of preference).

The most common rank coefficient is derived from Pearson's coefficient and is known as **Spearman's rank correlation coefficient**. The formula for this is:

$$r = 1 - \frac{6 * \sum d^2}{n(n^2 - 1)}$$

where: n = number of pairs of observations

d = difference between the rank of x and y.

The value of r is interpreted in a similar way to Pearson's correlation coefficient, however it is not really possible to say that one variable is affecting the other. The value of r is used to indicate the *level of agreement* between the two variables.

EXAMPLE 4.2

A large travel company produces a list of its top 10 travel destinations for the previous year every January. In the same month each year a national women's magazine also produces a similar list based on their annual reader survey. Calculate a suitable correlation coefficient and make appropriate comments on your result. The data collected are shown in the table below:

Destination	**Travel company rank**	**Magazine rank**
Florida	2	1
Canary Islands	5	6
Greek Islands	3	2
Germany	4	4
Spain	6	5
Caribbean	10	7
Australia	7	9
France	9	10
Canada	8	8
Russia	1	3

In order to calculate r a table that calculates the square of the differences between the ranks (d^2) is needed. Note that as the values are squared it does not matter which way round the differences are calculated.

Destination	Travel company rank	Magazine rank	d	d^2
Florida	2	1	1	1
Canary Islands	5	6	–1	1
Greek Islands	3	2	1	1
Germany	4	4	0	0
Spain	6	5	1	1
Caribbean	10	7	3	9
Australia	7	9	–2	4
France	9	10	–1	1
Canada	8	8	0	0
Russia	1	3	–2	4
				$\Sigma d^2 = 22$

$$r = 1 - \frac{6 * \Sigma d^2}{n(n^2 - 1)} = 1 - \frac{(6 * 22)}{10(100 - 1)}$$

$$r = 1 - \frac{132}{990}$$

$$r = 1 - 0.1333 = 0.867 \text{ (to 3 d.p.)}$$

As $r = 0.867$ this indicates there is quite a high level of agreement between the two publications.

In Example 4.2 both sets of data were already ranked. It is very likely that one set of data may require conversion into ranks. In such cases it is also very likely that the ranking will produce ties. An adjustment must be made so that the tied values equally share the ranks they would have occupied. This is shown by the following data:

Data:	39	28	28	20	17	17	17	15	13
Rank given:	1	2½	2½	4	6	6	6	8	9
		(share 2,3)			(share 5,6,7)				

Once ranked, the calculation would proceed as above, as shown in Example 4.3.

EXAMPLE 4.3

A florist franchise has recently set up an Internet site for the sale of its top five rated arrangements. Recorded in the table below are the numbers of orders received via the Internet for each of these arrangements. By calculating a suitable correlation coefficient, comment on the level of association between overall sales of the arrangements and sales made solely on the Internet.

Rating	Arrangement	Internet sales (£00s)
1	Lemon posy	29
2	Mixed blooms	35
3	Blue symphony	18
4	Pink carnival	29
5	Lover's knot	16

In this case only one set of data has been presented in the form of ranks, therefore before proceeding the data relating to Internet sales needs to be ranked appropriately.

For Internet sales it can be seen that the 'Mixed blooms' arrangement has the largest number of sales, thus a rank of 1 is allocated. There are then two arrangements with 2900 sales each, namely the 'Pink carnival' and the 'Lemon posy'. This means that in terms of ranks they are required to share 2 and 3 between them, giving the two arrangements a rank of 2½. The 'Blue symphony' arrangement is next with 1800 sales. As the second and third ranks have been allocated through the shared rank of 2½ 'Blue symphony' is given a rank of 4, with the final arrangement taking the rank of 5.

This information along with the subsequent differences (d) and values of d^2 is shown below:

Arrangement	Internet sales (£00s)	Internet rank	d	d^2
1: Lemon posy	29	2.5	−1.5	2.25
2: Mixed blooms	35	1	1	1
3: Blue symphony	18	4	−1	1
4: Pink carnival	29	2.5	1.5	2.25
5: Lover's knot	16	5	0	0
				$\Sigma d^2 = 6.5$

$$r = 1 - \frac{6 * \Sigma d^2}{n(n^2 - 1)} = 1 - \frac{(6 * 6.5)}{5(25-1)}$$

$$r = 1 - \frac{39}{120}$$

$$r = 1 - 0.325 = 0.675$$

Therefore we can see that there is a reasonable level of similarity between the best sellers on the Internet site and the florist's overall best sellers.

REVIEW ACTIVITY 1

Ten printers, suitable for use with personal computers and retailing at between £300 and £550, were evaluated by a number of volunteers. The volunteers were asked to award each printer percentage marks for 'speed' and 'print quality'. The assessments of these printers including an overall ranking are summarized as follows:

Model	1	2	3	4	5	6	7	8	9	10
Speed	20	45	25	10	30	25	35	30	20	25
Quality	65	35	55	85	15	25	45	25	55	35
Overall rank	5	3	8	7	4	10	1	2	9	6
Price (£)	410	396	350	530	399	353	430	404	350	375

(a) Calculate the product moment correlation coefficient between 'speed' and 'print quality' and interpret your answer.

(b) Calculate the rank correlation coefficient between overall ranking and retail price and interpret your answer.

Working:

Answers on pages 222–3.

4.5 Linear models

The construction of a linear regression model builds on a basic knowledge of linear equations. Hence to understand this work fully it is necessary to understand and to be able to construct linear equations. A brief summary of the knowledge required follows here, but readers may find it necessary to refer to other notes or textbooks to consolidate their skills before proceeding.

The general format for a simple linear equation is:

$$y = a + bx$$

(In some texts this is written as $y = mx + c$ where m is equivalent to b and c is equivalent to a).

- y is the *dependent* variable.
- x is the *independent* variable.
- a is a *constant* representing the point where the straight line cuts the y-axis (known as the *intercept*).
- b is a *constant* representing the *slope* (or gradient) of the straight line.

This is illustrated in Figure 4.7.

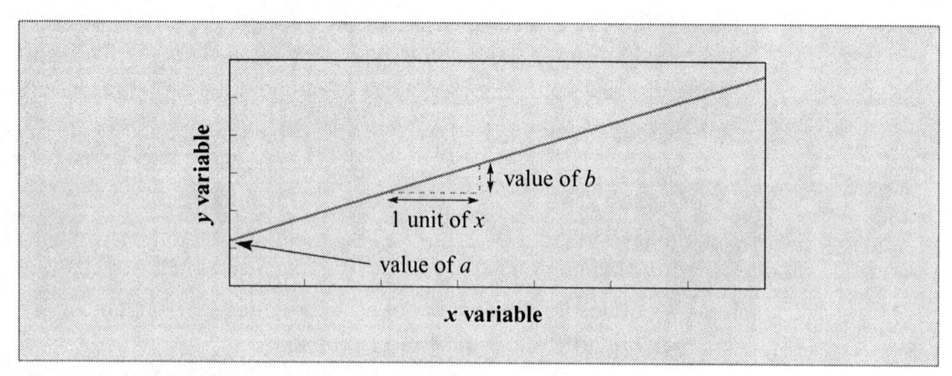

Figure 4.7 **General straight line: $y = a + bx$**

To consider how a linear model (as opposed to linear regression) is constructed, look at the following example.

EXAMPLE 4.4

An electricity company has a standing charge of £17.50 per quarter plus 8p per unit for electricity used. Find and graph a linear equation to model this situation for usage of up to 1500 units per quarter.

The equation will have the general form:

$$y = a + bx$$

- y must be *electricity charges* since this is the variable of interest.
- x must be *number of units used* since this determines the electricity charges.

(Also it may be said that charges *depend on* units used so electricity charge is *dependent* and number of units used is *independent*.)

To find a and b it is helpful to consider how the charges which arise at various levels of usage are made up.

For instance, if 10 units of electricity are used the charge is £17.50 + £0.08 * 10.

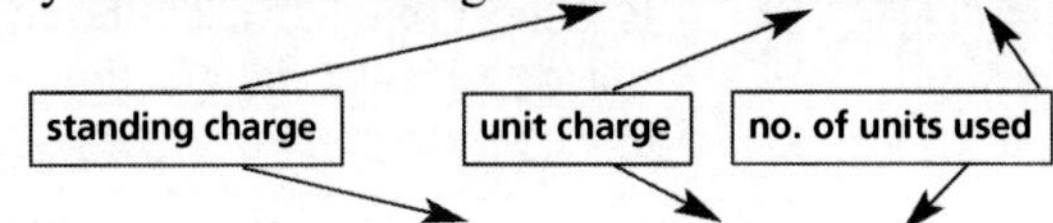

And if 20 units of electricity are used the charge is £17.50 + £0.08 * 20 ... and so on.

In general, therefore,

Electricity charges = £17.50 + £0.08 * units used

or, in the usual notation where y = electricity charges (£) and x = number of units used:

$$y = 17.5 + 0.08x$$

which is a linear model representing electricity charges in terms of units used.

There are a number of ways in which a known model can be presented on a graph. Perhaps the easiest of these is simply to choose a few values for x (two are sufficient but three allow a check for mistakes!), calculate the corresponding values of y and then plot the resulting pairs of points and join them together. Here the x values chosen are 0, 750 and 1500.

x	0	750	1500
$y = 17.5 + 0.08x$	17.5+0.08 * 0 = 17.5	17.5 + 0.08 * 750 = 77.5	17.5 + 0.08 * 1500 = 137.5

The resulting graph is shown in Figure 4.8.

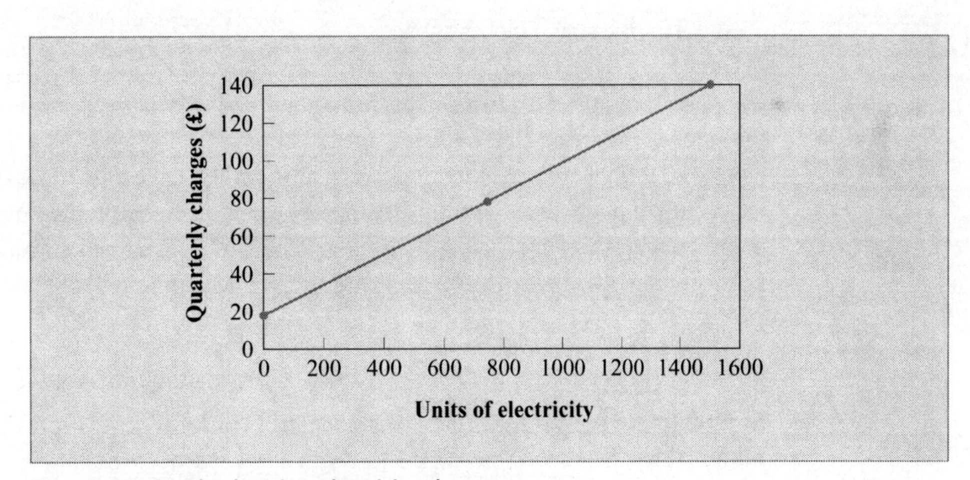

Figure 4.8 **Graph, showing electricity charges**

In order to check your understanding of linear models have a go at Review activity 2 before considering linear regression.

REVIEW ACTIVITY 2

Two local retailers are offering mobile telephones at different tariffs. Phoneyvode charge £15 per month plus 50p per minute for calls, while Purplecom charge £17.25 for rental but only 35p per minute for calls.

(a) Formulate equations for the call charges in each case.

(b) Produce a *single* graph showing the costs of each option if between 0 and 40 minutes of calls are made per month.

(c) Determine the level of calls at which Purplecom's tariff becomes the cheaper option.

(d) What is the overall cost per month at this level of calls?

Working:

Answers on page 224.

The linear equations in Example 4.4 and Review activity 2 are examples of a **deterministic** model i.e., if electricity usage were known then charges could be predicted exactly with no room for variation. In real life, it is often necessary to build a **probabilistic** model to deal with uncertainty. Simple linear regression, the technique which is described below, is an example of this latter type of model.

4.6 Simple linear regression

Consider Example 4.1 again (the sales and advertising data). It has been established that there is a strong link between advertising and sales, with a correlation coefficient of 0.948. However, due to the variability in the data it is impossible to find an exact linear model, as we did in Example 4.4 above. Nevertheless, given Figure 4.6 and the correlation coefficient there is evidence of a linear relationship between the sales and advertising expenditure. Therefore, the equation will still have the format

$$y = a + bx$$

but what is needed is a mathematical way of estimating the a and b values.

Simple linear regression (also known as least squares linear regression) is a technique which has been developed to do this. In essence, the aim is to find values of a and b (remember these are just constant values) which give the line which best fits the points. To do this requires more mathematical formulae:

$$b = \frac{n\sum xy - \sum x\sum y}{n\sum x^2 - (\sum x)^2}$$

and

$$a = \frac{\sum y}{n} - \frac{b\sum x}{n} \quad \text{or} \quad a = \bar{y} - b\bar{x}$$

(Note that these two formulae for a are equivalent and either may be used).

As with Pearson's correlation coefficient, most spreadsheets and scientific calculators have in-built functions that can be used to find these two values automatically (and their use is recommended).

Example 4.5 illustrates finding the linear regression coefficients using the full formulae.

EXAMPLE 4.5

Using the previous data on sales and advertising expenditure:

Sales (£000s)	25	35	29	24	38	12	18	27	17	30
Advert. expend. (£00s)	8	12	11	5	14	3	6	8	4	9

find the linear regression equation, add it to the original scatter graph, and produce forecasts for sales if advertising expenditure is:

(a) £700

(b) £1800

The value of b must be calculated first (since it is needed to work out the value of a). To do this, various numbers are needed:

$\sum x$ – the sum of all the x values;

$\sum y$ – the sum of all the y values;

$\sum x^2$ – the x values squared then added together;

$\sum xy$ – the sum of the x values multiplied by the y values;

n – the number of (expenditure, sales) pairs.

These were also required for the calculation of the correlation coefficient (r) which was completed in Example 4.1. Therefore the relevant figures can be extracted from that example i.e., $\sum x = 80$, $\sum y = 255$, $\sum x^2 = 756$, $\sum xy = 2289$ and $n = 10$.

(If r had not been previously calculated a similar table to the one in Example 4.1 would be required to calculate the summary values.)

Therefore

$$b = \frac{n\sum xy - \sum x\sum y}{n\sum x^2 - (\sum x)^2} = \frac{(10*2289) - (80*255)}{(10*756) - (80)^2}$$

$$b = \frac{22{,}890 - 20{,}400}{7560 - 6400} = \frac{2490}{1160}$$

$$b = 2.1465517$$

Example 4.5 *continued*

(Note that b has been left with a large number of decimal places at this stage to avoid errors in subsequent calculations. This would be achieved in practice by making use of a calculator's memory.)

Then

$$a = \frac{\sum y}{n} - \frac{b\sum x}{n} = \frac{255}{10} - 2.1465517 * \frac{80}{10}$$

$$a = 25.5 - 17.172413 = 8.327587$$

The final answers (rounded to three decimal places) are:

$$a = 8.32 \qquad b = 2.147$$

(Note that three decimal places were chosen as the data supplied were in thousands and hundreds.)

These give the linear regression equation

$$y = 8.328 + 2.147x$$

or, if preferred,

$$\text{Sales} = 8.328 + 2.147 * \text{Advertising expenditure}$$

When adding this to the scatter graph, the procedure is exactly as for graphing any other straight line: choose three x values and calculate y, then add the pairs of points to the graph. Here $x = 0$, 10 and 15 have been used to cover all of the values of x supplied in the original data. See Figure 4.9.

x	0	10	15
$y = 8.328 + 2.147x$	8.328	29.798	40.533

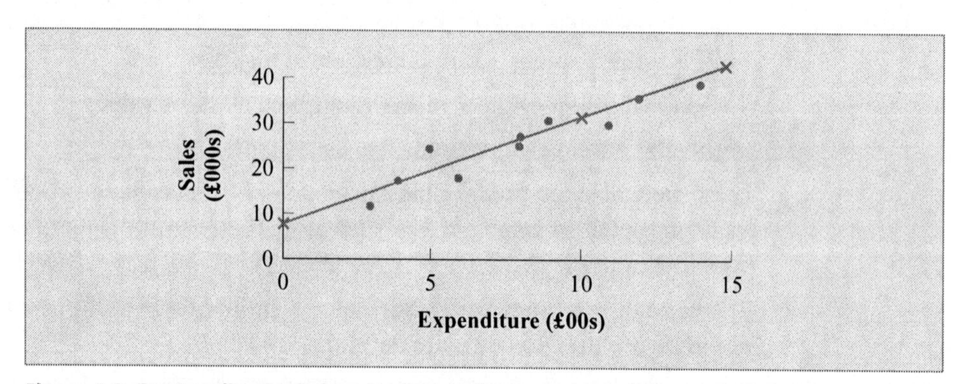

Figure 4.9 **Scatter diagram, showing expenditure versus sales**

To make forecasts, the values for x are simply substituted into the regression equation:

(a) Advertising expenditure = £700. As the figures used in the equation were given in hundreds, this means $x = 7$ giving

$$y = 8.328 + 2.147 * 7 = 23.357$$

As y is in thousands, 23,357 sales are forecast.

(b) Expenditure = £1800, so $x = 18$.

$$y = 8.328 + 2.147 * 18 = 46.974$$

i.e., 46,974 sales are forecast.

4.7 Assessing the accuracy of forecasts

Consider the two forecasts made at the end of the previous example in relation to the original data supplied.

In (a) the x value (7) fell within the range of the original data provided for x – which went from 3 to 14. This type of forecast is known as **interpolation**, and the forecast produced is likely to be accurate, since r is high and the model is considered to fit the data well.

However, in (b) the value of x used (18) falls outside the original data range, and it is not possible to be sure that the model continues to fit the data well. This is called **extrapolation** and it is necessary to be much more careful with forecasts made in this way. For instance, it might be that sales have reached a plateau level where more money spent on advertising has little or no effect. If this was the case the forecast would be inaccurate.

Therefore, when forecasts are made it is prudent to note whether interpolation or extrapolation is carried out and to consider the possible consequences.

As we have seen, the correlation coefficient (r) is often used as the first assessment of the model; a further measure, r^2, the **coefficient of determination**, can also be useful for further interpretation. Effectively, this is Pearson's correlation coefficient squared, but the term is generally used to describe the percentage of the variation in the y data that can be attributed to variation in the x data.

In the example above $r = 0.948$ so $r^2 = 0.899$. Thus it may be said that 89.9% of the variation in sales of the products is due to variation in the levels of advertising expenditure.

Finally, it should be noted that the sample size used may also have an important effect on the quality of the forecasts. In the example above only a small sample size – 10 pairs of points – were used, for ease of calculation. In reality, it is desirable to use at least 30 data points as, obviously, the larger the sample the more confidence can be placed in the accuracy of the model.

4.8 More complex regression models

The simple linear regression model discussed in this chapter has many other developments which are useful in modelling more complex situations. It may be desirable to add other factors which also have an effect on the dependent variable. For example, gas demand does not depend solely on the most obvious factor – temperature – but also on windchill and day of the week. It is possible to build **multiple regression models** which include all of these factors rather than just a single one.

In other situations the data may not exhibit the type of linear behaviour seen here (i.e., the graphs may be curved in some way) and so a **non-linear model** based on powers of x (x^2, x^3 etc.) or other transformations may be more appropriate. Although these developments are not discussed in detail here you should be aware that they exist and may be used in situations where simple linear models are inadequate.

REVIEW ACTIVITY 3

Mr Lillystone is the owner of a gift shop in a small town. He believes that the shop takings are related to the number of tourist coaches that stop in the town. He has collected the following data on takings and number of coach visits for a selection of recent days.

Day number	No. of coaches	Takings (£)
1	24	962
2	30	1181
3	9	578
4	48	1429
5	38	1324
6	15	752
7	5	542
8	38	1355
9	15	788
10	24	998
11	49	1462
12	10	650
13	17	862
14	11	719
15	16	828

(a) Determine which set of data represents the x (independent) and which the y (dependent) variable in this situation.

(b) Calculate values for a and b and write out the regression equation for this data.

(c) Forecast the takings for days where:

(i) 27 coaches
(ii) 55 coaches visit the town.

(d) How good do you expect the forecasts calculated in part (c) to be?

Working:

Answers on page 225.

Key points to remember

1. Correlation and regression are techniques which are used to see whether a relationship exists between two or more different sets of data. (In this book only two sets of data are considered.)
2. A graph known as a scatter diagram is used to identify the possibility and type of relationship. y is defined as the variable which it is believed is being influenced (dependent) and x is defined as the variable which is doing the influencing (independent).
3. The strength of a relationship between two sets of data is measured by Pearson's correlation coefficient (r). It is found by the following formula:

$$r = \frac{n\sum xy - \sum x \sum y}{\sqrt{[n\sum x^2 - (\sum x)^2][n\sum y^2 - (\sum y)^2]}}$$

4. The value of r can only take a value of –1 to +1 inclusive. Brief guidelines on the interpretation of this value are as follows:

+1	Perfect positive correlation exists between the data. As x increases y increases. If x is known y can be predicted exactly.
+0.8 < +1	Strong positive correlation exists between the data. As x increases y increases.
+0.4 < +0.8	Moderate positive correlation exists between the data. As x increases y increases.

$-0.4 < +0.4$	Very little correlation exists between the data.
$-0.4 < -0.8$	Moderate negative correlation exists between the data. As x increases y decreases.
$-0.8 < -1$	Strong negative correlation exists between the data. As x increases y decreases.
-1	Perfect negative correlation exists between the data. As x increases y decreases. If x is known y can be predicted exactly.

5. Regression is a technique which builds a straight line relationship between two sets of data. This relationship is of the form $y = a + bx$ where a and b are found by the following formulae:

$$b = \frac{n\sum xy - \sum x \sum y}{n\sum x^2 - (\sum x)^2}$$

and

$$a = \frac{\sum y}{n} - \frac{b\sum x}{n} \quad \text{or} \quad a = \bar{y} - b\bar{x}$$

6. Forecasts may be made using the resulting model. If the x (independent) value used falls within the original data set then this forecast is known as interpolation. If the x value falls outside the bounds of the original data then this forecast is known as extrapolation and care must be taken in its use.

7. The coefficient of determination (r^2) is another measure which may be used to assess the appropriateness of a regression model. This is found by squaring Pearson's correlation coefficient and then expressing it as a percentage. The resulting figure is then used to describe the percentage variation in the y data that can be attributed to the variation in the x data.

8. Spearman's rank correlation coefficient is used to measure the agreement between two sets of data, at least one of which has been presented in the form of ranks. The formula for its calculation is:

$$r = \frac{1 - 6 * \sum d^2}{n(n^2 - 1)}$$

where: n = number of pairs of observations

d = difference between the rank of x and y.

If one of the sets of data is not ranked, they must be allocated ranks and any identical values are to be allocated a shared rank.

9. Finally, you should be aware that other more complex regression models do exist. These can be either in the form of non-linear or multiple regression models. More details of these can be found in the books listed in the further reading section of the Introduction.

ADDITIONAL EXERCISES

Question 1

Pemberton's slimming club has decided to illustrate a theoretical approach to how aerobic exercise and calorie intake can affect weight. Twelve of the established club members have carefully recorded the number of minutes of aerobic exercise they have undertaken in one week along with their weekly calorie intake. This data is presented in the table below.

Weight loss (lb)	Aerobic exercise (mins)	Calorie intake
0.6	112	9560
2.8	190	7552
1.4	171	11,981
1.4	148	8338
2.6	193	10,202
3.8	235	7252
3.3	237	8097
2.5	176	8121
2.6	185	8300
2.0	186	11,216
3.3	228	7212
1.1	65	7631

(a) Construct two scatter diagrams to illustrate the relationship between weight loss and aerobic exercise plus weight loss and calorie intake. Describe the main features of the graphs and hence *estimate* possible correlation coefficients.

(b) *Calculate* the correlation coefficient for the weight loss and aerobic exercise relationship. Using this figure, calculate the coefficient of determination and define its meaning in this context.

(c) Given the following summary values for the relationship between weight loss and calorie intake, calculate r. By comparing this with the correlation coefficient found in (b) determine which of the two factors is the better contributor to weight loss, giving appropriate reasons for your choice.

$\Sigma x^2 = 9.5461103 * 10^8$ $\Sigma xy = 232{,}639.3$ $\Sigma x = 105{,}462$

Question 2

A group of students and a group of senior citizens were asked to consider seven yellow paint shades and rank them in order of preference. Using the results in the table:

Paint shade	Students preference	Senior citizens' preference
Luscious lemon	1	2
Mellow mustard	3	4
Buttercup	4	3
Sunrise	7	7
Mexican spice	6	5
Lemon sherbet	2	1
Banana boat	5	6

(a) Calculate a suitable correlation coefficient.

(b) Comment on the agreement between the two groups taking part in the survey.

Question 3 Parker's IT recruitment services hold regular interview days where candidates are required to undergo an interview and an IT aptitude test. The results for one particular session are presented below.

Candidate	*A*	*B*	*C*	*D*	*E*	*F*	*G*	*H*
Interview rank	5	1	3	2	6	8	7	4
IT aptitude score (out of 100)	70	85	80	75	60	60	60	80

Calculate a suitable correlation coefficient and use this to comment on the level of agreement between the interview and testing process.

Question 4 (This question assumes you have completed Question 1.)

Calculate a linear regression model which describes the relationship between weight loss and amount of aerobic exercise. Use this equation to predict the expected weight loss of a club member who has undertaken 150 minutes of aerobic exercise in the week.

Question 5 A transport company has provided the following data relating to a sample of journeys made, giving distance travelled and time taken. The company is interested in developing a model to predict time taken for a journey if distance to be travelled is known.

Distance (km)	Time (hours)
200	3.2
120	2.0
175	3.0
150	2.0
300	4.7
320	5.5
240	3.8
180	2.8
210	3.4
260	4.5

$\Sigma x = 2155$

$\Sigma y = 34.9$

$\Sigma x^2 = 501625$

$\Sigma y^2 = 133.67$

$\Sigma xy = 8175$

(a) Present the data using a suitable scatter diagram.

(b) Find the correlation coefficient and the equation of the line of regression and state them clearly.

(c) Two lorries are just about to leave the depot. One is to make a journey of 90 km while the other is to travel 220 km. Using your regression equation estimate the journey times for each lorry. How much confidence would you have in each of these answers?

Question 6

A supermarket chain is about to launch its own range of batteries and wishes to base its marketing on a campaign emphasizing that the price of a battery is not the most important factor in determining its reliability.

To assist in their publicity they have commissioned a small study into battery life. A sample of 50 batteries of various ages bought at varying prices have been tested (each under the same conditions) to see how long they would last.

Graphs and statistics as shown in Figure 4.10 have been produced.

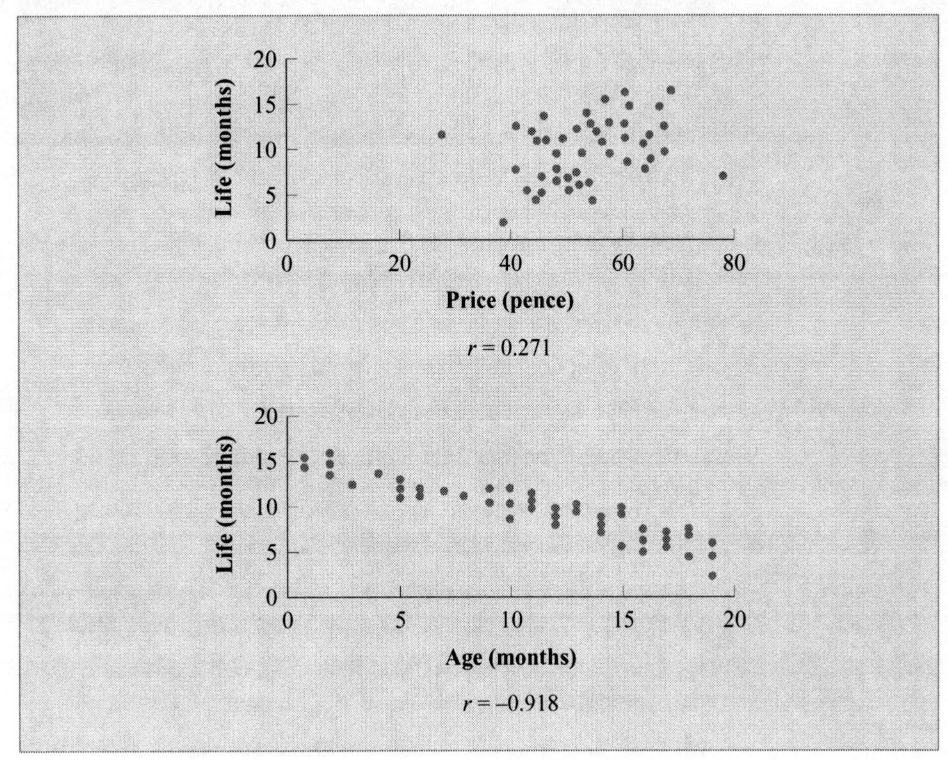

Figure 4.10 **(Top) Life and price of batteries and (bottom) age of battery when bought and life**

(a) Referring to the graphs and figures supplied as evidence, discuss which factors seem to affect battery life.

(b) Given the following extra information which has been calculated for you from the original data, find the most appropriate linear regression model which might be used to estimate battery life (i.e., one model only).

For age and battery life:

$\Sigma x = 508$ $\Sigma y = 499.3$ $\Sigma xy = 4256.9$ $\Sigma x^2 = 6682$

For price and battery life:

$\Sigma x = 2783$ $\Sigma y = 499.3$ $\Sigma xy = 28{,}217.2$ $\Sigma x^2 = 159{,}671$

(c) Comment on what the regression coefficients you have found tell you about battery life.

(d) Using your regression model, produce forecasts of how long the following batteries should last:

(i) cost 85p, 2 years old;

(ii) cost 50p, 6 months old.

(e) Comment on how confident you are about the accuracy of these forecasts.

SPREADSHEET EXERCISE

This exercise introduces the use of the Excel functions used in linear regression and correlation. As no Excel function is available to calculate Spearman's rank correlation coefficient automatically it has been excluded from the exercise.

The file SALES.XLS contains information about employees of a computer supply company. Data relating to mileage covered, number of sales made, period of time employed by the company and number of visits to customers made have been recorded for each of the 150 sales representatives for one month.

- column A contains an ID number for each sales representative;
- column B contains their mileage in a particular month;
- column C contains the number of sales they made;
- column D contains their length of service, recorded in months;
- column E contains the number of customer visits made in the month.

The company is interested in predicting the number of sales made.

(a) Construct three scatter diagrams to illustrate the possible relationships between the dependent variable and the three independent variables.

(b) Use an Excel function to find Pearson's correlation coefficients for the three pairs of variables graphed above.

(c) Make brief comments on the three relationships by referring to both the scatter diagrams and correlation coefficients. Which pair of variables exhibits the strongest relationship?

(d) Using this pair of variables and the relevant Excel functions, find the values of a and b which could be used to make up a linear regression equation to forecast sales. Write out the linear regression model and briefly interpret the values of a and b in this context.

(e) Construct an additional column of figures containing estimated sales figures, basing these on your linear regression equation from part (d) above. Add this set of estimated figures to your original scatter graph of the variables in your model to form a line through the data points.

Hints for completion

In Excel the three functions used in regression and correlation are:

=INTERCEPT(*y*-data range, *x*-data range)	Calculates the value of *a* in the linear regression model (i.e., the point at which the regression line crosses the *y*-axis)
=SLOPE(*y*-data range, *x*-data range)	Calculates the value of *b* in the linear regression equation
=CORREL(*y*-data range, *x*-data range)	Used to calculate Pearson's correlation coefficient
or	
=PEARSON(*y*-data range, *x*-data range)	
=RSQ(*y*-data range, *x*-data range)	Calculates the coefficient of determination

Figure 4.11 illustrates how these functions are applied in practice as well as giving the formula that would be required to answer part (e).

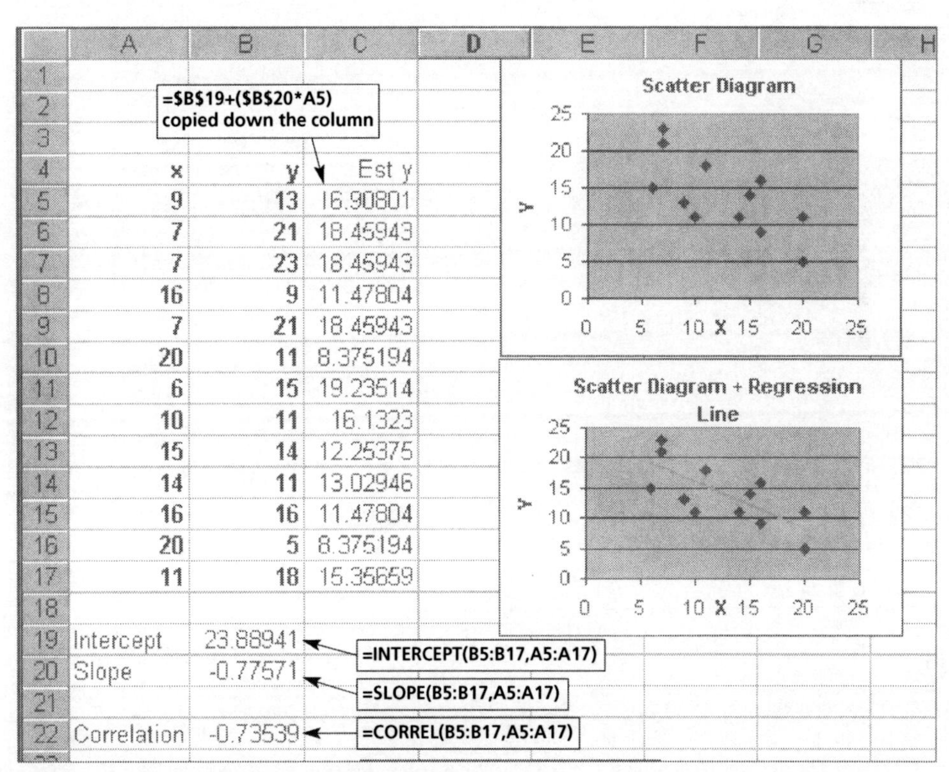

	A	B	C
4	x	y	Est y
5	9	13	16.90801
6	7	21	18.45943
7	7	23	18.45943
8	16	9	11.47804
9	7	21	18.45943
10	20	11	8.375194
11	6	15	19.23514
12	10	11	16.1323
13	15	14	12.25375
14	14	11	13.02946
15	16	16	11.47804
16	20	5	8.375194
17	11	18	15.35659
18			
19	Intercept	23.88941	
20	Slope	-0.77571	
21			
22	Correlation	-0.73539	

Figure 4.11 **Illustration of spreadsheet exercise**

Section 3
Uncertainty in Business

Chapter 7

A FIRM FOUNDATION: ELEMENTARY PROBABILITY

Chapter prerequisites

Before starting work on this chapter make sure you are happy with:

1 addition, subtraction and multiplication of fractions;

2 conversion of fractions to decimals or percentages and vice versa;

3 calculation of the arithmetic mean.

Learning outcomes

By the end of your work on this chapter you should be able to:

1 define probability in a given situation using *a priori* or empirical methods as appropriate;

2 solve problems involving the calculation of simple probabilities and their combination in 'or' and 'and' situations;

3 say what is meant by the expected value of a process, and calculate expected values for simple processes;

4 construct decision tables and trees, and make use of expected values to arrive at decisions;

5 know the limitations of this approach to decision-making.

Quantitative methods in practice

ACNielsen is one of the largest consumer research companies in the world. Among a wide portfolio of activities, they provide advice and support to companies intending to launch new products and services onto the market. Here is what one ACNielsen website has to say about the process of product launch (www.acnielsen.co.nz):

Getting New Product Launches Right

The key to the success of any product marketing company is largely dependent on the success of its brand portfolio. Over recent years brands have been introduced to some companies' balance sheets as a financial asset. At the same time, there have been countless seminars and books on how to effectively manage brands, and innovations in the measurement of brand equity and brand health.

Yet 70 per cent of all new product introductions still fail! (Source: ACNielsen BASES).

There are numerous reasons for this poor success rate. Some global companies simply throw onto the market their global products with a foreign ad. Others spend a fortune on product development but bypass consumer research. Some conduct exhaustive consumer research and product testing and then decide that despite poor results their gut feeling says it's going to be a winner. The reason for failure in all of these cases is a failure to understand or listen to the consumer.

Companies have to innovate and develop new products to survive, but new product development is expensive and risky and increasingly companies are looking to minimise risk by conducting thorough consumer research at the pre-launch and post-launch phase.

Let's focus in on a few specific points from this quote. We're told that 'new product development is expensive and risky', so clearly an important task for a company embarking on this process is to try to estimate the costs and the risks, in order to take decisions based on the fullest possible information. We have ways of measuring costs – it may not be easy to get agreement on actual figures, but we know that the resulting measurements will be in units of euros, dollars, rupees or another currency. But how can we measure *risk*? Does it even make sense to talk about 'measuring' it, or are we stuck with qualitative expressions such as 'very unlikely', 'almost certain' and so on?

There's a clue to how this question might be answered earlier in the quote: '70 per cent of new product introductions still fail'. Another way of interpreting this might be that 'there's a 70 per cent chance that a new product will fail on introduction'. Of course, that is a simple-minded way of looking at things – the chance of a *particular* product failing will depend on a whole bunch of other factors – but it suggests a possible way of measuring, or quantifying, the risk of failure.

The last significant phrase is the reference to those who, despite poor results from consumer research, trust their 'gut feeling' that the product will nevertheless be a winner – and generally come to grief as a consequence. There is nothing wrong with judgements based on informed management experience, but isn't there a better way to make decisions than on the basis of 'gut feeling' alone?

In this chapter, we will look at a number of ways in which the concept of 'chance' or 'risk' in the colloquial sense may be quantified or measured. The statistician's word for this quantification is 'probability', and so what we are really doing is laying the basis of probability theory, on which the next few chapters will build. We will also see how measurements of probability can be linked to costs and profits to produce a rational approach to decision-making.

The product development manager's problem

Let's stick with the product launch situation discussed by ACNielsen. Harold Black is responsible for the development of new product lines for Potters Toys Ltd, an old-established firm which manufactures dolls and other small plastic toys. He has recently been working on the development and promotion of a line of Asteroid Wars toys, which will be marketed to coincide with the UK opening in six months' time of a film of that name. However, he has recently heard a worrying rumour that the film has 'bombed' with preview audiences in the United States.

Although he reckons that this rumour only has about a 40 per cent chance of being true, it presents him with a difficult choice. If the product is launched to coincide with the film opening, then sales during the first month on the market had been expected to generate a profit of £120 000. However, if the film is not a success this could fall to as little as £20 000.

The alternative is to launch the product immediately rather than waiting for the film opening. In that case, he is fairly sure that a profit of £65 000 will result.

To make matters worse, there is a possibility that if the film succeeds, then a rival company, ToonToys, will enter the market with a very similar product, reducing Potters' profits to £60 000. Admittedly, the chances of ToonToys doing this are only believed to be about 50 per cent, but the possibility still has to be considered. Potters thus has to choose between delaying the product launch or going ahead now, taking into account both the doubts over the film's performance and the possible competition from ToonToys.

There are two clear requirements if Harold Black is to be able to tackle his problem logically. First, he needs to understand precisely what statements like 'a 50 per cent chance' and 'a 40 per cent chance' mean, and to be able to find the chances of the various sequences of events occurring. Second, he needs to have a way to link together the *chance* of something happening with the *financial outcome* if it does happen.

Reckoning the chances

Whether wittingly or unwittingly, we are making assessments of chances, or *probabilities* as statisticians prefer to call them, all the time. For example, when you look out of the window in the morning and decide not to wear a raincoat to go out, you are making a decision based on your estimate of the chance of rain during the day; if you learn that in past years 95 per cent of students on your course have passed the first-year examination, and accordingly feel somewhat encouraged, it is because you recognise that your chance of passing is presumably about the same; and of course, if you place bets on horses, you are making assessments of the chance that a particular horse will be successful.

Probably, in these cases, you would not like to be pinned down to an actual numerical statement of the chance involved, but in order to make use of probabilities in dealing with problems such as that outlined in the section above, that is just what we need to do. We will therefore begin by looking at the various ways in which a quantified probability might be defined.

Working it out in advance

Imagine that the Queen is coming to open a new factory for a firm with 600 employees, and that one employee is to be chosen to present her with a souvenir book. So that the selection of the lucky employee is done fairly, 600 pieces of paper, of which 599 are blank and one marked with a cross, are put into a hat, and each employee is invited to take one (you may be reminded of what we said about simple random samples in Chapter 3). Then I think you will agree that, if the hat is well shaken and all the pieces of paper are indistinguishable, the chances of any one individual, say Fred Smith, being chosen are 1 in 600 or 1/600.

In other words, we have found the probability of the event 'Fred Smith is chosen' by taking the number of ways this may happen – just one – as a fraction of the total number of possible events. We often denote the probability of an event occurring by writing $p(\text{event})$; so here we would say:

$$p(\text{Fred Smith chosen}) = 1/600.$$

We call this an *a priori* method of finding the probability, because we are able to assess the probability of the event *prior* to its actual occurrence simply by using our knowledge of the situation. Before generalising this definition to any event, however, we should look again at the assumptions we made in reaching our figure of 1/600. We said: '. . . the hat is well shaken and all the pieces of paper are indistinguishable'; in other words, the chances of each person being chosen are exactly the same, or, in statistical terms, all the outcomes are equally likely. Of course, if this were not the case – if the piece of paper bearing the cross were blue, say, so that the first person offered the hat could be sure of taking it – then, far from having a 1 in 600 chance of selection, poor old Fred, unless *he* were the lucky first, would have no chance at all!

With the provision, then, that all outcomes *are* equally likely, we can define a probability *a priori* as follows:

$$p(\text{event}) = \frac{\text{number of ways that event can occur}}{\text{total number of possible outcomes}}.$$

So if we know that out of the 600 employees, 250 are women, we can say that the chance of the chosen individual being a woman is given by:

$$p(\text{woman}) = \frac{250}{600},$$

since there are 250 ways in which the selected person could be a woman.

Doing an experiment

Unfortunately, there are many situations in which we just do not have the requisite prior knowledge to calculate probabilities in this way. Suppose, for example, that a firm wants to know what is the probability of an item produced by a particular automatic machine being defective. It is a perfectly reasonable question to ask: presumably a small proportion of defective items is unavoidable, whereas a large proportion would need to be remedied; but there is no way in which we can find this probability by *a priori* means. To ask

'How many ways can an acceptable item occur?' is a question no more meaningful than 'How long is a piece of string?' – the item either is defective or it is not, so the whole basis of the *a priori* method breaks down.

The obvious course to adopt here is to monitor the output of the machine over a reasonable period of time and actually find out how often it produces a defective item. Note that proviso 'over a reasonable period of time' – it is clearly no good just looking at two or three items; a sample of a few hundred items will give a much clearer picture of what is going on. If among 200 items, say, we found 12 defectives, then we might estimate the probability of a defective item being produced by the machine as 12/200. This is the experimental or *empirical* approach to probability, based on looking at what actually happens in practice rather than theorising ahead of the event. We might define probability in this way as:

$$p(\text{event}) = \frac{\text{number of times that event occurs}}{\text{total number of experiments}},$$

where we are using 'experiment' in a rather loose sense to mean the occasions on which the event *might* have occurred.

It might well happen, of course, that if we were to take a second sample of 200 items we would find 14 defectives, or perhaps only 11; for this reason a probability arrived at in this way can really only be regarded as an estimate. However, the larger the number of experiments, the more accurate we should expect the estimate to be. There are cases where we can actually verify this expectation by finding out how closely the experimental probability agrees with an *a priori* figure. For instance, we know that the chance of obtaining a six on a single throw of an unbiased dice is theoretically 1/6. If we perform the experiment of actually throwing the dice a number of times, we do not expect to get exactly 1/6 of the throws producing sixes, but the greater the number of throws, the nearer the proportion should get to the theoretical figure of 1/6. For this reason we say:

Experimental probability approaches theoretical probability as the number of experiments becomes very large.

Trusting to instinct

If you think back for a moment to the problem posed at the start of this chapter, you will realise that neither of the two definitions of probability given so far is likely to be the basis for a statement such as 'the chance of ToonToys getting away with piracy is 50–50'. A probability of this kind is almost certainly the product of someone's intuition – hopefully backed by experience and information – and in many business situations it is this third, *intuitive*, method of quantifying probabilities that we have to fall back on.

By whatever means we arrive at a probability figure, we will end up with something that is a fraction, either expressed as such (Fred Smith's chance of selection is 1/600), or as a percentage (like ToonToys 50–50 chance of getting away with piracy). Probabilities are thus measured on a scale from zero – representing, in terms of our three definitions, an event which cannot occur in any way, which has never been known to occur, or which we feel is impossible – to one – representing an event that is bound to occur, which has always happened so far, or which we feel to be inevitable.

This fact gives us a useful check on the correctness of our arguments in future, more complex probability calculations. An answer which is supposed to be a probability, and which is greater than 1, must be wrong!

Before we go on to consider how these definitions of probability apply to more complicated problems, let us apply them in a few simple cases. (You will often receive the impression in studying basic probability that statisticians are obsessed with gambling – all the problems seem to be about dice, cards and roulette wheels – but that is mainly because these are easy problems to consider.)

Some easy examples

Suppose first that you have a dice* which, instead of the usual numbered faces, has two green, two red and two yellow. What is the chance that, when it is thrown at random, a yellow face will show? The *a priori* definition gives two yellow faces out of six faces altogether, or 2/6. Notice, incidentally, that it often is not worth cancelling probability fractions like this one, particularly if you need to combine them later; you will often find yourself cancelling and then putting them over a common denominator, thus going round in circles!

If we had two such dice, and tossed them simultaneously, what would be the chance of obtaining one yellow and one green face? There are 36 combinations altogether, since any of the six faces of the first dice can be combined with any of the six faces of the second. Of these, how many fall into the category we are interested in? Either of the two yellow faces on the first dice could be combined with either of the two green ones on the second, so there are four possibilities there; or we could have either green face of the first dice combined with either yellow face of the second – another four possibilities. Altogether, then, there are eight possibilities in the category we are looking for, out of 36 possibilities in all, giving a probability of 8/36.

Now consider how you would determine the probability that it will be a wet day tomorrow. This is one which we need to approach via the experimental method, since there is no way we can count 'how many ways it might rain tomorrow'. If tomorrow is 28 February, then one way of approaching the problem would be to look up the weather records over the past, say, ten years, and find out, among all the February days in the ten-year period, what proportion have been wet. This will then give at least an approximate idea of the figure, though of course there is always the possibility that *this* year is exceptionally wet – or exceptionally dry!

Finally, what happens if someone asks you what you reckon to be the chance that you will pass the assessment at the end of your course. How would you reply? You *could* adopt an experimental approach, and look up the percentage of students on your course who have passed the assessment over the past few years; but ultimately only you know whether you have done sufficient work, written good lecture notes and so on, so your best bet is probably to give some kind of intuitive assessment of the probability based on that knowledge.

* Strictly, the singular term is die: one die, two dice, but I will adopt the popular usage of 'dice' for both singular and plural.

Quick check questions

1 A class contains 43 male and 27 female British students, plus 16 males and 24 females of other nationalities. What is the probability that if you pick a student at random from the class it will be a British male? A female student? Which definition of probability are you using here?

2 If you were asked to estimate the chance that you will be earning more than £40 000 per year within ten years of your graduation, how would you proceed? Which definition of probability would you be using?

3 The probability that it will rain tomorrow is estimated by forecasters to be 45 per cent. What is the probability that it will not rain? What fact about probability did you make use of in reaching your answer?

Answers:

1 *p*(British male) = 43/110; *p*(female) = 51/110. This uses the *a priori* definition of probaility, because we know the composition of the class.

2 Although you could try to find out what proportion of people who obtain degrees in your subject earn more than £40 000 within ten years of graduating, this would not necessarily give you a good idea of the position in relation to yourself. You would probably be better off simply making an informed estimate – using the intuitive approach.

3 Probability of no rain = 1 – probability of rain = 55 per cent. Here we are using the fact that the probability of a certainty is 1. Since 'it will either rain or not rain' amounts to a certainty, we can say that the probability of no rain is 1 – probability of rain. We will look at this kind of calculation in more detail below.

Putting probabilities together

If you glance again through our solution of the problem above concerning the two coloured dice tossed simultaneously, your reaction may well be 'There must be an easier way!' The business of counting the number of ways the thing we are interested in might happen is certainly very tedious. The problem is really a combination of two separate problems – throwing the first dice, and throwing the second – each of which is very easy on its own. So is there some way we can combine what we know about the two separate problems to give us the answer to the combined one?

There are actually *two* ways in which separate events may be combined in order to give a composite event, and fortunately there are ways of dealing with both forms of combination. If we refer to the two separate events as A and B, then we may ask what is the probability of either A *or* B happening, or alternatively what is the probability of A *and* B happening at once.

The 'or' rule

Taking the first of these forms of combination, let us ask what would be the probability, in throwing just one of our coloured dice, that we get either a yellow or a red face showing? The probability of a yellow face is 2/6, and that of a red one is 2/6 also, and since it is easy to see that altogether four faces fall into the category of 'yellow or red', the probability of this latter event is clearly 4/6. It looks, then, as if we have combined the separate probabilities in this case by adding them. In fact, it would appear that this is a general rule, for if we return to the *a priori* definition of probability, then:

Probability of A or B happening

$$= \frac{\text{number of ways A or B can happen}}{\text{total number of possibilities}}$$

$$= \frac{\text{number of ways A can happen + number of ways B can happen}}{\text{total number of possibilities}}$$

$$= \frac{\text{number of ways A can happen}}{\text{total number of possibilities}} + \frac{\text{number of ways B can happen}}{\text{total number of possibilities}}$$

= probablity of A happening + probability of B happening.

However, we must be a little careful when applying this result. The step we have taken in saying that the number of ways A or B can happen is the sum of the ways A can happen and the ways B can happen is only true if A and B cannot both happen at once – if, in statistical jargon, they are *mutually exclusive*. If A and B *can* occur simultaneously, then we will, in adding up the two sets of cases like this, be counting twice over those occasions on which both A and B happen.

This will be clear if we consider another example. If we throw an ordinary dice and ask what is the probability that an even number or one divisible by three will show, the addition rule in its simple form would suggest that the answer should be $p(\text{even}) + p(\text{divisible by three}) = 3/6 + 2/6 = 5/6$. In fact, of course, the answer should be 4/6: one of the even numbers – 6 – is also divisible by three, and so the events 'even' and 'divisible by three' are not mutually exclusive. The simple rule fails because it causes us to count 6 twice over.

There *are* ways of dealing with 'or' problems when the events are *not* mutually exclusive, as we will see later. For the time being, we state the rule in its simple form:

When A and B are mutually exclusive events

$$p(\text{A or B}) = p(\text{A}) + p(\text{B}).$$

The 'and' rule

Now consider the other type of combination, where we wish to find the probability of A *and* B happening at once. The problem discussed on page 146 of throwing the two coloured dice so as to obtain a combination of one yellow and one green face can be broken down into the probability of getting a yellow on the first dice *and* a green on the second, *or* vice versa. The first of these, a yellow on the first and a green on the second, we saw could occur in four ways, giving a probability of 4/36. Now the chance of a yellow on the first is 2/6, as is the chance of a green on the second, so it looks as if what we have done here is to *multiply* the two separate probabilities to get the combined one:

Probability of A and B happening = probability of A × probability of B.

But once again, there is a cautionary note to be sounded in the application of this result. In the example we have just looked at, the colour that showed on the second dice was clearly independent of what showed on the first; the fact that the first produced a yellow face did not make it any more, or any less, likely that the second would show a green one.

But situations arise quite frequently in which the outcome of the second event does depend on what has happened on the first attempt – where, in other words, the events are *dependent*. This, while it does not actually alter the form of the 'and' rule, does mean that we have to be careful to take into account the event which has already occurred in finding the probability of the other event.

Imagine, for example, that in a certain firm 40 per cent of the workforce are women – in other words, the probability that a worker chosen at random is a woman is 2/5. Only 25 per cent of the female workforce are management grade, whereas for male workers the figure is 30 per cent. What is the probability that a worker selected at random is both female *and* management grade? Here the probability of selecting a management grade worker varies according to whether the worker is male or female, so we must modify the 'and' rule slightly and say:

$$p(\text{female and management}) = p(\text{worker is female}) \times p(\text{worker is management } \textit{given that} \text{ worker is female})$$

$$= \frac{2}{5} \times \frac{1}{4} = \frac{2}{20} \text{ or } \frac{1}{10}.$$

With this reservation we can write the 'and' rule for combining probabilities as:

$$p(\text{A } \textit{and } \text{B}) = p(\text{A}) \times p(\text{B}).$$

These two rules are really all one needs to know in order to solve quite a wide range of probability problems. If you find it difficult to remember '*and* means multiply and *or* means add', which may seem a bit back to front at first – after all, it is usually 'and' that means add – ask yourself how big you would expect your combined probability to be, relative to the two separate probabilities. If we insist on two things happening at once – the 'and' case – this is surely less likely to occur than either of the separate events alone, so multiplying the two (fractional) probabilities gives an answer that is *smaller* than either of the figures being multiplied. If on the other hand we want one or another of two events to occur, and we are not fussy which it is, this is *more* likely to happen than either of the events alone, so adding the two separate probabilities gives an answer that is *bigger* than either of the individual figures.

Before we go on to solve some problems using our two rules, there is one useful consequence of the 'or' rule which should be pointed out: if we have a set of mutually exclusive events which between them cover all possible outcomes of a situation – let us call them A, B, C, . . . – then the probabilities of all these events together must add up to 1, for one or another of them is *bound* to occur – in other words it is a certainty, with probability 1. The probability of A or B or C or . . . happening is $p(\text{A}) + p(\text{B}) + p(\text{C}) + \ldots$, so this must be equal to 1. We call such events exhaustive, because between them they exhaust all the possible results of a process.

This fact can save a lot of arithmetic if recalled at the appropriate time. It is particularly useful if we want to find the chance of something *not* happening. Between them 'A happens' and 'A does not happen' are exhaustive events, and so:

$$p(\text{A happens} + p(\text{A does not happen}) = 1,$$
$$\text{whence } p(\text{A does not happen}) = 1 - p(\text{A happens}).$$

Thus, for example, if the probability that you will pass the examination at the end of your course is reckoned at 9/10, then the probability that you will fail (i.e. *not* pass) must be 1/10.

Tackling problems

Although the definitions of probability, and the two basic rules for combining probabilities, are very simple, it is only fair to recognise that many students find it quite difficult at first to deal with problems involving them. The English language is, I think, at least partly to blame for this difficulty. There are many different ways in which, for instance, an 'and' type of combination may be expressed – as 'both', 'neither' or 'also', to name but three possibilities. Unfortunately there is really no foolproof 'method' for tackling such problems – practice is the only way to acquire facility. So, here are a few illustrations to get you into the right frame of mind.

Example I

A production line involves the use of three machines consecutively. The chance that the first machine will break down in any one week is 1/10, for the second the chance is 1/20 and for the third 1/40. What is the probability that at least one of the machines breaks down in a certain week?

Here is a case where it pays to recall that exhaustive probabilities add up to 1. To count the number of ways in which at least one of the machines may break down is very time-consuming; it might be the first which breaks down, while the second and third are working; or the second could break down while one and three are working, or the third break down while one and two are working. But 'at least one' also includes the possibility that any *two* of the machines are broken down and only one is working – or, for that matter, that all three machines are broken down. So there are, in fact, seven different possibilities to examine. However, the *opposite* of at least one being out of action is that all three are working, in other words:

$$p(\text{at least one not working}) + p(\text{all three working}) = 1$$

so that:

$$p(\text{at least one not working}) = 1 - p(\text{all three working}).$$

Now the chance that all three are working is easily found, for this means that the first is working and the second is working *and* the third is working:

$$p(\text{all three working}) = p(\text{1st working}) \times p(\text{2nd working}) \times p(\text{3rd working}).$$

If the chance that the first is *not* working, as given in the statement of the problem, is 1/10, then the chance that it *is* working will, of course, be 9/10. Applying a similar argument to the other two machines, we have:

$$p(\text{all three working}) = \frac{9}{10} \times \frac{19}{20} \times \frac{39}{40} = \frac{6669}{8000}.$$

so

$$p(\text{at least one not working}) = 1 - \frac{6669}{8000} = \frac{1331}{8000}.$$

Of course, the solution could be written down in a much more abbreviated way; we have dotted the *i*'s and crossed the *t*'s rather laboriously here for the sake of illustrating the method.

Example 2

In a certain firm, when an employee arrives late there is a one in four chance that she will be caught by her manager. On the first occasion she is caught, she is given a warning; the second time she is dismissed. What is the probability that a worker who is late three times is not dismissed?

Here we have a situation involving conditional probabilities: what happens to the employee on the second and third occasions she is late depends on what happened the previous time. Such problems can often be presented most simply by means of a *probability tree*, as shown in Figure 7.1. The extreme left-hand branch of the tree stops after two stages because, since this corresponds to the case when the employee is caught on the first two occasions, she will then be dismissed and so the possibility of her being caught a third time does not arise.

The tree makes it easier for us to see the ways in which the case we are interested in – when the employee is late three times but caught at most once – may arise. There are in fact four possibilities: she may be caught just once, either on the first, second or third occasions, or she may not be caught at all. Each of these cases involves an 'and' combination of probabilities; for example:

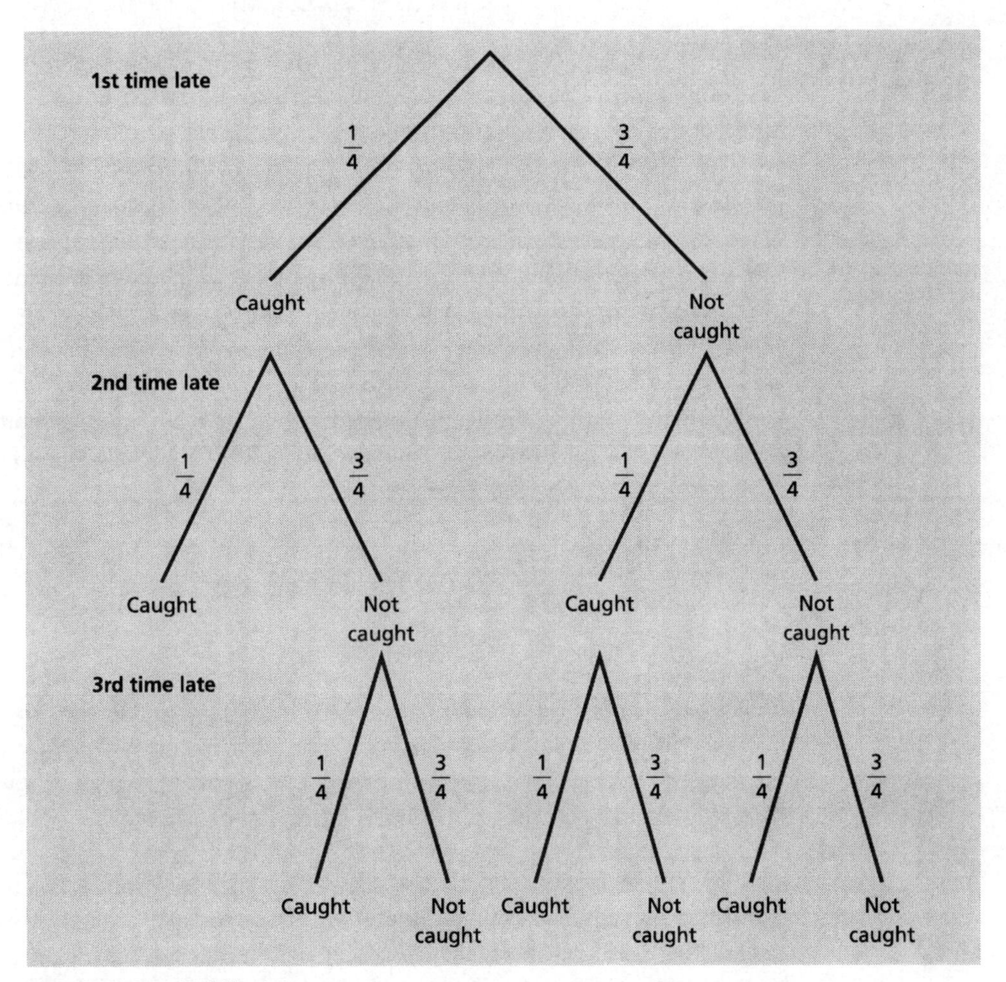

Figure 7.1 Probability tree

$$p(\text{caught the first time but not the second or third}) = \frac{1}{4} \times \frac{3}{4} \times \frac{3}{4} = \frac{9}{64}.$$

You should check that p(caught only on second occasion) and p(caught only on third occasion) are also equal to 9/64, while p(not caught at all) = 3/4 × 3/4 × 3/4 = 27/64. The four cases are linked together in an 'or' combination to give the answer we require:

$$p(\text{late three times but not dismissed}) = 9/64 + 9/64 + 9/64 + 27/64 = 54/64.$$

It might actually have been slightly quicker here to have worked from the opposite end, i.e. find the probability that she *is* dismissed, and take that away from 1 to find the probability that she is not – but there is little saving of effort.

Example 3

Two building contractors compete for contracts, and on past performance firm A has a probability of 3/4 of obtaining any one contract, while firm B has probability 1/4 (there are no other firms bidding). What is the probability that, when they bid for two contracts, firm A will obtain either the first or the second?

At first sight this looks like a straightforward 'or' combination:

$$p(\text{A gets first or A gets second}) = 3/4 + 3/4 = 6/4$$

which immediately tells us that something has gone wrong, because we cannot have a probability greater than 1. What has gone wrong is that we have ignored the restriction in using the 'or' rule – the events must be mutually exclusive – and of course in this case they are not. There is nothing to stop A getting the first *and* second contract. Our wrong 'method' has resulted in our counting twice over the occasions when this happens.

So what argument will give the correct answer? There are various possibilities: we may say, since we are looking for the probability that A gains the first or the second, *or both*, the only case we are *not* interested in is that in which B gets both the contracts. The probability of this is p(B gets first) × p(B gets second) = 1/4 × 1/4 = 1/16 (assuming that bids are independent). So p(A gets one or the other or both) = 1 – 1/16 = 15/16.

Alternatively, we can split up 'A gets the first or the second or both' into the three separate cases 'A gets the first but not the second' or 'A gets the second but not the first' or 'A gets both', which gives as before:

$$p(\text{A gets first or second or both}) = \left(\frac{3}{4} \times \frac{1}{4}\right) + \left(\frac{1}{4} \times \frac{3}{4}\right) + \left(\frac{3}{4} \times \frac{3}{4}\right) = \frac{15}{16}.$$

Example 4

Refer to the firm we discussed on page 149 where 40 per cent of the workforce are female, 25 per cent of the female workers are management grade and 30 per cent of the male workers are management grade. If a management-grade worker is selected at random from this firm what is the probability that she will be a female?

The first point to note here is that we are *not* asking 'What is the probability that a worker is a female management grade'; we are saying 'We *know* this worker is management; what's the probability that she is female?' In other words, rather than selecting our sample workers from the entire workforce, we are restricting ourselves to look at the management-grade workers only. The safest way of dealing with this situation is to draw up a table, with two dimensions representing the two quite separate divisions of the workers into male/female and management/non-management:

	Male	*Female*	*Total*
Management	18	10	28
Non-management	42	30	72
Total	60	40	100

In drawing up this table we have assumed for simplicity that the total workforce is 100 people, since this makes the calculations a bit easier. As we are only concerned with probabilities – that is, with proportions – it really does not matter what size workforce we assume.

It is now a simple matter to pick out of the table the figures we need: there are 10 female management workers out of 28 management workers altogether, so the probability that a management-grade worker is female is 10/28.

This tabular arrangement of the data is the one safe way of obtaining probabilities in this type of situation where we are looking, not at the entire population but at a restricted group within it. The key point to look for is that we are *given* some additional piece of information about the cases we are looking for, which enables us to narrow down our interest from the whole population to one of its subgroups – in this case, the management-grade workers.

Before reading the remainder of this chapter, you are strongly recommended to try Exercises 1–5 in order to practise handling probabilities. Although these examples may appear simple, probabilities for complex real-life scenarios can be built up using the principles we have established.

Quick check questions

1 A private equity company is bidding to purchase two businesses. The chance that the first bid will be successful is reckoned by analysts to be 1/4, while the chance that the second is successful is estimated at 1/5. The probability that neither bid is successful is (a) 3/5, (b) 1/20, (c) 9/20.

2 A bag of mixed fruitdrops contains 20 sweets, 6 of which are raspberry flavoured. If you select two sweets at random, the chance of getting two raspberry ones is (a) $6/20 \times 6/20$, (b) $6/20 \times 5/19$.

3 A company is running a promotion in which one packet in eight of the biscuits which it sells contains a token for a second free packet. The probability that if I buy 2 packets, neither will contain a token is (a) 1/4, (b) 63/64, (c) 49/64.

Answers:

1 (a) is correct – probability that neither is successful means probability that first is unsuccessful *and* second is unsuccessful = $3/4 \times 4/5 = 3/5$.

2 (b) is correct – if the first one you select is raspberry, then there are only 5 raspberry ones left out of the 19 remaining when you make the second selection.

3 (c) is correct – the chance that each individual packet does not contain a token is 7/8, so the chance that both packets do not contain a token = $7/8 \times 7/8 = 49/64$.

Giving probabilities a cash value

If you go back and re-read the problem posed at the beginning of this chapter, you will realise that, although we would now be in a position to advise Mr Black as to the probability of various combinations of events in which he might be interested, we still have no way of linking the probabilities of events with the financial results of those events. It is to this problem that we now turn our attention.

Let us begin with a very simple problem. A vendor sells cups of tea on a railway station at 35 pence per cup, and by keeping records of his sales over several weeks finds that they vary as follows in convenient multiples of 10:

No. of cups sold	*Percentage of days*
40	20
50	20
60	30
70	20
80	10

What can he expect his average takings per day to be, assuming that this pattern persists? He brews the cups of tea separately on demand, so that there is no problem of trying to predict the sales in advance of each day's business.

Clearly we can calculate his average takings per day by considering the distribution of takings over a period of, say, 100 days, and calculating the mean as in Chapter 5:

Taking (£) (x)	*No. of days (f)*	*fx*
14	20	280
17.50	20	350
21	30	630
24.50	20	490
28	10	280
		2030

So mean takings per day = 2030/100 = £20.30.

We call this the *expected value* of his daily takings, sometimes also called expected monetary value or EMV. Of course, he does not expect to get this precise amount on any one day – he gets either £14, or £17.50, or £21, or £24.50, or £28. But this is what he would expect, *in the long term*, his average daily takings to work out to.

Now we would have got exactly the same figure of £20.30 if, rather than taking an imaginary sample of 100 days as our averaging period, we had simply said that there is a 20 per cent chance that on any given day he will take £14, a 20 per cent chance that he will make £17.50, and so on. In other words, his expected average daily takings would be:

$$0.2 \times 14 + 0.2 \times 17.5 + 0.3 \times 21 + 0.2 \times 24.5 + 0.1 \times 28 = £20.30.$$

So the expected value of his daily takings can be calculated as:

Probability of selling 40 cups × financial result of selling 40 cups + probability of selling 50 cups × financial result of selling 50 cups + . . .

and we can generalise this to define the expected value of any process as follows:

$$\text{EMV} = \Sigma(\text{probability of outcome} \times \text{financial result of outcome})$$

where the Σ sign means 'added up all over all the possible outcomes of the process'.

Before going on to apply this idea to decision-making problems, let us see how it can be used in a couple of simple cases.

Example 1

Suppose an insurance company finds, by examining its past records, that on 80 per cent of its policies there is no claim, on 15 per cent there is a small claim, typically £50, and on the remaining 5 per cent there is a large claim, typically £500. In order to make a profit, it must make the premium per policy larger than the expected value of the claim per policy; but this, using the theory just developed, will be $0.8 \times 0 + 0.15 \times 50 + 0.05 \times 500 =$ £32.50. It is really a much-elaborated version of this calculation that insurance companies actually use in deciding how much their premiums should be.

Example 2

Imagine that you have watched people playing a fruit machine in a certain pub, and have noticed that over a long period it gave a £1.00 payout on average every 20 turns. Is it worth your while playing the machine, if the charge per turn is 10 pence?

Your expected winning per turn is

$$p(\text{winning}) \times \text{gain if you win} + p(\text{losing}) \times \text{loss if you lose} = 1/20 \times 90 + 19/20 \times (-10)$$
$$= 4.5 - 9.5 = -5.$$

So on the average, you stand to make a loss of 5 pence per turn, and therefore it is not worth playing.

Really, without saying so explicitly, we have moved here into the realm of decision-making, for you have to make a decision – to play or not to play – and on the basis of your expected winnings, the sensible decision would be not to play. The problem also highlights one of the defects of this approach to decision-making, in that someone with a well-developed gambling instinct would probably argue that it is worth something to him simply to have the *chance* of winning £1.00. The rather detached way in which we have looked at the decision takes no account of this; nor, being essentially a 'long-term' view of things, can it allow for the possibility that the machine will pay out on your very first turn, and you will have the strength of mind to quit at that point! Fortunately for the promoters of lotteries, very few people think in this way when deciding whether to gamble.

Decision tables

When we have a large number of possible courses of action among which a decision has to be made, and a large number of possible consequences to consider, the process can be made more systematic by drawing up a *decision table* (sometimes given the more technical-sounding name of decision *matrix*). To illustrate how it works, let us return to the problem of our railway-station tea vendor, and imagine that he has decided to diversify his business by also selling fruit pies. Unlike the cups of tea, however, these cannot be prepared on demand as each customer arrives; they have to be ordered in advance, and the supplier does not like the size of order changing from day to day – he will only accept orders for a week at a time. In other words, if our vendor decides to order 40 pies a day this week, he will be stuck with 40 per day for the whole week, and cannot change the number until next week.

Once again, the vendor begins by keeping a record of demand for the pies over a period of a few weeks and finds that it is as follows:

No. of pies demanded	*Percentage of occasions*
25	10
30	20
35	25
40	20
45	15
50	10

Of course, in practice there would probably be some kind of pattern of variation discernible from one day of the week to the next which might help him to plan his supplies. But for the moment, let us suppose that there is no such pattern and furthermore that the supplier insists that for the good of his reputation only fresh pies are sold; any left at the end of a day are to be returned to the bakery for a nominal refund of 5 pence. The vendor buys the pies from the supplier at 15 pence each, and sells them at 25 pence; thus every pie sold represents a profit of 10 pence, while every unsold pie represents a loss of 10 pence.

The vendor's problem is an example of decision-making *under uncertainty*; if he *knew* what the demand for pies each day would be, then he could buy just the right number and maximise his profits, but he does not have that knowledge. How then can he decide the 'best' number of pies per day to order?

The decision table for the vendor's problem is shown below: the possible decisions are at the left-hand side, and the uncontrollable factor – in this case, the demand for pies – across the columns of the table, the probability of each demand also being shown. There is clearly no point in considering buying fewer than 25 pies, since this number can *always* be sold; by the same token, as more than 50 are never required, to order such quantities would be pointless. So only the quantities actually demanded will be considered.

		Demand						*Expected*
		25(0.1)	*30(0.2)*	*35(0.25)*	*40(0.2)*	*45(0.15)*	*50(0.1)*	*value*
	25	2.5	2.5	2.5	2.5	2.5	2.5	2.5
	30	2.0	3.0	3.0	3.0	3.0	3.0	2.9
	35	1.5	2.5	3.5	3.5	3.5	3.5	3.1
Buy	*40*	1.0	2.0	3.0	4.0	4.0	4.0	3.05
	45	0.5	1.5	2.5	3.5	4.5	4.5	2.8
	50	0.0	1.0	2.0	3.0	4.0	4.0	2.4

The figures in the body of the table are arrived at as follows. Consider the occasions when 35 pies are demanded and only 25 have been bought; obviously in this case only 25 can be sold, which at a profit of 10 pence per pie will give a total profit of £2.50. The same will apply, in fact, to all other combinations in the top row (we are ignoring any question of the cost of lost goodwill through turning customers away). If, however, 35 pies are demanded and 40 have been bought, then although the sale of the 35 will produce £3.50 profit, we must offset against this the 5 pies that have to be returned at a loss of 10 pence per pie – a total loss of 50 pence. Thus the actual profit resulting from the '40 bought, 35 demanded' combination is only £3.00. You should verify in a similar way the calculation of the rest of the figures in the table.

The table, once completed like this, provides us with all the information we need to calculate the *expected value* of the vendor's profits resulting from each possible decision. For example, if he decides to buy 30 pies then his expected profit will be, using the method developed above:

$$0.1 \times 2 + 0.2 \times 3 + 0.25 \times 3 + 0.2 \times 3 + 0.15 \times 3 + 0.1 \times 3 = £2.90.$$

You can see the expected values of the remaining decisions in the right-hand column of the table.

Thus, if the vendor wishes to maximise his expected profits, he should choose to buy 35 pies per day. What this means is that if he persists in this strategy and the pattern of demand also remains as established, then in the long run this will give him an average profit of £3.10 a day – better than that achieved by any other choice.

This basis for decision-making is sometimes known as the *expected monetary value*, or EMV, decision criterion; we will return to a discussion of its suitability in particular cases, and alternative criteria that might be adopted, below.

Decision trees

We were able to deal with the problem in the last section by means of a simple decision table, because it involved only one set of 'uncontrollable circumstances' which applied with the same probabilities whatever the decision selected. Where there are different sets of consequences, with different probabilities, dependent upon which decision is made, such a method will not do and we must resort to drawing a decision *tree*. This, as its name suggests, is somewhat akin to a probability tree, with the incorporation of the financial outcomes which will result from each set of circumstances.

We will at last return to the problem posed at the start of the chapter to see how the decision tree method works. You will recall the choice faced by Harold Black at Potters Toys: whether to delay the launch of his new range of toys to coincide with the opening of the associated film, thus gaining profits of £120 000 if the film is a success but only £20 000 if it turns out to be a 'turkey', or to go ahead with the launch immediately and gain a definite £65 000. The probability that the film is a success was estimated at 60 per cent. He also has to deal with the possibility that, if the film does succeed, a rival company will enter the market and so reduce his profits to £60 000. The chance of this happening is 50 per cent.

In Figure 7.2 you can see the probability tree representing the various decisions and their consequence, without as yet the inclusion of any of the profits or costs. Notice that the tree *begins* with the decision to be made – this is the general rule – and that this *decision node*, as it is often called, is represented by a square box. This is in contrast to *chance nodes*, shown as circles. Of course, the decisions 'market now' and 'wait' do not

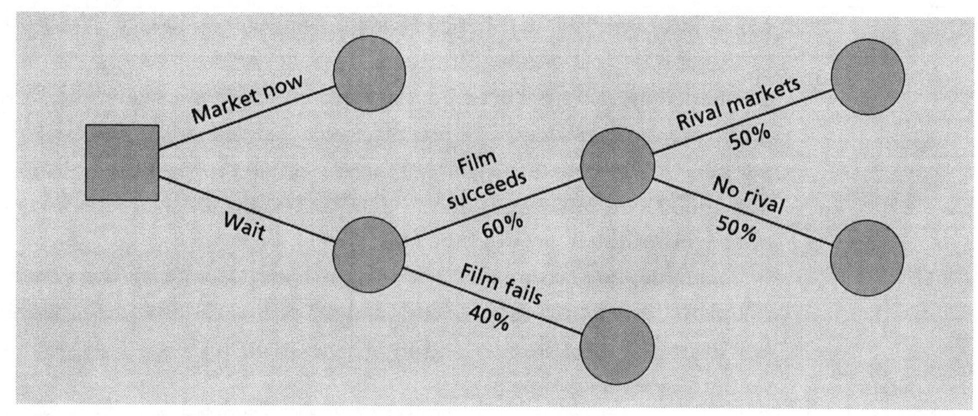

Figure 7.2 Decision tree: the first stage

have probabilities associated with them like the other branches of the tree, because unlike 'rival markets' or 'film succeeds' they are not subject to uncontrollable, probabilistic forces; one of them definitely *will* happen, and the other definitely will not, depending upon what choice is made.

We now begin to insert the profit figures into the tree, always starting from the *endpoints* of the branches, since it is these final consequences whose effects have been estimated. For example, the profit resulting from 'film succeeds, rival markets' will be £60 000. In the same way, 'film succeeds, no rival' yields £120 000, while 'film fails' gives £20 000. The result of the decision 'market now' is simply £65 000, since this is not associated with any further events.

We now use our definition of expected value to find the expected results of the various chains of events. First let's consider the expected value associated with the 'rival/no rival' chance node. This will be

$$\begin{array}{c}\text{chance of rival} \\ \text{marketing}\end{array} \times \begin{array}{c}\text{profit if} \\ \text{rival markets}\end{array} + \begin{array}{c}\text{chance that rival} \\ \text{doesn't market}\end{array} \times \begin{array}{c}\text{profit if} \\ \text{no rival}\end{array}$$

$$= 0.5 \times 60 + 0.5 \times 120$$
$$= 90 \text{ (using profits in £000 for simplicity).}$$

So the expected result of the event 'film succeeds', taking into account what the rival company might do, is £90 000. Now we work back once more, to find the expected value associated with the decision 'wait': this will be $0.6 \times 90 + 0.4 \times 20 = 62$ (make sure you can see where this calculation comes from).

Taking into account all the possible circumstances, then, we would advise Harold Black to market his product now, since the expected profit in that case – £65 000 – is a little higher than the expected result from waiting. The completed tree is shown in Figure 7.3. The decision in this case is quite marginal, since the profits associated with the two decisions are very close.

To summarise the process for constructing a decision tree:

- draw the tree representing the logical sequence of events, always beginning with the decision to be made;
- insert the financial result of each sequence of events at the corresponding terminal node of the tree;
- work back towards the decision node, using the expected value.

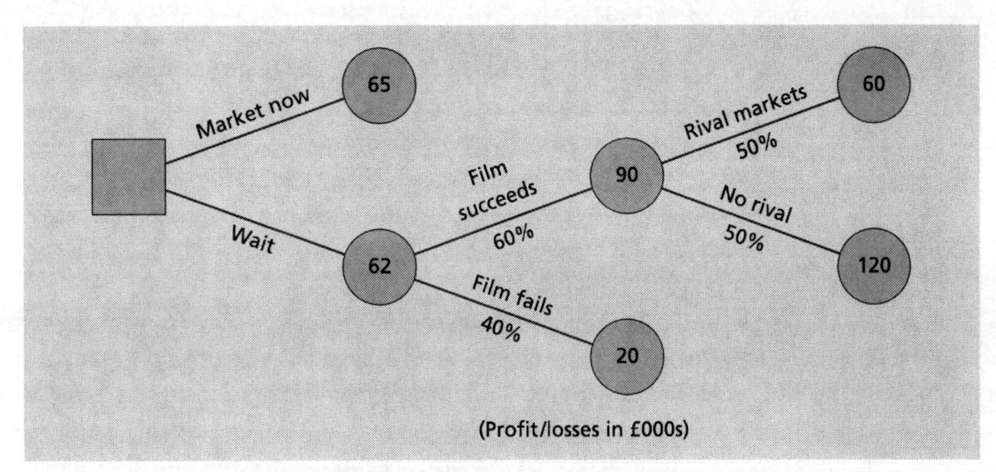

Figure 7.3 The completed decision tree

Example

We will finish this section with another example of a decision tree. I am about to buy a new calculator, and have the choice of a cheap unbranded model at £4.50, or a well-known make at £7.50. There is no guarantee with the cheap model, so if it breaks down during the first year of use I will simply have to buy another, at the same price. Friends who have similar calculators tell me this happens with about 1 in 5 of them. The more expensive calculator is much less likely to break down – the manufacturer states that the proportion which do so is only about 1 in 50 – and if it does, the guarantee means that I will only have to pay the 50 pence postage to return it to the factory. Is it worth buying the dearer machine?

The tree for this problem is shown in Figure 7.4, starting at the left with the decision 'dearer' versus 'cheaper' machine. The total cost to me of having a cheap machine which breaks down is £9, since I have no choice but to buy another at £4.50. The cost of an

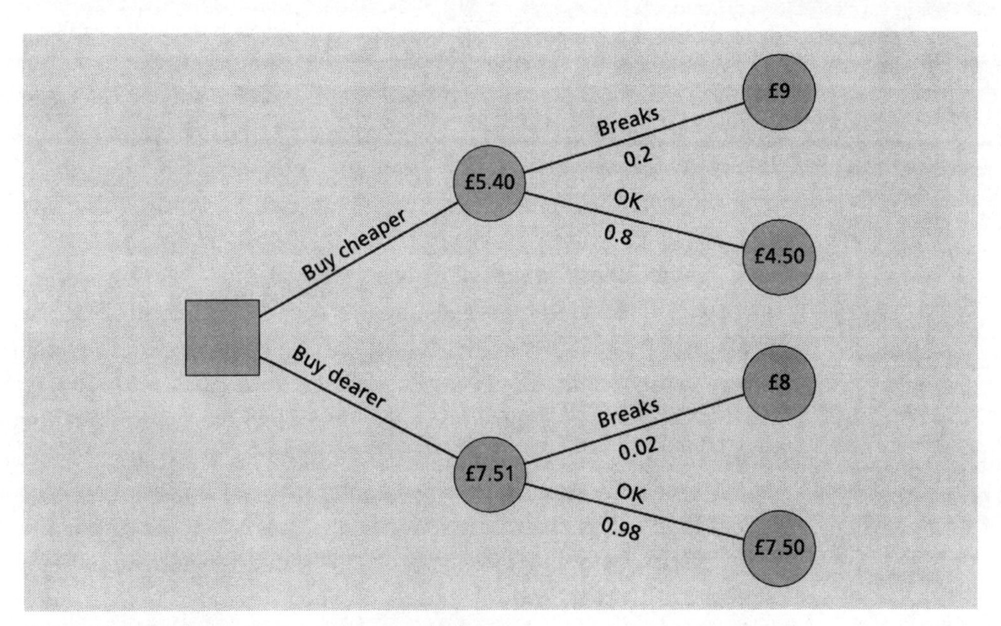

Figure 7.4 Decision tree: buying a calculator

expensive machine which breaks down is only £8 – the initial cost of £7.50 plus the 50 pence postage. If the machine does *not* break down, of course, then in either case the cost is merely the initial purchase price.

As you can see, the expected cost of buying a cheap machine is $0.2 \times 9 + 0.8 \times 4.5 =$ £5.40, whereas for the dearer machine it is $0.02 \times 8 + 0.98 \times 7.5 =$ £7.51. So it would appear that the cheaper machine is the better bet – though of course you might ask, since the chance of a breakdown is so high in this case, what is the chance that your replacement machine will break down – and so on!

Both the examples we have considered here involve only a single decision. However, many real decision problems involve sequences of decisions; they can be tackled in the same way as our simpler examples. When the decision tree becomes very large and complex, it is often necessary to use computer software for the analysis; this will generally speaking be a 'dedicated' package specifically designed for decision analysis, rather than an application of a multi-purpose package such as Excel.

Such packages often offer additional facilities to the user. They may allow a manager to give a range of options, such as 'most likely, pessimistic, optimistic', rather than a single figure as the financial consequence of a decision. They may also help to answer questions such as 'How much should I be prepared to pay for further information about this situation which will help to improve my decision-making?'

Drawbacks of the method

Strictly speaking, decision theory belongs in a later section of this book, since it is definitely 'a tool of planning', and a very important one at that. However, we have really only scratched the surface of the topic here, to illustrate how probability theory can be applied to some very real problems. In practice, problems would rarely be as simple as the ones we have solved, and would often involve not just one decision but a whole sequence.

It would not be fair to leave this topic without mentioning some of the defects of this whole approach to decision-making. We have already touched on this in the section on decision tables, where we mentioned that the EMV as a decision criterion is really most appropriate in a situation where the process is going to be repeated numerous times, since it is in such a case that the EMV can guarantee us the best possible overall return. In a 'one-off' type of situation – such as the marketing decision discussed in the section on decision trees – it is by no means clear that EMV will give the 'best' solution.

The other major drawback to using EMV as our criterion is that it requires at least estimated values for the probabilities of the various uncontrollable circumstances which may arise. Where no such estimates are available, the whole method fails, and other criteria have been developed for coping with such cases. For example, in the case of the vendor's problem examined on pages 155–7, had the vendor had no idea of the pattern of demand for fruit pies, other than that the most he would ever be asked for was 50 in one day, and the least 25, he might adopt the pessimistic viewpoint that, if the worst comes to the worst, he will sell 25 pies in a day. From that standpoint, his best decision would clearly be to buy 25 only, as this gives him the maximum possible profit if 25 are demanded. This 'pessimistic' strategy is sometimes referred to as 'maximin', since it maximises his profits in, as it were, the 'minimum' circumstances.

An optimistic vendor, on the other hand, would hope that he might sell 50 pies – the maximum that has ever been demanded of him in one day. His choice therefore would be to buy 50, since that will give him the maximum profit under the circumstance he is hoping for. The 'optimist's' strategy is often called 'maximax', since it maximises profits under the 'maximum' circumstances that may arise.

This by no means exhausts the possible choices of decision criteria, but unfortunately, in the absence of any idea what the probabilities of various contingencies may be, some of them are little more than shots in the dark. A further defect of the method as a whole is that we need to be able to put at least an approximate cash figure on the outcome of various sequences of events, but some of the figures used may be no more than inspired guesses. How, for instance, does Mr Black of Potters Toys *know* that his profit will be £65 000 if he markets now? And if he has got his estimates wrong, will he end up by making a disastrously wrong decision? It is easy to visualise a situation in which the expected results of two or more possible decisions could be so finely balanced that just a small change to one of the profit estimates – or, for that matter, to one of the probabilities – would completely alter the decision. You will have a chance to think about this question of the *sensitivity* of the decision to changes in the figures a bit more in some of the Exercises at the end of the chapter, and this whole topic of how small errors in the data of a problem may alter the solution is one that will become familiar as you read Part 4.

Finally, as pointed out earlier, we have taken a very cold-bloodedly financial point of view throughout our decision-making. But frequently where business decisions are concerned there are other, less quantifiable, but equally important, factors to be considered. Suppose a firm is considering re-siting its plant on a green-belt industrial estate; how can it measure in cash terms the benefits to its workers of a healthier working environment, or the inconvenience of being more distant from a railway station, or the effect on production of workers having much longer journeys to reach the plant? And yet these are precisely the kind of questions the firm *should* be considering when trying to decide whether to make the move. There are ways of attempting to attach nominal cash values to factors of this kind, but naturally the subject is much less cut-and-dried, and much more open to controversy than anything we have considered in this chapter.

EXERCISES

Further examples on the work of this chapter can be found on the ***companion website****.*

1 A public health inspector is visiting the PQR supermarket, and inspects the staff washroom. The manager knows that one day on average out of every three the sink is blocked, and two days out of five there is no towel available. If the inspector will only pass the premises if the sink is clear and a towel is available, what is the chance that he will do so?

2 Half the workers in a certain factory are women, but among part-time workers they represent a much higher proportion, in fact four-fifths. A quarter of the overall workforce consists of part-timers. What is the probability (a) that a worker is male; (b) that a part-time worker is male; (c) that a male worker is a part-timer?

→

3 The probability that Martin Moribund will die during the ten-year term of a life insurance policy is assessed by the insurance company at 1/5. Arthur Average's probability of living to the end of the ten-year period is reckoned at 95 per cent. What is the probability that at the end of the ten years (a) both and (b) one or the other, but not both, is living?

4 As part of a very strict auditing procedure, every audit document is examined first by an articled junior accountant, then by a qualified accountant, and finally by one of the partners in the accounting firm. If there is an error in the document the chance that the junior will detect it is 4/5: if he finds the error, he will not bother passing on the document to his senior. The chance of the qualified accountant detecting an error in the documents he examines is 3/5, and once again he passes on only those documents that appear to him to be correct. Finally, when the partner examines the documents that reach him, his chance of detecting an error is 1/2.

(a) What is the probability that an erroneous document will be detected by one or other of the three examiners?

(b) Do the three probabilities for the three personnel quoted suggest that the junior is better at detecting errors than the partner?

5 An unscrupulous manufacturer knows that in a box of a dozen lightbulbs which he is selling to a customer, four are in fact not working. He watches nervously as the customer insists on removing three and testing them. What is the probability that only one of the three tested fails to work?

6 I am trying to decide whether to move house or stay in my present one. I must decide immediately, but unfortunately there is an element of uncertainty in the situation, as my firm is in the middle of reorganisation, and may shortly move me to another site, closer to my present home than to the house I am considering buying. I reckon the chances of my being moved at about 40 per cent. If I am moved, I estimate that annual fares from my present home would cost £200, as opposed to £250 from the new house. To reach the site where I work at present, on the other hand, currently costs me £300 per year from my present house, but would cost only £200 a year from the new house. If there is no price difference between the two houses, so that I make neither a profit nor a loss on the transaction, what would you advise?

7 If I do not put any money in a parking meter when I park, there is a one-in-ten chance that a warden will notice, and I will be fined £25. If I pay now, it will cost me 20 pence. Is it worth trying to get away without paying?

8 I have an old tea set inherited from my great-aunt. At the moment I would get £50 for it if I sold it, which can be invested to give me £65 in a year's time. If I hang on to the tea set for a year, an antique dealer friend tells me there is a 1/5 chance that this particular type of pottery will become fashionable and I will be able to sell the tea set for £125. Otherwise the value will remain the same, though my cleaning lady is very clumsy and there is always the chance, if I do decide to keep the tea set for another year, that she will smash it during that year. On past performance I assess the chance of this happening at 10 per cent. What should I do?

9 Discuss how you would assess the probability that:

(a) a candidate of a given party, standing in a by-election in a given constituency, will be elected;

(b) the baby your elder sister is expecting will be a girl;

(c) a consumer, presented with two otherwise identical packages, will take the red one in preference to the blue;

(d) the aeroplane on which you are flying to Majorca for your holidays will crash on the way.

10 Demonstrate for yourself how the probability given by the experimental approach becomes closer to that given by the *a priori* approach as the number of experiments becomes larger. You can do this by tossing a coin over and over, keeping a running record of the cumulative number of heads obtained, and the cumulative probability, and seeing how the latter figure approaches 0.5 (assuming, of course, that the coin is fair!).

As an example, suppose your first ten tosses gave H, H, T, H, T, T, H, T, H, H. Then your running total of heads would be 1, 2, 2, 3, 3, 3, 4, 4, 5, 6, and the cumulative probabilities would be as follows:

$$1/1 = 1,\ 2/2 = 1,\ 2/3 = 0.67,\ 3/4 = 0.75,\ 3/5 = 0.6,$$
$$3/6 = 0.5,\ 4/7 = 0.57,\ 4/8 = 0.5,\ 5/9 = 0.55,\ 6/10 = 0.6.$$

If you choose to plot the cumulative probabilities on a graph against the number of experiments, you will see in an even more striking way how as the number of experiments becomes larger, the probability tends to 'home in' upon 0.5.

11 Referring to the problem posed on page 159 and the decision tree in Figure 7.3, all other things being equal, how small would the chance of the rival marketing have to be before it would be worthwhile abandoning the project?

12 In Exercise 7 what chance of discovery by the traffic warden would make it worth your while trying to get away without paying the meter? Given the probabilities as in the question, what increase in the standard charge for the meter would convince you that it is worthwhile not to pay?

(In Exercises 11 and 12 we are investigating the sensitivity of our decision to changes – a topic to which we will be returning in later chapters.)

13 At the moment there is much discussion in the serious media about the wisdom and efficacy of 'screening' programmes for various potentially fatal diseases. At first sight the issues seem clear-cut: if there is a test which can tell you whether or not you have a disease at an early stage, so that if you have, you can be given treatment, surely that is a good thing?

That would certainly be true if such tests were infallible, but unfortunately that is rarely the case: they can wrongly return negative results for a person who actually has the disease, and sometimes also register as positive someone who does not have it. Suppose, for example, that historic data suggest one person in 200 000 suffers from Gauss's Disease, and that a new test has just been developed that can detect this unpleasant complaint before any symptoms appear. However, early results indicate that the test returns a false positive (i.e. it indicates someone has the disease when they have not) in 2 per cent of cases, and also that it gives a false negative (indicating that someone is free of the disease when they actually have it) in 5 per cent of cases.

(a) If you have just been tested for Gauss's Disease and given a positive result, what is the chance that you actually have the disease?

(b) What is the implication of your answer to (a) for the introduction of widespread screening for the disease?

(c) What assumptions are being made in our approach to this problem, and to what extent do you think they are realistic?

Further reading

For further reading on the topic of probability and decision making, the following book may be useful:

Goodwin, P. and Wright, G. (2003), *Decision Analysis for Management Judgment*, 3rd edn, Wiley.

Chapter 8

PATTERNS OF PROBABILITY
SOME DISTRIBUTIONS

Chapter prerequisites

Before starting work on this chapter make sure you are happy with:

1 the definitions of probability and the rules for combining elementary probabilities;

2 the ideas of frequency distributions and histograms;

3 the definition and meaning of mean and standard deviation;

4 the conversion of decimals to percentages and vice versa.

Learning outcomes

By the end of your work on this chapter you should be able to:

1 recognise problems that can be modelled by the binomial, Poisson and normal distributions;

2 solve such problems with the use of the appropriate tables;

3 recognise when the use of these distributions involves approximations in the original problem;

4 outline the connections between these three distributions.

Quantitative methods in practice

The *Risks Digest*, subtitled 'Forum on Risks to the Public in Computers and Related Systems', is an electronic journal published by the Association for Computing Machinery's Committee on Computers and Public Policy (go to www.acm.org and search for Risks Digest). A sample from the contents list of the April 2007 edition will give you an idea of the flavour of the journal:

- Gov't straining to secure computer systems
- Don't let your navigation system fool you
- 'System problems' on a departing airline flight?
- Elections bring down foreign Web sites

In other words, tales of computer disasters. Actually, when you consider the extent to which every aspect of our lives today depends on computer-based systems, the proportion of failures is remarkably small – but of course, the consequences can be enormously inconvenient or even disastrous when a system does fail.

After our discussion in the previous chapter, you may find yourself wondering how the risks of such failures are assessed. Given the complexity of the systems involved, the 'first principles' approach adopted in Chapter 7 is clearly not a realistic option – when a computer program may contain thousands of lines of code, and may have been written by a team involving many people, we can hardly ask 'how many ways might an error occur?'! And yet it is essential to be able to assess the chances that various kinds of system failure may occur.

In this situation, rather than working 'from scratch', we generally resort to using well-established patterns of probability which can be shown to model the problem effectively. These patterns have a theoretical basis; they have been studied and tabulated, and their behaviour is well understood. The technical name for these models is probability distributions (for reasons that we will explore later). Dozens of theoretical distributions exist; in this chapter we will look at three of the most important.

The quality manager's problem

Bennetts is a small firm which manufactures 'wholefood' cakes and confectionery. Originally something of a 'cottage industry', started in the premises behind a wholefood retail store by the proprietor, the business has expanded rapidly in line with the entire wholefood business, and now employs some 30 people manufacturing around two dozen product lines and distributing to wholefood and healthfood stores over quite a large area.

When the business was started, the control of the quality of the product presented no problems, as output was so small that every item could be individually checked. With expansion, however, it has been increasingly difficult to maintain this standard of checking, particularly since some automatic packing machinery has been purchased. Moreover, the requirements of trading standards in relation to weights and measures need to be considered. One of the staff has therefore been designated – along with his several other job functions – 'Quality Manager', and has been given overall responsibility for ensuring that products generally come up to scratch, that the packing machines are not producing large numbers of underweight packs, and so on.

We will concentrate on just three of the problems he has encountered in his new role. First, there is the Crunchy Flapjack situation: these rather fragile biscuits are packed by machine in boxes of half-a-dozen; in the interests of customer goodwill, Bennetts will replace any box in which more than half of the biscuits are broken. The quality manager has monitored the machine and found that it tends to break, on average, 1 biscuit in every 20. So what sort of proportion of returned boxes is Bennetts likely to have to deal with? He is assuming, of course, that the biscuits are so well packed that once they get inside the box, no more will be broken – in other words, all breakages can be ascribed to the packing machine.

The second problem concerns the Natural Molasses Coated Toffee Apples. These are supplied to retailers packed in boxes, but as the boxes are filled by weight, and of course the weight of individual apples varies, there is no knowing exactly how many are in a given box (though it is a pretty large number – around 144). Inevitably, now that the apples are produced in large numbers, the occasional one is not properly dipped in the toffee. One important customer has suggested that, if as the apples are being unpacked in his shop there appear to be an exceptionally large number with faulty toffee coatings, he should have the option of returning the whole box for replacement. While Bennetts agrees to this in principle, the quality manager would like to know just what should be agreed on as 'an exceptionally large number'. He knows that the average number of faulty apples per box is 6, and he would like to fix the agreement in such a way that he will only need to replace one box in 100.

Finally, the machine that fills bags of Carrot Candy has been causing problems. The nominal weight of these bags is 500 g, but of course in practice there is a certain variation in the exact weights produced by the machine. The current procedure is to set the machine to an average weight slightly higher than 500 g – at present 510 g – and then check-weigh the bags and refill by hand any which are underweight. However, this is wasting a great deal of time as it turns out that about 20 per cent of all the bags have to be manually refilled. So the quality manager would like to know what setting he should use for the average weight on the packing machine if he wants to cut this proportion down to 5 per cent.

You will not be surprised to learn that all three of these problems are connected with probability. The manager wants to know, for example, what is the probability that a box of Crunchy Flapjacks will contain more than three broken out of six; he wants to know what the probability is of various numbers of faulty toffee apples per box, so that he can make an informed decision about the agreed number for an automatic replacement of the consignment; and if he knew the probability, for a given setting of the packing machine, that a bag of Carrot Candy weighing less than 500 g will be produced, then he could adjust the setting to give the required proportion of underweight bags.

But, like the computer problems mentioned in the introduction to this chapter, these are not the sort of probability questions with which we have dealt in Chapter 7. The first one *could* be dealt with 'from scratch', as it were, since we know the probability of a single biscuit being broken, and want to find the probability that more than three biscuits out of six will be broken. Even this, however, would be very tedious, since we would have to work out all the different ways in which four biscuits out of six might be broken (there are in fact 15 of them!), or five out of the six might be broken, or all six might be broken

– rather a daunting task. And when it comes to the remaining two problems the methods we have used so far fail completely.

However, what these three problems have in common is that each belongs to a well-established *pattern* of problem – patterns that recur so often and in so many different situations that to save our having to develop the theory for such a problem every time it is encountered, the required probabilities have been calculated once for all, and provided in the form of tables. Thus all that you, the user of the established theory, need to be able to do is, first to recognise *which* of the established patterns your problem conforms to – or can be made to conform to, since sometimes a bit of approximation is needed – and second to make use of the appropriate set of tables in the context of your problem to obtain the probability you need.

These standard patterns of probability are called *probability distributions*, which may ring a bell in your mind; we have already come across that word distribution, though in a different context, in Chapter 5. There we were discussing frequency distributions; is this one of those confusing cases where the same word is used to mean different things in two different contexts?

There is actually a very close link between the idea of a probability distribution, which will form the main topic of this chapter, and the familiar frequency distribution; but in order to establish this link, we will have to abandon for a moment the *theoretical* probability distributions – the standard patterns of probability which we have just been talking about – and take a look at a more practical example.

The idea of a probability distribution

We will return, for this section, to the frequency distribution which became very familiar in Chapter 5 – the wage distribution of the Grimchester motor-workers, which for convenience is repeated here:

Weekly take-home pay (£)	*No. of Grimchester workers*
300 but under 310	3
310 but under 320	7
320 but under 330	33
330 but under 340	26
340 but under 350	24
350 but under 360	20
360 but under 370	18
370 but under 380	15
380 but under 400	4

Suppose we now ask, not how many of the workers in this sample earn between £300 and £310 per week, but what is the *probability* of a Grimchester motor-worker earning between £300 and £310 per week? Then, assuming this sample of workers is representative, we can easily calculate the required probability using the familiar definition:

$$\frac{\text{number of workers in the £300–£310 bracket}}{\text{total number of workers in the sample}} = 3/150 = 0.02.$$

In the same way we could convert all the other frequencies to probabilities simply by dividing by 150, and so convert our frequency distribution into a probability distribution – a table which tells us how the probabilities are distributed between the various wage-groups:

Weekly take-home pay (£)	*Probability*
300 but under 310	0.02
310 but under 320	0.047
320 but under 330	0.22
330 but under 340	0.173
340 but under 350	0.16
350 but under 360	0.133
360 but under 370	0.12
370 but under 380	0.1
380 but under 400	0.027

This is an example of an *experimental* probability distribution, since it was obtained by actually taking a sample of workers and noting their wages. Many of the features with which we are familiar in the frequency distribution carry over into the probability distribution. It will, for instance, have a mean and a standard deviation, which are identical to those we calculated in Chapter 5 (can you see why?). Just as the frequencies in the original distribution added up to 150, the total number of workers in the sample, so the probabilities in the new distribution add up to 1; between them they cover all the possible wages for the sample.

We can also convert the diagram that represented the frequency distribution – the histogram – into one which represents the probability distribution. You can see this in Figure 8.1 – apart from the vertical scale, the diagram is identical to Figure 5.1(a). But whereas in the ordinary histogram the area of each block represented the frequency of

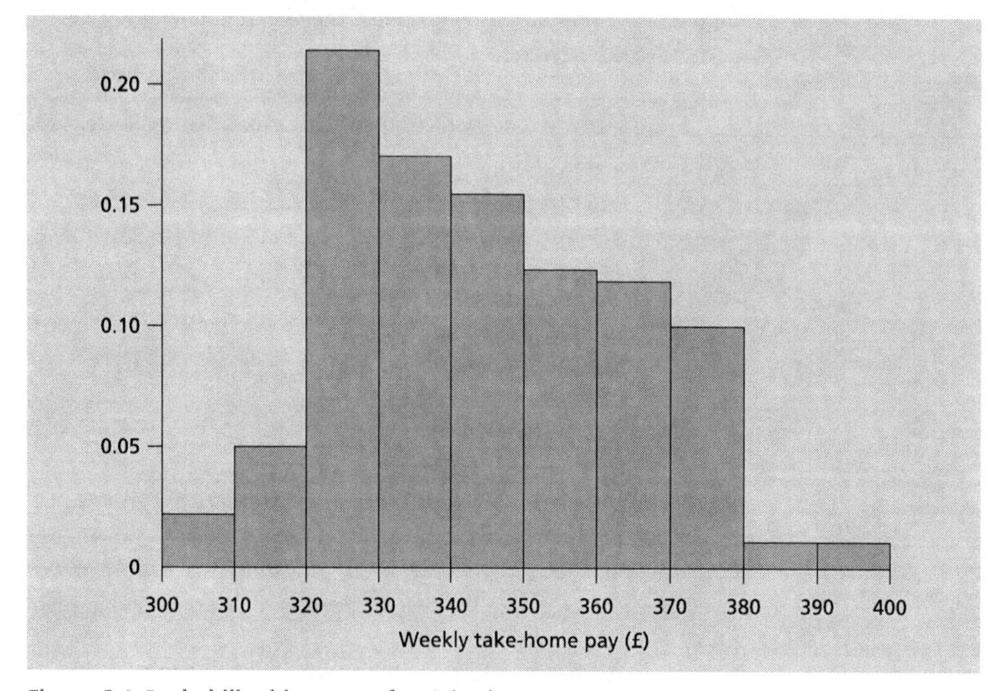

Figure 8.1 Probability histogram for Grimchester wages

the corresponding class, in what we might call the probability histogram the area of the blocks represents the probability that a value falls in the corresponding class. It follows from this that the overall area under the probability histogram must add up to 1, the sum of the probabilities. This is a point we shall be returning to later.

Although this experimental probability distribution serves quite well as an introduction to the idea of a probability distribution, it is not very useful in terms of working out probabilities, since it applies only to the particular sample of 150 workers included in the survey (although if the survey was well designed it presumably has some degree of applicability to the population from which the sample was taken). But far more useful in general terms are the *theoretical* probability distributions which relate to the kind of experimental distribution we have just looked at rather as the *a priori* definition of probability relates to the experimental definition. They are distributions worked out on general, theoretical grounds, which retain many of the features we have observed in the experimental distribution, but which are applicable to a much wider class of problems.

The binomial distribution

Recognising the pattern

The first of the quality manager's problems was, you will recall, concerned with the fragile Crunchy Flapjacks. He has determined that the packing machine breaks, on average, 1 biscuit in 20 – which is another way of saying that the probability of a biscuit being broken is one-twentieth or 0.05. What he needs to know is the proportion of boxes which will contain more than three broken biscuits; this is, again, equivalent to knowing the probability that a box of six biscuits will contain more than three broken.

Let us try to summarise the things we know about this problem. The most obvious, perhaps, is that we are concerned with a situation in which there are only a finite, discrete number of possibilities: there could be 0, 1, 2 . . . up to 6 broken biscuits in a box, but it does not make any sense to think of the probability that there are, say two-and-a-half broken ones! Furthermore, we are in an either/or situation: either a biscuit is broken or it isn't – there is no such thing as a partly broken biscuit. The remaining information with which we are supplied is: first the number of biscuits in a box, which is known and fixed; and second the probability of an individual biscuit being broken by the machine, which presumably if the machine is warmed up and running steadily will again be fixed.

The facts about this problem which we have just summarised make it a typical example of a *binomial* probability situation, which can be tackled with the aid of the binomial distribution. The name *bi*nomial gives a clue as to one major feature of this distribution; it applies in cases where there are just two possible outcomes to a process – here, the individual biscuit is broken or it isn't. We could summarise the requirements for a problem to fit this binomial pattern as follows:

Conditions for a binomial problem:

1 either/or situation;
2 number of trials (usually called n) is known and fixed;
3 probability of success on each trial (usually called p) is known and fixed.

We are using the terms 'trials' and 'success' fairly loosely here, to mean respectively the number of times a thing might have a chance of occurring, and the times when it actually *does* occur. This means that, in the problem of the biscuits, a 'success' consists of a biscuit being broken by the machine!

Before looking at the actual probabilities obtained in binomial situations, it is a good idea to practise recognising a binomial problem when you see one. We will look at three further examples.

Problem 1

Five coins are tossed simultaneously; what is the chance of obtaining three heads?

The either/or requirement is clearly met here, since each coin must come down showing either heads or tails. The number of 'trials' is the number of coins being tossed, so $n = 5$; and if the coins are all fair ones, then the probability of 'success' (i.e. getting a head) each time is 0.5. All the requirements for a binomial problem are thus present.

Problem 2

By looking up weather records for the past ten years I have discovered that the proportion of wet days in the current month of the year has been 60 per cent. What is the probability that next week there will be five or more wet days?

If a day is defined as wet (it rains sometime during the day) or dry (it doesn't), then we have our either/or situation. We can use the 60 per cent figure to give an approximate value of 0.6 for p, the probability of 'success' (a wet day), but there is a certain amount of approximation here in assuming that p is fixed; wet days, corresponding to periods of atmospheric low pressure, tend to come in twos and threes, so you might argue that if it rained today the probability of rain tomorrow is higher than if it had been dry today. However, we will not be making too serious an error if we treat p as having a fixed value of 0.6. Of course, n will be 7, the number of days in the week.

Problem 3

An unscrupulous shopkeeper has packed lightbulbs into crates of 144 and is selling them at a bargain price; what his customers do not know is that in each box, 24 are in fact faulty bulbs which will not work. A customer insists on trying a sample of six bulbs before he buys; what is the probability that they will all work?

Here the either/or corresponds to the bulbs working/not working, and n is 6, the number being tried. As for p, it is clearly 24/144 – or is it? When the first bulb is taken, there are 24 ways of picking a dud bulb out of 144 bulbs altogether. But presumably the customer will not replace the first bulb before taking a second one, so that on his second choice the chance of getting a dud is either 23/143 – if the first was a dud – or 24/143 if the first was working. So the requirement that p is known *and fixed* appears to break down again. However, the difference between 24/144, which as a decimal is 0.167, and 23/143 (0.161) or 24/143 (0.168) is so small that in practice we would not be making too sweeping an approximation if we took $p = 24/144$ and used the binomial distribution.

This is only the case, however, because the 'population' of bulbs from which we are sampling is relatively large (144). If the whole case of bulbs contained only, say, 30 bulbs, then the differences between the values of p as successive bulbs were taken would be a good deal greater, as you can easily verify, and the use of the binomial distribution would hardly be justified; see also Exercise 5, Chapter 7.

From this it should be clear that frequently, in 'squeezing' our practical problem slightly to fit the binomial pattern, we are using the theoretical distribution as a reasonably good but easier-to-handle imitation of the real-life situation. We are in fact using the binomial to *model* the practical problem, a process with which you will become increasingly familiar as you read later sections of this book.

Using the tables

As mentioned earlier, we could in principle solve problems of the binomial pattern by means of the basic rules for combining probabilities introduced in Chapter 7. To see how this can be done, and also how much simpler the process is with the aid of the tables of the distribution, let us return to the first of the problems examined above. If five coins are tossed simultaneously, what is the probability of obtaining three heads? We can, somewhat laboriously, write down all the different ways in which three heads out of five coins might occur:

HHHTT	HHTHT	HHTTH	HTHHT	HTHTH
HTTHH	THHHT	THHTH	THTHH	TTHHH

In other words, there are ten different ways in which the case we are interested in might arise. The probability of any one of these will be 1/32; for example, $p(\text{HHHTT}) = \frac{1}{2}\times\frac{1}{2}\times\frac{1}{2}\times\frac{1}{2}\times\frac{1}{2}$, and so on. So the probability we are looking for will be $10 \times 1/32$ or 10/32, which as a decimal is 0.3125.

In fact, we could say that in general for a binomial problem, the chance of getting r successes out of n trials will be given by the following formula:

> p(r successes in n trials) =
> probability of r successes $\times$ probability of the remaining ($n - r$) failures $\times$ the number of ways in which r successes out of n trials can happen.

However, as you can see, the process of working out binomial probabilities in this way, particularly the business of determining the number of different ways in which a certain number of successes can occur, is quite complicated, even though there are short-cut methods which can help. We will therefore rely for our solution of binomial problems on the tables in Appendix 3.

You will find the tables headed '*Cumulative* binomial probabilities' – in other words, they give the probability of getting r *or more* successes out of n trials in a binomial situation. The values of n – from 1 to 10 – correspond to the main blocks of the table, while the values of p – from 0.05 to 0.5 – are to be found at the heads of the columns. Where there are blanks in the table, for instance for $n = 5$ with $r = 4$ and $p = 0.05$, this simply means that the probability is so small that it would not show up in these tables (which are given only to four decimal places).

To see how the tables are to be used, let us first deal with the coin-tossing problem we have just been looking at 'by hand'. We had $n = 5$ and $p = 0.5$, and we were interested in the chance of getting three heads. Now if we look in the block $n = 5$ of the tables, under the column $p = 0.5$ and in the row $r = 3$, what we find – namely 0.5000 – is the probability of getting three or more heads. This, of course, is not exactly what we want. However, the figure opposite $r = 4$ – 0.1874 – is the probability of getting four or more heads. Now 'four or more' heads out of five means four heads or five heads, whereas 'three or more' means three or four or five. So the difference between these two figures must give the probability of getting *exactly* three heads.

Thus p(three heads in five throws) = 0.5000 – 0.1874 = 0.3126, just as we calculated at the beginning of this section.

You may wonder *why* the tables are arranged in this way, which means we have to perform subtraction sums to find the probability of getting an exact number of successes. But in practical situations it is often more useful to answer such questions as 'What's the chance of more than three eggs being smashed?' or 'What's the probability this sales representative will make at least six sales?', so on balance, I think this cumulative method of presenting the tables is preferable.

Another example

Let us now solve problem 2 posed on page 170, where the probability of rain on a particular day is 60 per cent, giving $p = 0.6$, and we wish to know the probability of five or more wet days next week, so $n = 7$. It is easy enough to find the block of tables headed $n = 7$, but where is $p = 0.6$? The values of p at the heads of the columns only go as far as $p = 0.5$ so how are we to deal with the remaining values between 0.5 and 1? The answer is by turning the problem on its head and asking not what is the probability of five or more wet days if p(wet day) = 0.6, but rather what is the probability of two *or fewer* dry days if p(dry day) = 0.4 – which of course amounts to exactly the same thing. Because of the either/or nature of binomial problems, a problem involving a value of p greater than 0.5 can always be re-expressed in terms of the *opposite* situation, for which p is less than 0.5. That is why the tables need only go as far as $p = 0.5$.

To solve this problem, then, we want p(2 or less dry days out of 7) with p(dry day) = 0.4; we are still not quite home, however, for the tables are arranged to give the probability of r or more events, not r or less. But here the fact that probabilities add up to 1 comes to our rescue:

$$p(\text{2 or less dry days}) + p(\text{3 or more dry days}) = 1$$

because between them the two situations cover all possibilities, so we have:

$$p(\text{2 or less dry days}) = 1 - p(\text{3 or more dry days}).$$

If we look in the $n = 7$ block of the tables, under $p = 0.4$ and opposite $r = 3$, what we find is the probability of three or more dry days, which turns out to be 0.5800. So p(2 or less dry days) = 1 – 0.5800 = 0.4200, which is therefore also the chance of five or more wet days in the week.

You will realise by now that one often has to do a certain amount of juggling with a problem before it appears in the right form for use with the tables. Here again, as with the elementary probability problems in Chapter 7, I am afraid the English language is very much to blame. It is worth spending a little time looking at the various ways in which questions of this kind can be posed, and how they relate to each other. For this purpose it is useful to make use once more of the 'number line' which we encountered in Chapter 1 and which is repeated below:

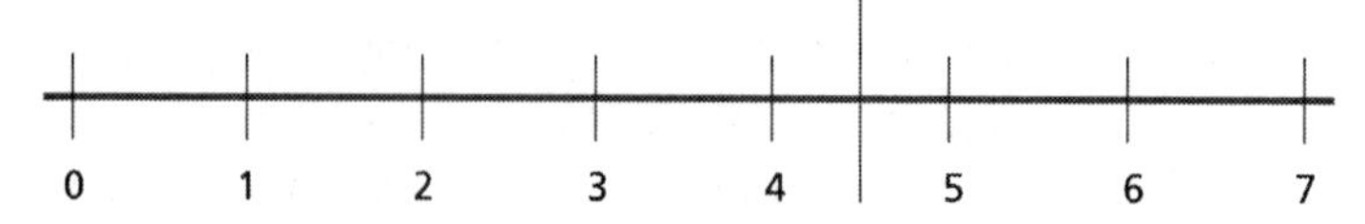

The probabilities given directly by the tables are, as we have seen, of the 'or more' variety – for example, five or more wet days out of seven. The *opposite* of this can be found from the number line by drawing a division which cuts off the '5 or more' cases from the rest, as shown; then it is clear that the remaining possibilities are '4 or less'. (The precise position of the division does not matter since we are dealing with a discrete situation where values between 4 and 5 cannot occur.) But there are other ways of expressing these two fundamental cases: '5 or more' is the same as 'more than 4', or 'not less than 5', or 'at least 5', while '4 or less' can also be stated as 'less than 5', 'not more than 4' and 'at most 4'. So you really need your wits about you in untangling this sort of problem, and the use of the number line, though it may seem a bit infantile, can be a great help. You can always write it on a scrap of paper and throw it away afterwards, so no one need know you resorted to such basic methods!

Some general features of the tables

There are two other points about the binomial tables worth noting. First, you have probably observed that the figures in the $r = 0$ row for every block of the tables are all 1.0000. This is not surprising, if you recall that these figures represent the probability of 0 or more successes out of n; there are *bound* to be 0 or more successes, so this probability corresponds to a certainty, whatever the value of n. Hence it is always equal to 1.

The second fact is that the set of tables provided in Appendix 3 is very limited. There are larger sets of published tables, but most people now would make use of Excel or a similar computer-based resource to give them the necessary values; we will look at how this works later in the chapter. Meanwhile, here are two more examples to help familiarise you with the use of the tables.

Example 1

Information is transmitted electronically in the form of *bits*. Suppose that a message consisting of eight bits is to be transmitted, and that the chances of any one bit being transmitted erroneously is 0.1. What is the chance that the entire message is transmitted correctly?

Here we have $n = 8$, $p(\text{error}) = 0.1$, and we want to find $p(\text{exactly 0 errors})$. This will be

$$p(0 \text{ or more errors}) - (1 \text{ or more errors}) = 1 - 0.5695 = 0.4305,$$

that is, about a 43 per cent chance, which is not very satisfactory. Of course, in practice the chance of an error in one bit would be very much smaller – perhaps of the order of 10^{-10} or 0.000 000 000 1!

We have assumed here that the errors occur randomly, which is an important assumption not always met in practice. For example, if the information were being transmitted over a telephone line which was subject during the transmission to a burst of electronic 'noise', then it is likely that several consecutive bits would be corrupted; in this case, the binomial model would not apply.

Example 2

A certain type of orthopaedic surgery works successfully for about 75 per cent of patients with a particular condition. What is the probability that in a randomly selected group of nine patients with the condition who have this type of surgery, it is successful in at least seven cases?

Here $n = 9$ and $p(\text{success}) = 0.75$. However, because this is greater than 0.5 it does not appear among the tabulated p-values, so we need to turn the problem round and express it in terms of the number of failures, noting that $p(\text{failure}) = 0.25$.

We are interested in at least 7 successes – that is 7, 8 or 9 successes, which is the same as 2, 1 or 0 failures. Thus in terms of failures we want $p(2 \text{ or less})$. But the tables are not arranged to give probabilities of this kind – instead we need to note that $p(2 \text{ or less failures}) = 1 - p(3 \text{ or more failures})$. Now the tables show that $p(3 \text{ or more})$ with $n = 9$ and $p = 0.25$ is 0.3993. So finally we can say:

$$\begin{aligned} p(\text{at least 7 successes}) &= p(2 \text{ or less failures}) \\ &= 1 - p(3 \text{ or more failures}) \\ &= 1 - 0.3993 = 0.6007 \text{ or about 60 per cent.} \end{aligned}$$

This may seem a long and convoluted process; it will be easier to follow if you try to think your way through it step by step, rather than attempting to turn it into some system of 'rules'. It is always safer to *understand* what you are doing!

We will now conclude our use of the binomial tables by returning to the quality manager's problem with the Crunchy Flapjacks: given $n = 6$ and $p = 0.05$, what is the probability of more than three broken biscuits in a box? $p(\text{more than } 3) = p(4 \text{ or more})$, so we should be looking up the block $n = 6$, the column $p = 0.05$ and the row $r = 4$; the probability then turns out to be 0.0001 within the accuracy of the tables, so apparently the proportion of replacements demanded will be only 1 in 10 000. This is not too surprising if you ask what would be the average number of broken biscuits you would expect to find in a box; if the proportion of broken ones is 1 in 20, and boxes contain six, then the average proportion broken per box will be one-twentieth of six, which is 0.3. So the chance of getting a box with more than three broken will indeed be very small.

Quick check questions

1 One in three shops in a particular area of a city is unoccupied at any given time. You need to find the probability that in a row of ten shops, only one is unoccupied. Identify n and p assuming that you want to solve this problem using the binomial distribution. Do you think the distribution is a good model in this case?

2 In a group of 12 people, saying 'at least 3 are female' is the same as saying (a) 'at least 9 are male'; (b) 'no more than 9 are male'; (c) 'less than 9 are male'?

3 Work out from first principles (that is, without using the tables) the probability that two students in a randomly selected group of three at Stratford University are Business Studies students, if the proportion of Business Studies students in the (large) student population of the University is 20 per cent.

Answers:

1 $n = 10$, $p = 1/3$ or 0.33. The distribution probably isn't a very good model in this case, because it's likely that groups of unoccupied shops might occur together – thus the distribution is not random.

2 The correct answer is (b) – if you can't see why this is, try using the number line to display the situation.

3 The probability is $0.2 \times 0.2 \times 0.8 \times 3 = 0.096$ – there are three different ways in which the situation could arise, since it could be any one of the three students who is the non-Business student.

The Poisson distribution

Recognising the pattern

If you were approaching the second of the quality manager's problems from scratch, you might well, armed with your new knowledge of the binomial distribution, try to fit it into that pattern. Remember that the difficulty with the toffee apples was that small number with faulty toffee coating – an average of three per box. The number of apples in a box was not known exactly, since they are packed by weight, but it is fairly large.

We certainly have the binomial-type either/or situation here: either an apple has a faulty coating or it hasn't. But we look in vain for the other two requirements, n and p: we do not know n, as we have just observed; nor do we know what the probability of an individual apple being faulty may be. All we have is the average or *mean* number of faulty apples per box. What we can say, however, is that the faulty ones are pretty unusual – there are only six of them in a box containing round about 144 – so the value of p, whatever it may be, must be quite small.

The information which we have here characterises a *Poisson* problem, for which probabilities are given by the Poisson distribution (called after its French discoverer). These characteristics may be summarised as follows:

For a Poisson problem we require

1 either/or situation;
2 mean number of successes per unit, m, known and fixed;
3 p, chance of success, unknown but small (the event is 'unusual').

As with the binomial problems, we will begin our study of Poisson problems by learning to recognise this pattern in particular cases.

Problem 1

Attendance records at a large factory show that on average there are seven absentees on any day. What is the probability that on a certain day there will be more than eight people absent?

Here the either/or situation is provided by absent/present. The mean to be used is clearly seven, and if the factory is large and only seven people per day on average are absent, the chance of an individual being absent is clearly small. The only assumption we need to make is that the average number of absences is fixed, in other words it does not vary with, for instance, the day of the week or the time of year. This might lead to slight inaccuracies if we are actually interested in a day in February which falls in the middle of a 'flu epidemic, or the day after a public holiday when some workers may decide unofficially to extend their time off.

Problem 2

An automated production line breaks down on average once in every two hours. A certain special production run requires uninterrupted running of the line for eight hours. What is the probability that this can be achieved?

Our two-way outcome here is breakdown/no breakdown, but when we come to identify the mean we have to be a bit careful about the relevant unit over which to average. As stated in the problem, there is a breakdown every two hours; that is an average of 0.5 breakdowns per hour. But we are actually interested in the numbers of breakdowns over an *eight*-hour period, so the mean relevant to this period will be *four* breakdowns. At this rate, the chance of the machine breaking down at any particular point in time is pretty small, so we have the 'unusual event' requirement.

Problem 3

It is known that an automatic packing machine produces, on average, 1 in 100 bags that is underweight. What is the probability that a case of 500 bags filled by the machine will contain fewer than 3 underweight?

Although the magic word 'average' occurs in this problem, it is, strictly speaking, a binomial problem. We have the bags classified as either underweight or not; we know n, which is the 500 bags per box; and p, the probability that a bag is underweight, is 1/100 or 0.01. However, we certainly cannot use the tables in Appendix 3 to solve the problem since they do not go anywhere near $n = 500$.

What we *can* do though, is to make use of the Poisson distribution as an approximation to the binomial. As $p = 0.01$ is certainly small, the 'unusual event' requirement is satisfied, and the mean number of underweight bags per crate is easily calculated as 5 (1 in 100 is underweight, and there are 500 in the crate). So we have the necessary conditions for using the Poisson distribution.

You may say 'Well, in that case where does the approximation come in?' It arises from the fact that, in a binomial problem, there is an *upper limit* to the number of successes that can occur; there is no way we could have 501 underweight boxes if the crate only contains 500. But strictly speaking, in a Poisson situation, as we do not know n there is *no* upper limit to the number of successes which might occur. It is pretty unlikely, in problem 2, that the machine would break down 20 times, or even 100 times, over the eight-hour period; nevertheless, it just *might* happen and the Poisson distribution takes account of this.

However, in a case like the present one, where n is very big and p is very small, these probabilities at the 'top end' of the range of possibilities are going to be so tiny that the difference between the two distributions, over the range of practical interest, is not important.

From what has been said it will be clear that in many cases, as with the binomial problems, we are using the Poisson pattern as a model, which *may* fit our problem exactly, or may involve a certain amount of approximation.

Using the tables

Tables of the probabilities which apply to problems of the Poisson pattern are given in Appendix 4. In many respects these resemble the binomial tables: they are cumulative, giving the probability of *r or more* successes; the probabilities are quoted to four decimal places, so that a blank does not indicate that something is impossible, merely that the chance of its occurrence is too small to show up in the tables; and all the entries for $r = 0$ are 1.0000, since '0 or more successes' is an event that is bound to occur. The tables are, however, simpler in that, as the Poisson pattern only requires the knowledge of a single quantity m, they are arranged throughout in columns corresponding to the various values of m.

You can see, too, how the point made above about the absence of an upper limit to the number of successes shows up in the tables. The column of the table with $m = 2.0$, for instance, stops at $r = 9$ only because that is where the probabilities cease to show up in four-figure tables. There is no reason why, given more accurate tables, the possibility of $r = 10$ or higher values should not be considered.

So much for the theoretical aspects of the tables; we can now make use of them to solve the problems posed in the preceding section. Let us start with problem 1 where we had $m = 7$, and wished to know p(more than 8 people absent). Before the tables can be used, 'more than 8' has to be rephrased as '9 or more'; then all we need do is look in the column $m = 7$ and the row $r = 9$ to obtain a probability of 0.2709.

For problem 2, we found that the relevant mean, the number of breakdowns per eight-hour period, was equal to 4, and we were interested in the chance of obtaining such a period with no breakdowns. We can find this in a manner similar to the one we used on page 173 with reference to the binomial tables:

$$\begin{aligned} p(\text{no breakdowns}) &= p(0 \text{ or more breakdowns}) - p(1 \text{ or more}) \\ &= 1.000 - 0.9817, \text{ looking under } m = 4 \\ &= 0.0183. \end{aligned}$$

Finally, problem 3 had $m = 5$, and we need the chance of fewer than three underweight bags: p(less than 3 underweight) + p(3 or more underweight) = 1, so p(less than 3 underweight) = 1 – p(3 or more underweight). Looking in the tables under $m = 5$ and $r = 3$ we find the figure 0.8753, so

$$p(\text{less than 3 underweight}) = 1 - 0.8753 = 0.1247.$$

Having practised the use of the tables with these examples you will realise that many of the points raised in connection with the binomial tables – particularly the way in which the wording of a question may need adjustment to the precise form given in the tables – apply equally well here.

Let us now return to the quality manager's second problem which concerned the faulty toffee apples. These were averaging out at six per box – in other words $m = 6$. But he does not want to know a probability; rather he has *decided* what probability he is interested in – the 1-in-a-100 replacement rate which he is prepared to accept – and needs to know what number of faulty apples that probability corresponds to. That is, he wishes to find the value of r, with an m of 6, such that the probability of r or more 'successes' (i.e. faulty apples) is 1/100 or 0.01.

We are, in effect, using the tables 'backwards' here; we look under $m = 6$ and run down the column of probabilities until we meet 0.01. Actually that precise value does not occur; the probability of 12 or more 'successes' is 0.0201, while that of 13 or more is 0.0088. Thus if the quality manager agrees to replace the entire box if 13 or more badly coated apples are encountered, he can be confident that he will have to do this with a probability of only 0.0088, which represents fewer than 1 box in 100.

As with problems 1 and 3 above, strictly speaking the Poisson is only an approximation here, since there is an upper limit to the possible number of 'successes'. However, since this limit is large, the approximation will be good.

Quick check questions

1 Name two differences between a problem which could be modelled by the binomial distribution and one which would require the Poisson distribution to be used.

2 The mean number of customers per week at a travel agent who book Business Class flights is 15. The agent is open five days per week. What value of m would you use to find the probability that on a particular day five passengers book Business Class? What would you be assuming in using the Poisson model here?

3 In the tables of Appendix 4, when $m = 2$, what numbers of occurrences have a probability of less than 20 per cent?

Answers:

1 For the Poisson, we don't know n and p separately, and there is no upper limit to the number of possible 'successes'.

2 We should use $m = 3$, 15 Business Class travellers over a 5-day week averages to 3 per day. It might, however, be the case that Business Class travellers are more likely to book on certain days of the week, in which case the distribution is not random and the Poisson might not be a good model.

3 Four or more occurrences (because the probability falls below 0.2000 between $r = 3$ and $r = 4$.

The normal distribution

Spotting the pattern

When we turn from the two distributions we have looked at so far in this chapter to consider the quality manager's last problem concerning the weight of bags of Carrot Candy, one major difference should strike you immediately. Whereas with both binomial and Poisson problems we were talking about either/or situations where the number of times a thing occurred could be *counted*, in the Carrot Candy problem we are talking about something – weight – which is not being counted but *measured*. The distinction is more or less the same as the one made in Chapter 3 between discrete and continuous variables, and so the binomial and Poisson distributions are referred to as *discrete* probability distributions. What we need to deal with the Carrot Candy problem is a *continuous* probability distribution – one that will tell us (given of course a certain amount of data) what is the probability that a continuous variable, such as the weight of a bag of Carrot Candy, will take certain values.

We approached the idea of a probability distribution in the section 'The idea of a probability distribution', page 167, by way of frequency distributions, so let us try to shed some light on the current problem by doing the same thing. If the quality manager were to take a sample of 100 bags filled by an automatic machine (assume it is a different one from the one causing his problems), he might get the following frequency table:

Weight of bag (g)	*No. of bags*
503 but under 505	2
505 but under 507	12
507 but under 509	21
509 but under 511	29
511 but under 513	23
513 but under 515	11
515 but under 517	2

This could, of course, be turned into an experimental probability distribution by dividing all the frequencies by 100. The probability histogram for this distribution is shown in Figure 8.2(a). It shows a certain degree of symmetry, as we might expect, the machine apparently producing roughly equal proportions of bags above and below the average weight. It is also clear that weights a very long way from the centre of the distribution occur much less often than those close to the central value.

This histogram, however, is not likely to be very representative of the entire output of the machine since it applies only to one particular sample of 100 bags. Were the sample to consist of 1000 rather than 100 bags, we could expect to find a good deal more regularity in the behaviour of the distribution, resulting in something like the histogram in Figure 8.2(b). You can see that as there is so much more data, it has been possible to subdivide it into classes with a width of only 0.5 g rather than the 2 g interval used in Figure 8.2(a). Altogether the histogram exhibits a much smoother appearance, though the feature of symmetry about a central peak value is still noticeable.

By now you should find it quite easy to imagine that, were we to take more and more bags in the sample and subdivide the intervals of the histogram with increasing precision, we would ultimately obtain a histogram with steps so small and so close together as to be almost indistinguishable from the smooth curve shown in Figure 8.3. This is what is known as the *normal distribution* curve, and it will become very familiar to you in the course of the next few chapters.

How the normal distribution works

Before proceeding to ask how the normal distribution can help us in calculating probabilities, we should take note of some of its important features. The symmetry which we noticed in the histograms is apparent also here; if the curve were folded down the centre the two halves would lie exactly on top of each other. The curve is often described as 'bell-shaped', expressing the fact that it drops on either side of a central peak. But it never actually touches the horizontal axis though it gets closer and closer to it the further away from the peak we go. And here is where the element of 'modelling' comes in again – the normal distribution is a *theoretical* distribution, so we cannot expect that our real-life distributions will conform to it exactly. The weight distribution, for example, will have a lower limit; the samples of 100 and 1000 bags contained no bags weighing less than 500 g, and even if we admit the possibility that the machine may occasionally omit to fill a bag at all, thus producing an item with zero weight, it certainly cannot produce negative weights. Yet the theoretical distribution carries on, in principle, indefinitely to the left as well as to the right, so clearly it does not fit our real-life situation very well at these extremes. However, over the part that matters – the bit between about 500 and 520 g – it fits very

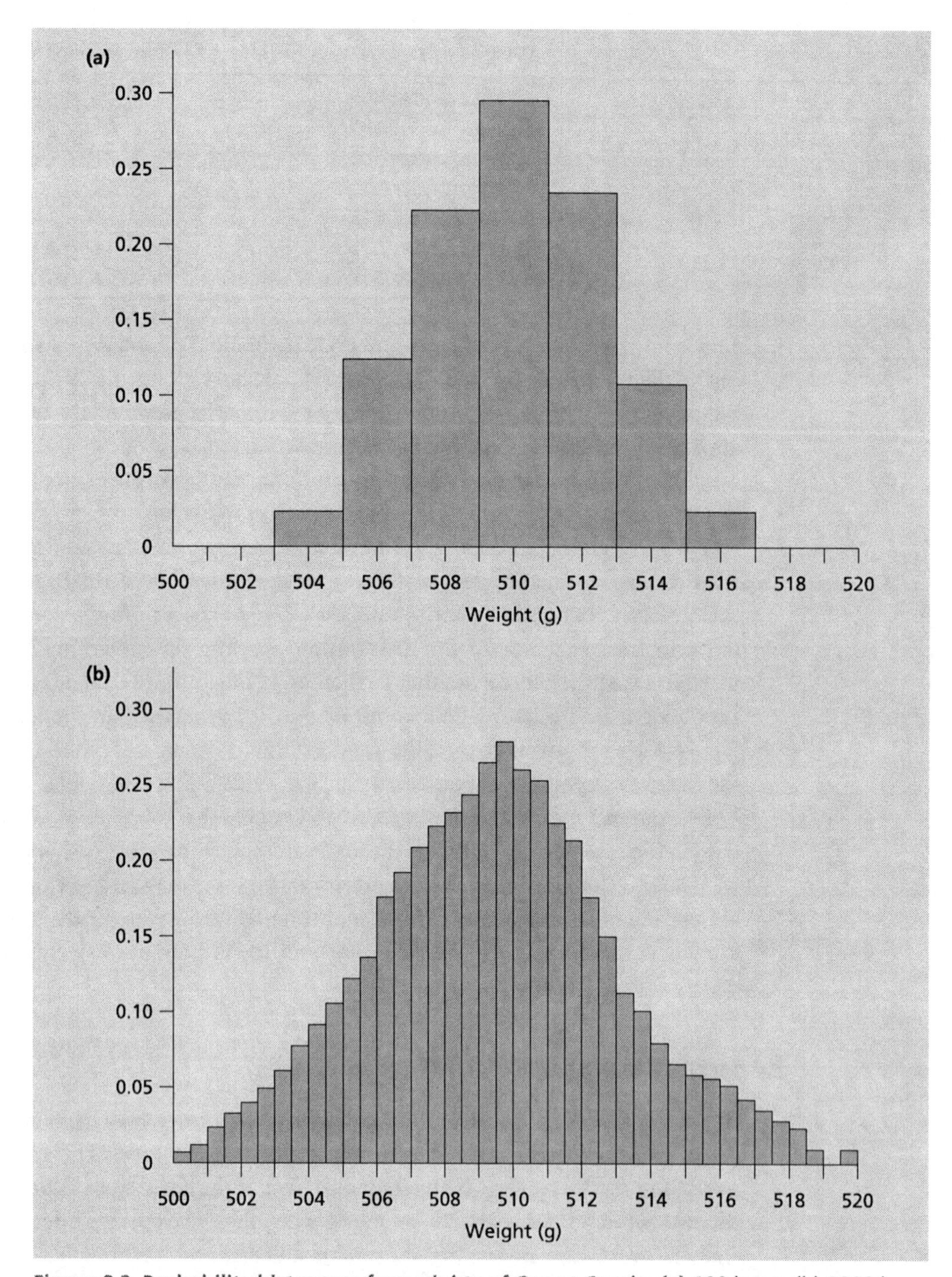

Figure 8.2 Probability histogram for weights of Carrot Candy: (a) 100 bags; (b) 1000 bags

well, and the part of the distribution in the region where it *does not* fit is so tiny that it is not very important. We will be returning to this question of how well a particular practical case fits the theoretical normal curve later on.

Two very important facts about the probability histogram which were noted in the section 'The idea of a probability distribution', page 167, apply equally well to the smoothed-off histogram which gives the normal curve. First, the *area* occupied by the histogram represented probability; so it is for the areas under the normal curve. Second, the total area of the histogram was 1; similarly with the total area under the normal curve.

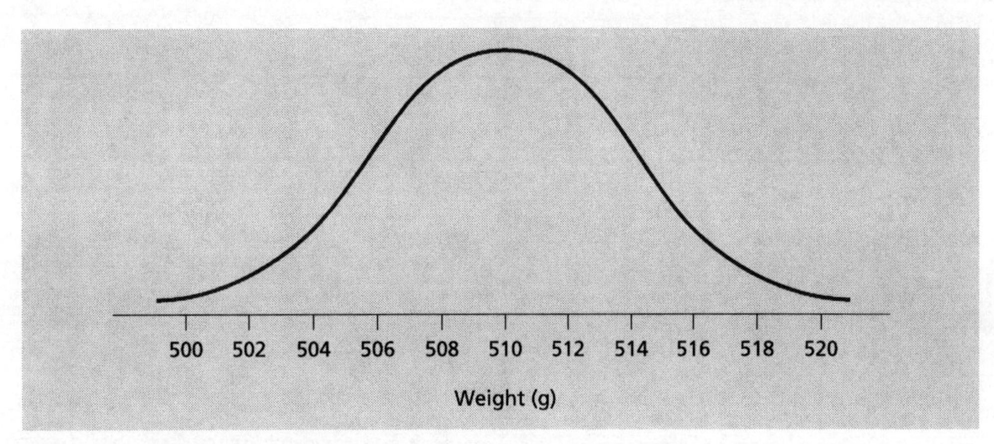

Figure 8.3 Normal distribution curve

We are happily talking about 'the' normal curve, but of course what we have got in Figure 8.3 is only one of an infinite number of possible normal curves, all basically the same shape, but varying in their position and amount of spread; several such curves are shown in Figure 8.4. So what information do we need in order to distinguish one normal curve from another? If we know the *mean* of the relevant distribution we will know the position of the 'peak' of the curve, while the standard deviation is the easiest way of characterising how spread out the distribution is. For the weight distribution in Figure 8.3 the mean is 510 g as shown, and the standard deviation, as you can check from the distribution for 100 bags, is about 2.5 g.

Now that we know how the normal distribution behaves and have the mean and standard deviation to describe our particular normal distribution, we can begin to ask questions about probabilities. Suppose, for example, that we want to know what proportion of these bags weighs more than 515 g; this will be given by the proportion of the area under the curve to the right of 515 g, as shown in Figure 8.5(a). (You are strongly recommended always to draw such a diagram when tackling normal distribution problems.)

But how are we to determine this area? True, we know that the total area is 1, but that does not help us to find exactly what fraction of the area falls to the right of 515. We could try plotting the curve accurately on graph paper and finding the area by counting squares, but apart from being very slow, that would require a knowledge of the equation of the curve, which is so unpleasant that I will not alarm you by writing it down. Anyway, such an answer would not be very accurate. So we resort to the expedient which has come to

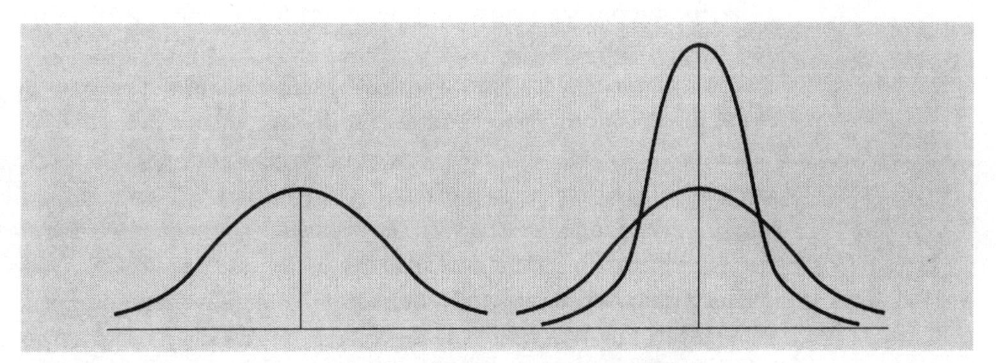

Figure 8.4 Normal curves with different means and spreads

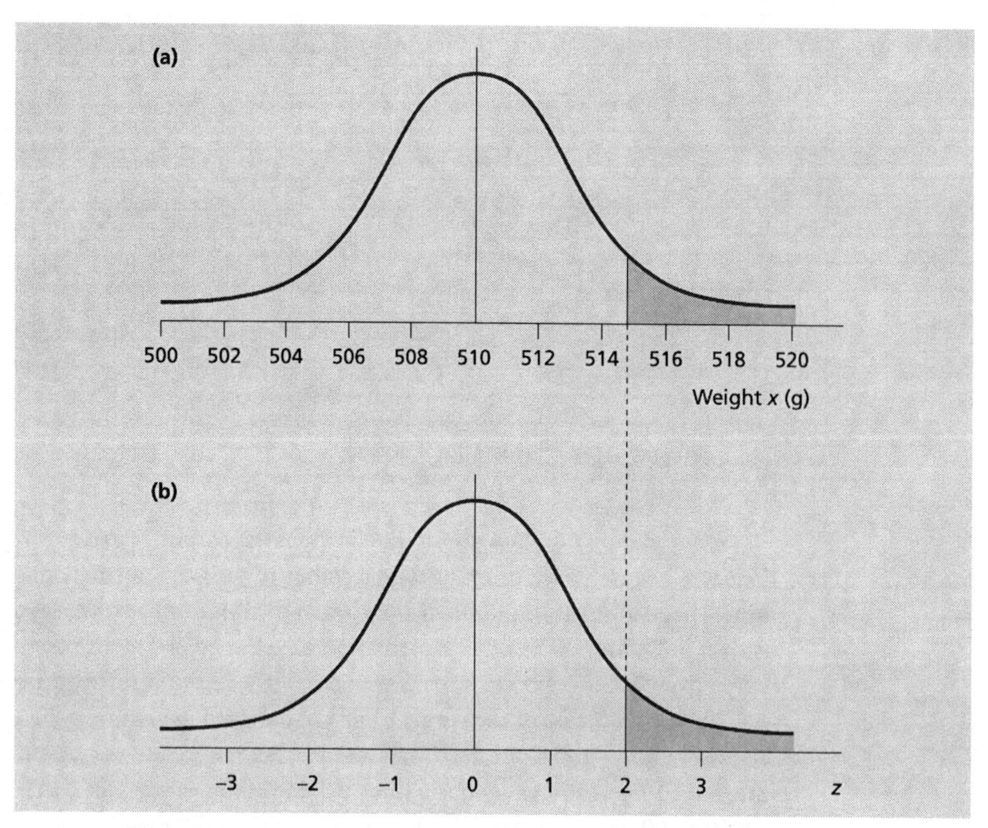

Figure 8.5 Relating a distribution to the standard normal distribution

our aid with the previous two distributions: we make use of a set of tables of the areas under the normal curve, which have already been computed accurately by someone else. All we need know, once again, is how to use them.

Using the tables

That insidious phrase '*the* normal curve' has slipped in again in the last paragraph, but we now know that there are any number of normal curves with different means and different standard deviations. This is rather a depressing thought: does it mean we need an infinite, or at least a very large, set of tables to cope with all the different combinations of mean and standard deviation which we might come across? Happily the answer is no. Since all these different normal curves are the same fundamental *shape*, tables are provided for just one such curve, called the *standard* normal distribution, and all other normal distributions are then related to that.

You will find a table of areas under the standard normal curve in Appendix 5. It really is the simplest normal distribution that one could have since its mean is 0, as shown in the sketch at the top of the tables, and its standard deviation is 1. The table, as its heading tells us, gives the areas in the 'tail' of the distribution – the bit to the right of a given value. The horizontal axis is called the z-axis, and z is often referred to as the *standard normal variable*. So, the tables work like this: to find the probability, say, that z is greater than 2 – perhaps more meaningfully interpreted as finding the proportion of the values in the standard distribution which are bigger than 2 – we simply look down the left-hand side of the tables until we find $z = 2$, and then read off the probability under the column headed 0.00. This tells us that the probability of a value greater than 2.00 is 0.022 75. Had we wanted a value greater than 2.05 we would have located 2.0 in the left-hand column first, and then proceeded across the tables to the column headed 0.05 to obtain a probability of 0.020 18.

This, you may say, is all very well, but how does this highly theoretical distribution, referring to nothing in particular, help us to answer questions about the weight distribution of bags with a mean of 510 g and a standard deviation of 2.5 g? How can we connect our practical distribution with the standard one in the tables? The clue is provided in Figure 8.5(a) and (b). Remember that the *shape* of the two normal distributions is the same; all that varies are their means and standard deviations. So the necessary connection will be provided if we can determine what points in the theoretical distribution – on the z-axis – correspond to what points in the practical distribution on the x-axis. For instance, to take a concrete case, what z-value lies directly under $x = 515$?

It is easy enough to see that $z = 0$ will coincide with $x = 510$, these being the peak values, that is the means, of the two distributions. As we move out from the means, it is the standard deviation that indicates how far from the mean the rest of the values in the distribution tend to be. By the time we reach $x = 515$, we are two standard deviations away from the mean of the weight distribution (the standard deviation was 2.5 g, remember). Thus $x = 515$ must correspond to a point on the z-axis two standard deviations away from the mean. But the standard deviation of this distribution is 1; so $x = 515$ will correspond to $z = 2$. In other words, z tells us *how many standard deviations away from the mean* the point we are interested in lies.

If you like formulae rather than words, we can translate this fact as follows: the distance from the mean, 510 g, to the value we are interested in, 515 g, is 515 – 510; then z is the number of standard deviations in this distance, so:

$$z = \frac{515 - 510}{2.5} = 2$$

as before. In fact for *any* point x in a distribution with a mean m and a standard deviation s, we can define the corresponding standard normal variable z thus:

$$z = \frac{x - m}{s}.^{*}$$

The process of calculating z from x is sometimes called *standardisation*.

Once we have made this transition from x to z, the rest is easy. We set out to find the proportion of the bags which have weight in excess of 515 g, represented by the area under the standard curve to the right of $z = 2$, which we have already looked up in the tables and found to be 0.022 75. Because five-figure decimals do not say much to most people, I prefer to convert this to a percentage and say that 2.275 per cent of all bags filled by this machine will weigh more than 515 g.

Using the normal distribution in practice

Setting up the machinery for using the normal tables has taken rather a long time, but really the process is quite simple: we sketched the normal distribution for our problem,

* You will also encounter this formula with the Greek letters μ and σ used in place of m and s in other textbooks and sets of statistical tables.

and identified on it the mean and the particular value we are interested in. Then we made the transition from our x-distribution to the standard z-distribution by using the fact that z is the number of standard deviations from the mean up to our x-value. Finally, we used the tables to tell us the required probability. When we apply this process to a few more sample problems you will see how quick it is. For simplicity we will stay with the weight distribution, mean 510 and standard deviation 2.5 g.

Problem 1

What percentage of the bags filled by the machine will weigh less than 507.5 g?

The area we require is shown in Figure 8.6(a); it is the shaded area beyond one standard deviation to the *left* of the mean, so that it corresponds, as the sketch at the top of Appendix 5 shows, to a *negative* value of z. (You should find the same thing if you use the formula for calculating z.) But there are no negative values of z given in the tables, and a minute's thought should suggest why not. The symmetry of the distribution means that if the areas at the left-hand end of the distribution, where z is negative, *were* tabulated, they would be exactly the same as those at the right-hand end, so the exercise would be a bit of a waste of time.

We can, then, find the area we are interested in, to the left of $z = -1$, by ignoring the fact that z is negative and looking up the area to the *right* of $z = +1$, which is 0.1587. So 15.87 per cent of bags weigh less than 507.5 g.

Problem 2

What is the probability that a bag filled by the machine weighs less than 512 g?

As you can see from Figure 8.6(b), the area we want here is not the right shape for looking up directly in the tables. What we *can* find directly, though, is the probability that a bag weighs *more* than 512 g. The z-value corresponding to $x = 512$ is

$$\frac{512 - 510}{2.5}$$

or 0.8, and the tables give the area to the right of 0.8 as 0.2119.

So p(bag weighs more than 512 g) = 0.2119. But of course p(bag weighs more than 512 g) + p(bag weighs less than 512 g) = 1, so p(bag weighs less than 512 g) = 1 − 0.2119 = 0.7881.

At this point you may feel a bit worried about the bags that weigh *exactly* 512 g, which seem to have got left out of our analysis. In fact the normal distribution cannot deal with the probability of obtaining a single exact value, as for instance $p(x = 512\text{ g})$. In terms of the diagram it is not too difficult to see why this is: the 'area' corresponding to a single value such as this is zero. In practical terms this can be interpreted by saying that, when there is an infinite range of possible weights for the bags, as there is with any continuous distribution, the chance of any one precise value occurring is so small as to be effectively zero; we might get a bag which we think weighs 512 g, but no doubt if we weighed it more accurately we would find it actually weighed 511.97 g, or 512.01 g. So whether we write p(bag weighs less than 512 g) or p(bag weighs less than or equal to 512 g) is really immaterial.

Problem 3

What percentage of the bags will weigh between 512 and 515 g?

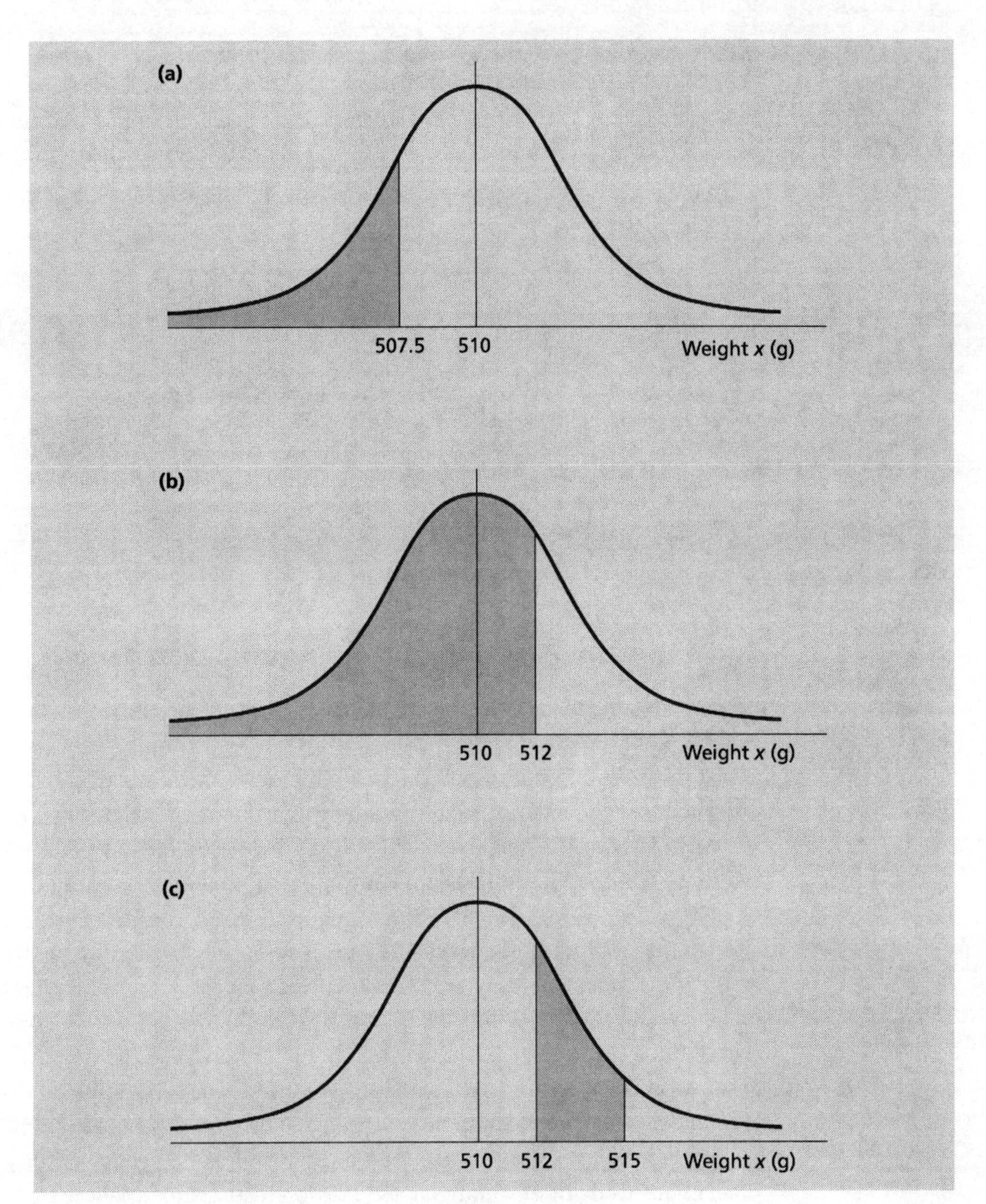

Figure 8.6 Areas under the normal distribution curve

Again, the area as illustrated in Figure 8.6(c) cannot be looked up directly. What we have to do in this case is express the required area as the difference of two areas which *can* be looked up: namely, the area to the right of 512 and that to the right of 515. We have just found, under 2, that the area to the right of 512 is 0.2119, and earlier in this section we determined the area to the right of 515 as 0.022 75. So *p*(bag weighs between 512 and 515 g) = 0.2119 − 0.022 75 = 0.189 15, which means nearly 19 per cent of bags fall between these two limits.

These examples do not cover all the possible types of area which may arise, but by now you should realise that the way to tackle any area which is not suitable for direct use with the tables is to split it into several that *are* suitable, not forgetting the useful facts that the total area under the curve is 1 and the areas on either side of the mean are each 0.5.

Quick check questions

1 In a normal distribution with a mean of 12 and standard deviation 1.5, what is the probability of the value of the variable being more than 15? Less than 9.5?

2 What z-value cuts off the top 2 per cent of values in the standard normal distribution?

3 A normally distributed variable has a mean of 20 mm, and 5 per cent of its values are above 24 mm. What is its standard deviation?

Answers:

1 When $x = 15$, $z = (15 - 12)/1.5 = 2$, so tables give the probability as 0.022 75 or 2.275 per cent. When $x = 9.5$, $z = (9.5 - 12)/1.5 = 1.66$, so the probability is 0.0485 or 4.85 per cent.
2 Look for a value as near as you can find to 2 per cent or 0.02 in the main body of the normal tables. The nearest is 0.02018, corresponding to a z-value of 2.07.
3 The z-value which cuts off the top 5 per cent of the normal distribution is about 1.65. Thus $1.65 = (x - \text{mean})/\text{s.d} = (24 - 20)/\text{s.d.}$ This can be solved to give s.d. = 4/1.65 = 2.42 mm.

Some general points about the normal distribution

Before returning to and solving the quality manager's third problem, there are a few more general points worth making about the normal distribution. The first takes us back to Chapter 5, where in our efforts to get a 'feel' for the meaning of the standard deviation, we noted that most of the values in a fairly symmetric distribution will lie within three standard deviations either side of the mean. The reason for this becomes clear if we now interpret 'reasonably symmetric' as meaning 'approximately normal', and examine the normal tables. Three standard deviations away from the mean gives $z = 3$, and sure enough the tables show that only 0.135 per cent of the distribution lies beyond this point. At the same time, you can verify the statement made earlier in this chapter that the normal curve never actually hits the z-axis. By the time we get out to $z = 4$, only 0.003 per cent of the distribution is excluded, but no matter how large the value of z, we would find, given sufficiently accurate tables, that there would always be a tiny bit 'left over'.

Another question which may have occurred to you is 'How do we know that the normal distribution is a good model for a given problem?' After all, we have been careful to note, in our study of the binomial and Poisson distributions, where we have had to make assumptions in order to use the distributions. The fact is that we rather tend to *assume* that distributions of continuous variables such as weights, people's heights, IQs and so on will be normal. The very name of the distribution reflects this assumption: it is what we 'normally' expect to occur; and in most of these cases the assumption is fairly well justified, as long as we are talking about a pretty big population. Take IQs, for example. The majority of people have IQs somewhere near the mean; the further away from the mean an IQ is, the less likely one is to encounter someone with that IQ, and the proportions of the population with IQs above and below the average are, in principle, roughly the same – the numbers of Einsteins being balanced by people at the other end of the distribution. Thus we would expect the shape of this distribution to be something close to the normal. The same will apply to *any* variable that is the result of the accumulative effect of a large number of random influences (this can actually be demonstrated mathematically).

Nevertheless, there *are* other continuous distributions of importance – we will encounter one of these in Chapter 10. There are even other symmetrical distributions with infinite tails on either side, looking to the naked eye indistinguishable from normal curves. So it does not do to be *too* ready to assume that a variable is normally distributed, but a method of deciding whether this is the case or not will have to wait until Chapter 10.

Solving the original problem

As the grand finale to our discussion of the normal distribution, we will now tackle the quality manager's third problem. The machine filling bags of Carrot Candy is set to a mean weight of 510 g, but this setting is producing rejects – bags weighing under 500 g – at a rate of 20 per cent of total production, which is unacceptably high. So what should the new average setting of the machine be if the rate of rejects is to be cut to 5 per cent?

We will assume that the weights of bags as filled by the machine are normally distributed with a mean of 510 g. A sketch of the distribution is given in Figure 8.7. But this problem differs from all those we have solved so far in that we are not trying to find a probability, or percentage, or whatever one likes to call it. Instead we are *given* the proportion of bags weighing less than 500 g – in other words, we are told that the shaded area in Figure 8.7 is 20 per cent of the whole or 0.2. So what *do* we need to find?

What we do not know at this point is the variability of the weights being produced by this machine as measured by the standard deviation. However, we can deduce this via the known proportion of rejects being produced. The problem is the reverse of the ones solved earlier, in that we know the area and want to work backwards from there. So when we consult the tables, we look among the areas – the figures in the body of the table – for something as near as possible to 0.2000. The nearest is 0.2005, corresponding to a z of 0.84 (you should be following this in the tables).

Recalling that z tells us 'how many standard deviations from x to the mean', we can therefore deduce that from 500 to 510 is 0.84 standard deviations. That means 10 g is $0.84 \times s$, so that s must be 10/0.84 or 11.9 g. (If you find this hard to follow, try asking yourself how you would work out s if 10 g had turned out to be two standard deviations.)

This is a rather high value for the standard deviation. However, it is generally much more difficult – and expensive – to adjust the variability than the mean. So we therefore ask: given this degree of variability, what should the mean setting on the machine be if only 5 per cent of the bags are to fall below 500 g?

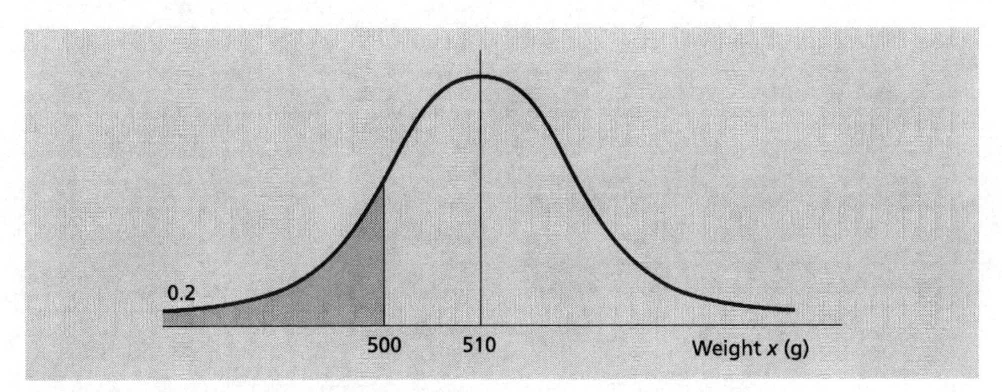

Figure 8.7 Present distribution of weights

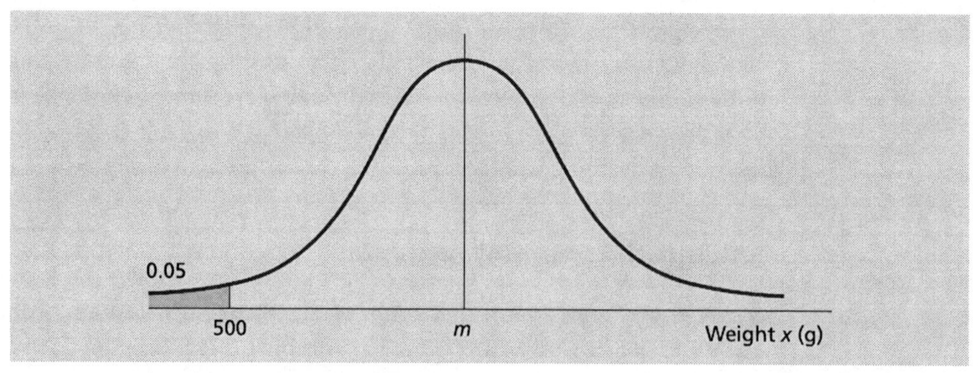

Figure 8.8 Required distribution of weights

A new sketch is required, since the distribution produced by the adjusted machine will centre on the new, unknown mean, m, as shown in Figure 8.8. Again, what we know is the area to the left of 500 g, but now this area is reduced to 5 per cent or 0.05. The same 'backward' use of the tables as before shows that such an area is cut off by the value $z = 1.65$ (this actually gives an area of 0.0495, but that is the nearest we can get within the accuracy of these tables). So the distance from 500 to the mean must be 1.65 standard deviations, hence the mean is 1.65 standard deviations above 500:

$$m = 500 + 1.65 \times 11.9 = 519.64 \text{ g}$$

This is therefore the average weight to which the machine would have to be set to give only 5 per cent of bags below 500 g, with its existing variability.

One final point about all these problems. You will find that many textbooks and sets of tables use notation in such situations which bristles with Greek letters, brackets, < and > signs. It is quite unnecessary for you to try to use such notation; as long as you explain what you are doing clearly, and do not just produce numbers like rabbits out of a hat with no indication as to whether they are areas, standard deviations or what, there is no one 'right' way of writing out these problems.

Quick check questions

1 What is the probability that a normally distributed quantity will be more than 1.2 standard deviations above the mean?

2 In the tables of Appendix 5, what value of z is exceeded in only 5 per cent of cases?

3 The amounts of petrol purchased by customers of a filling station are normally distributed with a mean of 40 litres and a standard deviation of 8 litres. What value of z would you use to find the probability that a customer purchases less than 26 litres?

Answers:

1 0.1151 or about 11.5 per cent.

2 Between $z = 1.64$ and $z = 1.65$.

3 $z = (26 - 40)/8 = -1.75$. We would actually look up $z = 1.75$ in the tables, using the fact that they are symmetric.

Some further points

The distributions – two discrete and one continuous – that we have studied in this chapter are only three, though arguably the three most important, out of the large number of probability distributions which have been investigated and tabulated. As already mentioned, we will be coming across two other continuous distributions, called the *chi-squared* distribution and the t-distribution, in Chapter 10, and a glance through a book of statistical tables will show several others. With all of them, however, the same two-stage process is needed: first the recognition of the type of situation to which the distribution in question applies, and second the use of the tabulated probabilities associated with the distribution.

The normal as an approximation to binomial and Poisson

Although we have made the distinction between the continuous normal distribution and the discrete binomial and Poisson, there are in fact links between them. We have already seen how the Poisson can be used as an approximation to the binomial, but both of these can be approximated by the normal under certain circumstances. If you recall how we approached the normal curve in the first place by taking histograms with larger amounts of data and smaller class intervals, you should not be surprised to learn that when n becomes large and p is not too far from 0.5 the binomial is approximated quite well by the normal; the requirement that n should be large means that 'smoothing off' the histogram does not introduce too much inaccuracy, while the need for p to be near to 0.5 is occasioned by the symmetry of the normal curve. It is impossible to lay down hard and fast rules as to how large is large, but roughly speaking if p is between 0.1 and 0.9, and $n \times p > 5$, the approximation is a reasonable one. Figure 8.9 shows a binomial distribution histogram resulting from tossing 20 coins together 1000 times and recording the number of heads (so $n = 20$, $p = 0.5$). You can see from the superimposed normal curve how closely the approximation works.

Normal approximation to the binomial

A sample of 400 adults is randomly chosen by a market researcher from a large population; members of the sample are asked to give their views on the taste of a new minced

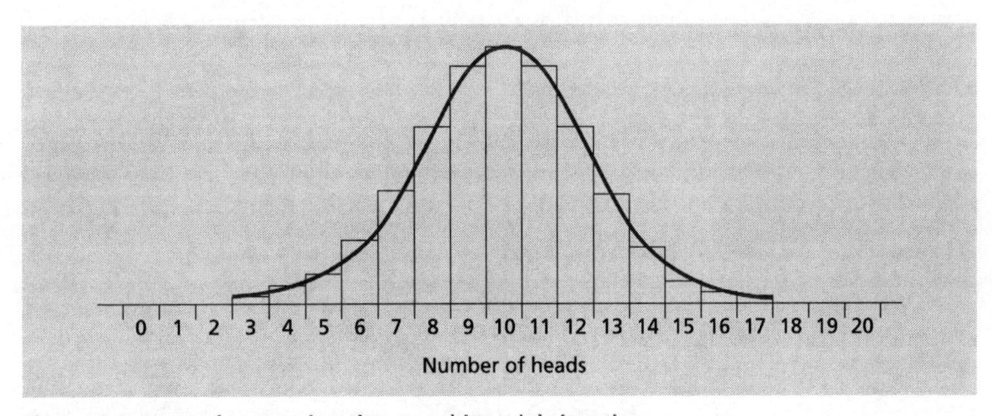

Figure 8.9 Normal approximation to a binomial situation

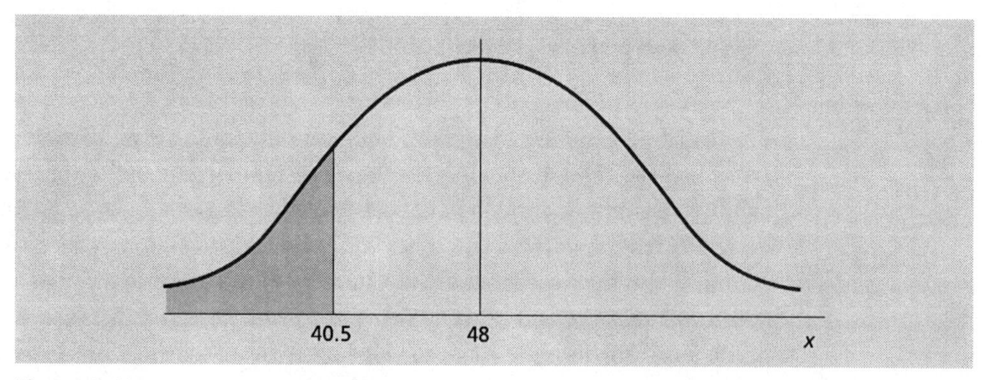

Figure 8.10

chicken product. However, 12 per cent of the population is vegetarian, though the researcher cannot identify the vegetarians in advance. What is the chance that at least 360 of the sample will agree to taste the product? (We have to assume that the only people who will refuse are the vegetarians.)

Here we have a binomial problem with $n = 400$ and $p = 0.12$, but this value of n is far too big to allow us to use binomial tables. Fortunately, $p > 0.1$ and $np = 48$, so we can use the normal approximation instead. The mean will be 48 (this is just the average number of vegetarians we would expect to find in the sample of 400 people), and the standard deviation is given by

$$\sqrt{np(1-p)} = \sqrt{(400 \times 0.12 \times 0.88)} = 6.5.$$

Before we can use the normal distribution to work out the required probability, we need to decide precisely what value of x we are interested in. We are using a continuous normal curve here to approximate a discrete binomial situation, and so we need to think rather carefully about the appropriate value of x to use. If we want to find the chance that 40 or fewer people agree to taste the product, then we need to ask 'What value of a continuous variable would be rounded off to 40 as the nearest discrete value?' The answer is, of course, 40.5; so the probability we are looking for is $p(x < 40.5)$, not $p(x < 41)$ as you might think. The process we have gone through here is called a *continuity correction*, and should always be used when approximating a discrete variable with a continuous one.

Having decided on the value of x, we can plot the relevant normal curve as shown in Figure 8.10, where the required probability is represented by the shaded area:

$$p(40 \text{ or less}) = p(x < 40.5) = p\left(z < \frac{40.5 - 48}{6.5}\right) = p(z < -1.15) = 0.1243,$$

from normal tables.

So the researcher has about a 12.5 per cent chance of getting at least 360 non-vegetarians in his or her sample. And in case you are interested, the 'true' answer calculated using the binomial formula (rather a tedious process!) would be 0.1227, so the approximation is quite good in this case.

Normal approximation to Poisson

The Poisson, too, can be approximated by a normal curve if m, the average number of successes, is large (bigger than about 30); Figure 8.11 shows how well the normal curve fits

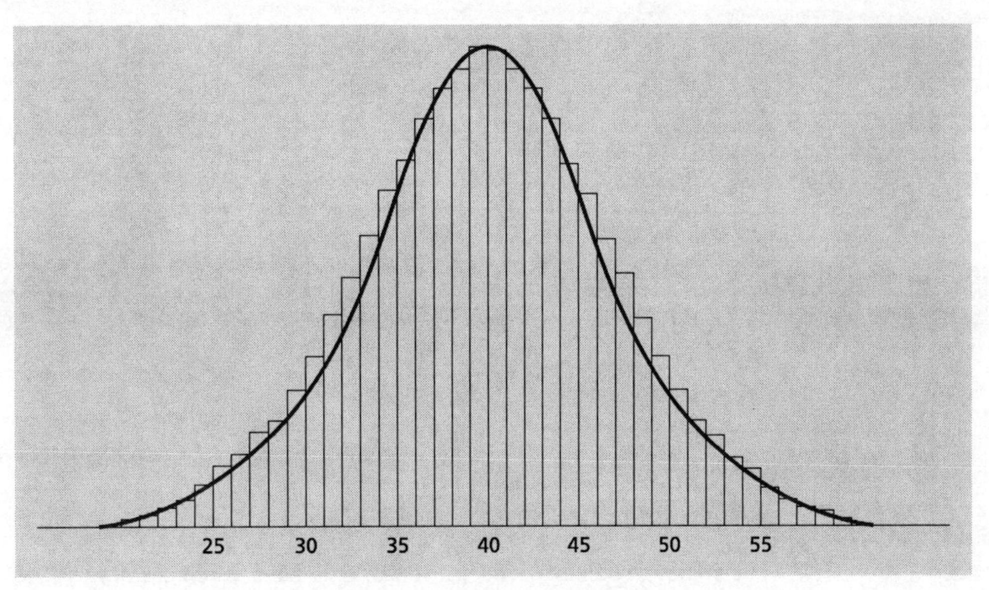

Figure 8.11 Normal approximation to a Poisson situation

a Poisson probability histogram with $m = 40$. This is why most tables of binomial and Poisson probabilities do not cover a very wide range; over a large part of the range the normal approximation is quite adequate. This tendency of other distributions to become normal when large amounts of data are involved is one reason why the normal is so important, and explains why it crops up again and again in more advanced statistical work.

To see how the normal approximation to a Poisson distribution works, consider the following situation. An environmental scientist is studying a plant whose presence in an area indicates that the area is free of certain pollutants (this is one way in which the recovery of industrially polluted land can be studied). He divides up the area of interest in a large number of squares, each 10 m × 10 m, and counts the number of specimens of the plant in each square; the average turns out to be 52. If the distribution were random, what proportion of the squares would you expect to contain more than 60 specimens?

On the assumption that the distribution is random, we can use a Poisson distribution to model this situation. However, because the mean is large – 52 – we cannot use the tables in the appendix; instead we have to use the normal approximation, with mean = 52. It can be shown mathematically that the standard deviation of a Poisson distribution is always equal to the square root of its mean, so in this case it will be $\sqrt{52}$ or 7.21. Just as with the normal approximation to the binomial, we need to use a continuity correction here when choosing the value of x; in this case, we are interested in all discrete values over 60, so we choose $x = 60.5$ (because all values above this would round up to 61 or more). Thus the probability we want is given by the shaded area in Figure 8.12, and can be calculated as:

$$p(x > 60.5) = p\left(z > \frac{60.5 - 52}{7.21}\right) = p(z > 1.18) = 0.1192,$$

so that nearly 12 per cent of squares would be expected to contain more than 60 plants. Since the exact answer, using the Poisson distribution formula, would be 0.1208, the approximation here is quite good.

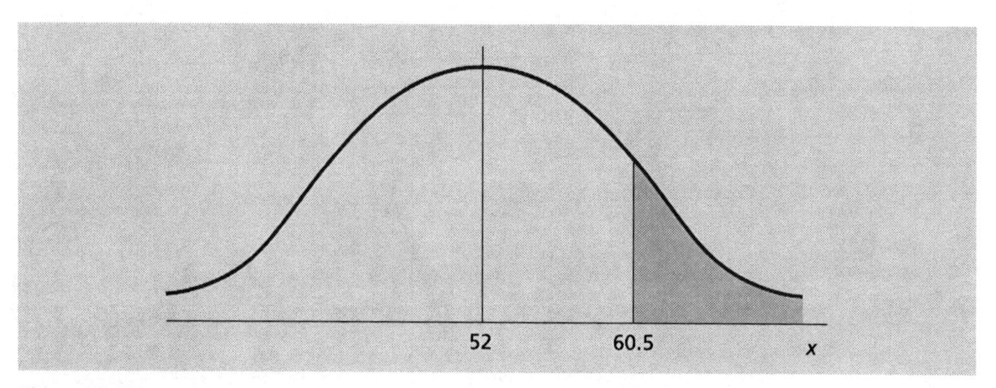

Figure 8.12

Which distribution should I use?

The major problem which most students have when tackling probability distribution problems for the first time is deciding on the appropriate distribution to use in a given situation. The critical question is 'What information do I have?', since this will generally determine the distribution to be used, even if some approximation is called for. You may find the diagram in Figure 8.13 helpful in dealing with this difficulty.

Probabilities from the computer

Excel has a large number of statistical functions, a list of which can be obtained by searching for HELP on STATISTICAL FUNCTIONS. For example, the function =NORMDIST(16.7,15,0.8,TRUE) will give the cumulative normal probability for a value of 16.7 in a normal distribution with a mean of 15 and a standard deviation of 0.8 – in other words, the probability of getting a value less than or equal to 16.7 from this distribution, which turns out to be 0.983 207. The role of the TRUE parameter in this function is to indicate that we want the cumulative probability – if any other value is entered, Excel returns instead the probability density function, whose use need not concern us.

In a similar way, =NORMINV(0.92, 15, 0.8) gives us the inverse distribution, equivalent to looking up the normal tables 'backwards' as described earlier in this chapter. The value returned is 16.124 06, indicating that 92 per cent of values in a normal distribution with mean 15 and standard deviation 0.8 are less than 16.12.

The function =BINOMDIST(2, 10, 0.2, TRUE) will give the cumulative probability of up to two successes in a binomial situation with $n = 10$ and $p = 2$ (which is 0.6778), while =BINOMDIST(2, 10, 0.2, FALSE) gives the probability of *exactly* two successes. However, Excel will not give the inverse for a discrete distribution.

Likewise the function POISSON(4, 2, TRUE) gives the probability of up to 4 occurrences of an event, where the mean number of occurrences is 2; the value returned by Excel is 0.947 347. As with the binomial, POISSON (4, 2, FALSE) gives the probability of *exactly* 4 occurrences.

Try experimenting with these functions in Excel, and check your results against the tables in the Appendices.

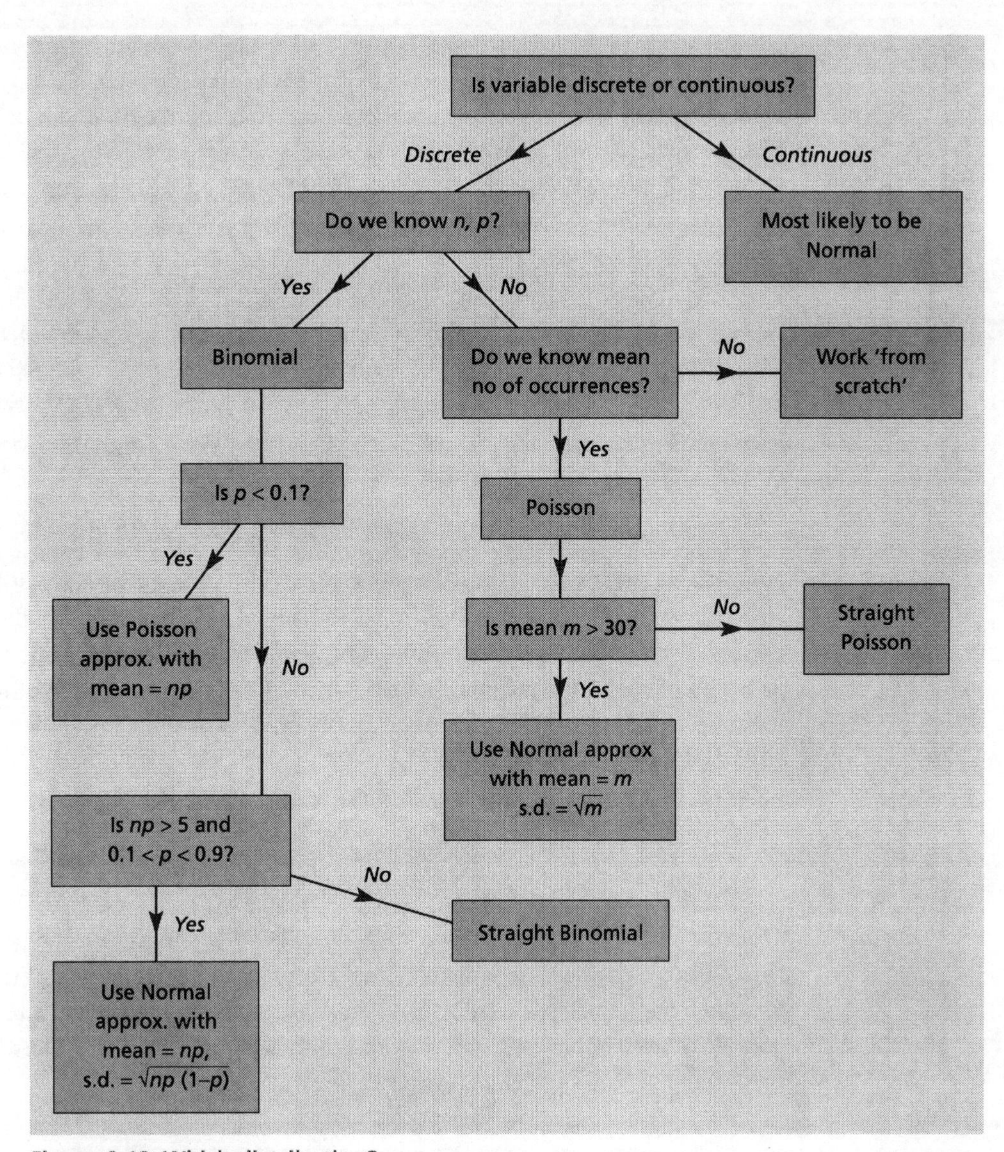

Figure 8.13 Which distribution?

Thinking again about computer failures

We began this chapter by considering the question 'How do people assess the risks of computer failure?'. We will end by examining one aspect of this question which can be tackled with the aid of the distributions we've been studying.

When a computer reads data from a disk or CD – or for that matter, when you listen to music on a CD, download music to your iPod or watch a DVD – millions of 'bits' of encoded information are being individually read. An error in reading any one of those bits may result in a problem – a 'glitch' in the sound you're hearing, a wrong figure in a bank's records, or something more serious. So it's vital for manufacturers of computer hardware and other electronic equipment to be able to guarantee a very low error rate.

Let's suppose that a particular floppy disk drive has a stated error rate of 1 error in every 20 000 bits read, and that a particular set of data involves reading 100 000 bits (in reality the error rate would be much lower and the volume of data much higher, but we will use these figures so as to get manageable calculations). The question 'What is the chance that all the data is read without any errors?' is clearly an important one. But can we model this, and obtain an estimate of the probability, by using the distributions we've looked at in this chapter?

As usual, start by identifying what information we've got. We know the number of bits being read is 100 000 – that's the value of n, the number of 'opportunities for an error'. We know the chance of an error in reading any one bit – it's 1 in 20 000 or 0.000 05, and it's what we have called p earlier in the chapter. If we are prepared to assume that errors occur randomly and independently (which in practice may not always be the case), then we have an example of a binomial situation:

$$n = 100\,000,\ p(\text{error}) = 0.000\,05, \text{ and we want } p(\text{zero errors}), \text{ so } k = 0.$$

However, we certainly can't use the tables provided in the Appendix to solve the problem, since the value of n is far too big, and p too small. But this is exactly the case where the Poisson approximation to the binomial becomes applicable. The *mean* number of errors in reading 100 000 bits will be $100\,000 \times 0.000\,05$ or 5; another way of looking at this is to say that if there is, on average, one error in every 20 000 bits read, then in 100 000 there will be five errors.

So we use the Poisson tables with mean = 5 to find p(exactly zero errors):

$$\begin{aligned} p(\text{exactly zero errors}) &= p(0 \text{ or more}) - p(1 \text{ or more}) \\ &= 1 - 0.9933 = 0.0067. \end{aligned}$$

Thus there is only a small chance of reading the 100 000 bits without any errors occurring. With a more realistic probability of error – say, one in a million or 0.000 001 – it can be shown mathematically, using the formula for the Poisson distribution, that the chance goes up to over 90 per cent, and of course the lower the chance of an error, the bigger the probability of reading the data without any errors at all.

EXERCISES

Further examples on the work of this chapter can be found on the ***companion website***.

Here is a hotch-potch of problems of all three types, so that you get used to recognising each distribution.

1 A greengrocer has checked six trays of tomatoes and found that they contain respectively 2, 0, 1, 4, 3 and 2 bad fruit. What is the probability that a tray will contain (a) 2 or more; (b) no bad fruit?

2 A manufacturer of Christmas crackers knows that 3 crackers in every 20 do not contain a paper hat and a customer complains that his box of 10 crackers contained 3 without paper hats. What is the probability of this occurrence?

3 A machine produces small metal components whose lengths are normally distributed with a mean of 5 cm and a standard deviation of 0.2 cm. What is the probability that a component will have a length (a) less than 4.7 cm; (b) more than 4.8 cm; (c) between 4.6 and 5.3 cm?

4 A worker is late, on average, one morning in four. If he works a five-day week, what is the probability that he will be late less than three times next week? What is the most likely number of times he will be late?

5 A work-study engineer times a certain operation, and discovers that the average time it takes is 10 minutes, but on 15 per cent of occasions it takes more than 13 minutes. Assuming that times for the operation follow a normal distribution, what is its standard deviation?

6 Nine times out of ten a quotation made by a firm to a customer leads to a definite order. What is the probability that a batch of five quotations leads to four definite orders?

7 A small internal switchboard can cope with up to six incoming calls per minute. The average number of incoming calls received is 12 every five minutes. What is the probability that in a two-minute interval the switchboard receives more calls than it can cope with?

8 An automatic packing machine is filling bags of sugar to a nominal weight of 1 kg. Fifty thousand bags per week are produced by the machine, which at present is set to a mean of 1005 g. All bags below the nominal weight are rejected, this policy resulting at present in a reject rate of 1500 bags per week. (a) What is the standard deviation of the bags filled by the machine? (b) To what mean should the machine be re-set if the standard deviation cannot be changed, if each rejected bag costs the company 8p, and a saving of £40 per week is to be made?

9 Ten coins are tossed together and the number of heads is counted.

(a) Using the binomial distribution, find the probability of getting six or more heads.

(b) Now see how close to this figure the normal approximation comes. The appropriate mean to use will be 5, since that is the average number of heads we would expect to get in 10 tosses of a fair coin. It can be proved that the standard deviation of a binomial distribution is $\sqrt{np(1-p)}$, so here it will be $\sqrt{10 \times 0.5 \times 0.5}$ which is 1.58. You need to be careful, too, as to what '6 or more' means in terms of a continuous distribution like the normal. Everything from 5.5 upwards has to be included, since 5.5, 5.6, etc., would all be rounded off to 6 when treated as discrete; this is the 'continuity correction', mentioned earlier in the chapter.

10 Now try the same sort of thing with the Poisson as an approximation to the binomial. Suppose 5 per cent of items produced by a machine are defective in some way, and a sample of ten items is taken.

(a) Use the binomial to work out the probability that at least one of the ten is defective.

(b) Now use the Poisson to work out the same thing. The mean to use is, of course, 0.5, since if 5 per cent of the items are faulty, the number of defectives to be expected out of ten would, on average, be 5 per cent of ten.

11 Very large reels of electrical cable may have quite large numbers of small flaws without their usefulness being seriously impaired. Suppose the average number of such flaws per 2000 metre reel is 36. What is the probability that if you purchase such a reel it will have fewer than 30 flaws? This is strictly a Poisson problem, but since the mean is large (36) we can use the normal as an approximation. It can be proved that the standard deviation of the Poisson is the square root of its mean, so that here standard deviation $= \sqrt{36} = 6$. Use normal tables to solve the problem (remember that, as in Exercise 9, we are approximating a discrete situation by a continuous one).

12 Companies that rely on external suppliers to provide essential components often operate what is called Sampling Inspection. Under this system, a sample is taken from every batch which arrives

→

from the supplier, and tested. If the sample meets certain acceptance criteria, the whole batch is accepted; if not, the whole batch is sent back to the supplier.

For example, a company that retails fizzy drinks in plastic bottles obtains the bottles from an external supplier. In the past, the quality of bottles sent by this supplier has not been entirely satisfactory, with an average of 5 per cent of bottles sent being faulty and likely to explode when subjected to the pressure of gas in the drink. To avoid problems that will occur if faulty bottles get through on to the filling line, it has been agreed that the following sampling scheme will operate: from every batch of 500 bottles received from the supplier, a sample of 10 will be selected at random, and put through a pressure-testing procedure. If any bottles in the sample fail the test, this will be regarded as a signal of unsatisfactory quality, and the whole batch will be returned to the supplier.

(a) If in fact 5 per cent of the batch is faulty, what will be the chance that the sample contains no defectives, and therefore the batch will be accepted?
(b) What is the chance of accepting the batch if 10 per cent of the batch is faulty?
(c) Repeat the calculation above for defective rates 15 per cent and 20 per cent. Hence sketch a graph of the probability of accepting the batch against the percentage of defective items in the batch, and comment on your results. (This graph is called an *operating characteristic* for the sampling scheme; we will be returning to the topic of operating characteristics and sampling in Chapter 11.)

Answers

Solutions to selected exercises

in Morris

CHAPTER 1
Answers to test of basic mathematical skills

1. (+)1	If you got any of these wrong, read pp. 9–11.
2. −2.5 or $-2\frac{1}{2}$	
3. 47/40 or $1\frac{7}{40}$	Problems with any of these? See pp. 11–12.
4. $\frac{21}{40}$	
5. 4	
6. 0.125	If you got any of these wrong, read pp. 13–16.
7. 40	
8. 0.416 66 . . .	
9. 28/100 or 7/25	
10. 67.5	See p. 14 if you got this wrong.
11. 1.28	These three are covered on pp. 15–16.
12. 28.125%	
13. £30	
14. x^6	See pp. 16–18 if either of these is wrong.
15. x^8	
16. $5a + 4b$	See pp. 18–19 if you got this wrong.
17. £$\frac{24}{k}$	See pp. 21–22 if either of these is wrong.
18. £$m/12$	
19. $f + m < 150$	This is covered on p. 22.
20. $x = 5$	See pp. 19–21 if these caused problems.
21. $y = 32/7$	
22. $p = 4, q = -1.5$	See pp. 22–24 if you couldn't do this.
23. At $t = -5/3$ or $-1\frac{2}{3}$	See pp. 25–28 if you got this wrong.
24. (c)	See pp. 28–29 if you got these wrong.
25. Below and to the right	

Exercise 1

1. -16 2. 0 3. 2 4. 32 5. 14 6. -3
7. -12 8. -6 9. (+)24 10. -9 11. (+)2 12. 25

Exercise 2

1. $\frac{7}{48}$ 2. $-\frac{1}{12}$ 3. $\frac{3}{22}$ 4. $\frac{1}{8}$ 5. $\frac{18}{7}$ or $2\frac{4}{7}$
6. $\frac{14}{20}$ or $\frac{7}{10}$ 7. 20 8. $\frac{15}{64}$ 9. $-\frac{9}{32}$ 10. $\frac{1}{6}$

Exercise 3

1. 0.444 2. 70 3. 14.4 4. 120 5. 17 000
6. $\frac{85}{100}$ or $\frac{17}{20}$ 7. 4.2 8. 0.1 9. 1 10. 0.02

Exercise 4

1. 3.2 2. 0.17 3. 42% to the nearest whole number 4. £15
5. £16 6. 952 7. 91% 8. 16% 9. 22.9 tonnes
10. Two years' interest will have been added, giving a total of £220.50

Exercise 5

1. y^2 2. $x^{-\frac{1}{3}}$ 3. x^2 4. p^3q^3 5. n^{-3}
6. $\frac{b}{a}$ or $a^{-1}b$ 7. 1 8. $\frac{x}{3}$ or $\frac{1}{3}x$ 9. $x^{\frac{11}{2}}$ 10. $\pm 4x^2$

Exercise 6

1. $6x^2 - 18x$ 2. $a^2 + a - 2$ 3. $3xy + xz$
4. 32, 256 5. -33.75 6. $2x^3 - 2xy^2 - x^2 + y^2$
7. $5b - a$ (remember that the – sign in front of the second bracket multiplies everything inside the bracket).
8. The brackets are needed to show that the $B + F$ must be worked out first – giving the cost of one sandwich – and then multiplied by the number of sandwiches.
9. The 2 should have multiplied both terms in the first bracket, and the terms in the second bracket should both be multiplied by $-x$. The correct version is

$$2(x + y) - x(x + y) = 2x + 2y - x^2 - xy$$

10. $x[2x - 3(y - 2)] = x[2x - 3y + 6] = 2x^2 - 3xy + 6x$

Exercise 7

1. $x = -5$ 2. $x = \frac{1}{2}$ 3. $x = 3$ or -3 4. $x = 1$
5. $f = \frac{v - u}{t}$ or $\frac{1}{t}(v - u)$ 6. $x = -2.5$ 7. $V = \frac{R - P + F}{n}$
8. $a = \pm 4\sqrt{c} - b$ 9. $y = \frac{27z^3}{x^2}$ 10. $x = 2$

Exercise 8

1. Cost = $(50 + 5m)$ pence 2. $1.5h + 1.25s < 12$
3. £1.60 4. $25 + (y - 12) \times 3$ pence or $(3y - 11)$ pence

Exercise 9

1. $x = 3, y = -3$
2. $x = 1, y = 2$
3. Equations are the same
4. $x = 1.5, y = -2$
5. $x = 3, y = 0$
6. The numbers are 6 and 12 (call the numbers x and y and solve the equations $x = 2y; x + y = 18$.)
7. $a = 8, b = 3$
8. The equations are inconsistent, so there is no solution.
9. Peter is 17. Call the ages of the two boys A and P in an obvious notation. Then $P = A + 3$, and $P + A = 31$.
   Solving simultaneously gives $P = 17, A = 14$.
10. The first equation can be multiplied by y to give $x = 5y$. Solving $x = 5y$. Solving $x = 5y$ and $2x + y = 33$ gives $11y = 33$ so $y = 3$, whence $x = 15$.

Exercise 10

1. (a), (c), (d)
2. (a) slope = 2; (c) slope = 6; (d) slope = 5/2

3.

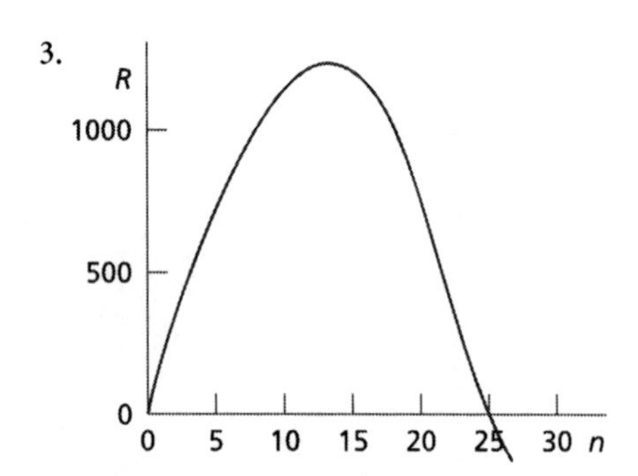

4.

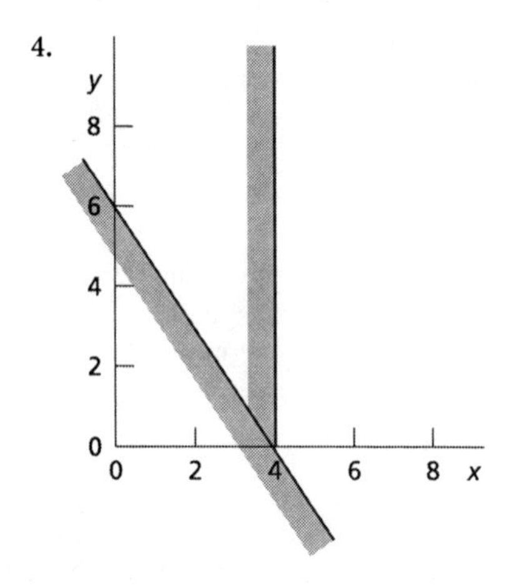

5. The graph is a straight line, passing through the y-axis at $y = 1$, with a positive slope of 2.
6. The graph crosses the x-axis where $y = 0$, giving $x = 3.5$.
7. If $y = x(x - 3)$, then when $x = 0$ $y = 0$ also. Thus the graph passes through the origin.
8. The graph crosses the n-axis when $p = 0$, gibing $n = 4000$. In practical terms this means that if the price of the item were zero, so that it was being given away, then 4000 items would be demanded.
9. The region which satisfies the inequality lies below a line through $x = 10$ on the x-axis and $y = 4$ on the y-axis.
10.

n	0	1	2	3	4	5	6	7	8	9	10	11	12	13	14	15	16	17	18	19	20
C	0	−36	−64	−84	−96	−100	−96	−84	−64	−36	0	44	96	156	224	300	384	476	576	684	800

Exercise 11

1. Break-even at 1667 items approximately.
2. $x = 1$ and $x = 5$
3. 500 items

Exercise 12

1. 1394	2. 1096	3. −10
4. 11.45	5. 20.608	6. 239
7. 3.93	8. 869	9. 9.9
10. 11.3	11. £14.04	12. 3.15, 10.63, 12.99, 19.29, 28.35
13. 82.5	14. 29, 46, 55, 74, 91	15. £297
16. £19.98	17. 2.69	18. 0.64
19. 5.11	20. 6.2	21. 3.68
22. 0.18	23. −16	24. £431.52

CHAPTER 7

1. $\frac{2}{3} \times \frac{3}{5}$ or $\frac{2}{5}$ (assuming independence)

2. (a) $\frac{1}{2}$; (b) $\frac{1}{5}$; (c) $\frac{1}{10}$.

3. (a) $\frac{4}{5} \times \frac{95}{100}$ or 0.76; (b) $\left(\frac{1}{5} \times \frac{95}{100}\right) + \left(\frac{4}{5} \times \frac{5}{100}\right)$ or 0.23.

4. (a) $\frac{4}{5} + \left(\frac{1}{5} \times \frac{3}{5}\right) + \left(\frac{1}{5} \times \frac{2}{5} \times \frac{1}{2}\right)$ or 0.96;

   alternatively $1 - p(\text{no one finds error}) = 1 - \left(\frac{1}{5} \times \frac{2}{5} \times \frac{1}{2}\right)$.

   (b) No – he weeds out the easy ones.

5. $\frac{4}{12} \times \frac{8}{11} \times \frac{7}{10} \times 3$ or 0.51.

6. Move – expected cost £220, as against £260 for staying.
7. No – expected cost of not paying is £2.50.
8. Sell now – expected result of keeping it is only £58.50.
11. Chance of rival marketing must be less than 5/12.
12. 2/250; standard charge would need to be > £2.50.
13. (a) The easiest way to deal with this problem is via a table. Assume that a random sample of 4 000 000 people has been taken (this number is chosen simply to make the arithmetic easier, but any total could be used). Then we would expect the situation to be as shown below.

	Has disease	*Does not have disease*	*Total*
Test + ve	19	79 999.6	80 018.6
Test – ve	1	3 919 980.4	3 919 981.4
Total	20	3 999 980	4 000 000

The chance that you have the disease if you have just tested positive is thus 19/80 018.6 or about 0.000 24. In other words, because of the comparative rarity of the disease, and the relative unreliability of the test, there is only a small chance that someone chosen at random who tests positive does in fact have the disease.

(b) Widespread screening for the disease with such an unreliable test and such a rare complaint will result in a great many people being unnecessarily worried, since the vast majority of those with a positive test do not in fact have the disease. Screening is probably only worthwhile if the reliability of the test can be substantially increased (you might like to think just how much it would need to be increased in order to give a better than 50 per cent chance that someone testing positive has the disease).

(c) The argument above will only apply if the test is given totally at random. If it is only given to those who have some reason to believe that they are likely to have the disease (such as exhibiting definite symptoms), then the position may be very different, since the proportion of people in the tested group with the disease may well be greater than that in the population at large.

CHAPTER 8

1. (a) 0.5940; (b) 0.1353 (Poisson, mean = 2).
2. 0.1298 (binomial, $n = 10, p = 0.15$).
3. (a) 0.0668; (b) 0.8413; (c) 0.910 45.
4. 0.8965; once (binomial, $n = 5, p = 0.25$; 'most likely' = having greatest probability).
5. 3 minutes approx.
6. 0.328 (binomial, $n = 5$, use p(no order) = 0.1).
7. 0.0014 (Poisson, mean = 4.8).
8. (a) 2.66 g; (b) 1005.45 g.
9. (a) 0.3770; (b) 0.3745.
10. (a) 0.4013; (b) 0.3935.
11. 0.1393 (using all values below 29.5).
12. (a) This is binomial, $p = 0.05, n = 10$.
    p(accept batch) = 0.599.
    (b) Here $p = 0.1, n = 10$, and p(accept batch) = 0.349.
    (c) $p = 0.15, n = 10, p$(accept) = 0.197.
    $p = 0.2, n = 10, p$(accept) = 0.107.
    The operating characteristic decreases rather slowly, indicating that this is not a very good inspection scheme – even very poor-quality batches have quite a high chance of being accepted. For a more discriminating scheme, a larger sample size would need to be used.

Answers

in Sharpe

Chapter 2

1. Answers will vary.
3. *Who*—50 recent oil spills; *What*—date, spillage amount (no specified unit) and cause of puncture; *When*—Recent years; *Where*—United States; *Why*—To determine whether or not spillage amount per oil spill has decreased since Congress passed the 1990 Oil Pollution Act and use that information in the design of new tankers; *How*—not specified; *Variables*—There are 3 variables. Spillage amount and date are quantitative variables, and cause of puncture is a categorical variable.
5. *Who*—existing stores; *What*—sales ($), town population (000), median age (years), median income ($), and whether or not they sell beer/wine; *When*—not specified; *Where*—United States; *Why*—The food retailer is interested in understanding any association of these variables to help them determine where to open their next store; *How*—collection from their stores; *Variables*—Sales ($), population (000), median age (years), and median income ($) are all quantitative variables. Whether or not the store sells beer/wine is categorical.
7. *Who*—Arby's sandwiches; *What*—type of meat, number of calories (in calories), and serving size (in ounces); *When*—not specified; *Where*—Arby's restaurants; *Why*—These data might be used to assess the nutritional value of the different sandwiches; *How*—Information was gathered from each of the sandwiches on the menu at Arby's, resulting in a census; *Variables*—There are three variables. Number of calories and serving size are quantitative variables, and type of meat is a categorical variable.
9. *Who*—385 species of flowers; *What*—date of first flowering (in days); *When*—over a period of 47 years; *Where*—Southern England; *Why*—The researchers believe that this indicates a warming of the overall climate; *How*—not specified; *Variables*—Date of first flowering is a quantitative variable; *Concerns*—Hopefully, date of first flowering was measured in days from January 1, or some other convention, to avoid problems with leap years.
11. *Who*—students; *What*—age (probably in years, though perhaps in years and months), race or ethnicity, number of absences, grade level, reading score, math score, and disabilities/special needs; *When*—current; *Where*—not specified; *Why*—Keeping this information is a state requirement; *How*—The information is collected and stored as part of school records; *Variables*—There are 7 variables. Race or ethnicity, grade level, and disabilities/special needs are categorical variables. Number of absences, age, reading score, and math score are quantitative variables; *Concerns*—What tests are used to measure reading and math ability, and what are the units of measure for the tests?
13. *Who*—customers of a start-up company; *What*—customer name, ID number, region of the country, date of last purchase, amount of purchase (probably in dollars), and item purchased; *When*—present time; *Where*—not specified; *Why*—The company is building a database of sales information; *How*—Presumably, the company records the information from each new customer; *Variables*—There are 6 variables. Name, ID number, region of the country, and item purchased are categorical variables. Date and amount of purchase are quantitative variables; *Concerns*—Region is a categorical variable, and it is potentially confusing to record it as a number.
15. *Who*—vineyards; *What*—size of vineyard (in acres), number of years in existence, state, varieties of grapes grown, average case price (in dollars), gross sales (probably in dollars), and percent profit; *When*—not specified; *Where*—not specified; *Why*—Business analysts hoped to provide information that would be helpful to producers of U.S. wines; *How*—not specified; *Variables*—There are 5 quantitative variables and two categorical variables. Size of vineyard, number of years in existence, average case price, gross sales, and percent profit are quantitative variables. State and variety of grapes grown are categorical variables.
17. *Who*—1,180 Americans; *What*—region, age (in years), political party affiliation, whether or not the person owned any shares of stock, and their attitude toward unions; *When*—not specified; *Where*—United States; *Why*—The information was gathered for presentation in a Gallup public opinion poll; *How*—phone survey; *Variables*—There are 5 variables. Region, political party affiliation, and stock ownership are categorical variables. Age and opinion about unions are quantitative variables.
19. *Who*—every model of automobile in the United States; *What*—vehicle manufacturer, vehicle type, weight (probably in pounds), horsepower (in horsepower), and gas mileage (in miles per gallon) for city and highway driving; *When*—This information is collected currently; *Where*—United States; *Why*—The Environmental Protection Agency uses the information to track fuel economy of vehicles; *How*—The data is collected from the manufacturer of each model; *Variables*—There are 6 variables. City mileage, highway mileage, weight, and horsepower are quantitative variables. Manufacturer and type of car are categorical variables.
21. *Who*—states in the United States; *What*—state name, whether or not the state sponsors a lottery, the number of numbers in the lottery, the number of matches required to win, and the probability of holding a winning ticket; *When*—1998; *Where*—United States; *Why*—It is likely that this study was performed in order to compare the chances of winning the lottery in each state; *How*—Although not specified, the researchers probably simply gathered data from a number of different sources, such as state lottery website and publications; *Variables*—There are 5 variables. State name and whether or not the state sponsors a lottery are categorical variables, and number, matches, and probability of winning are quantitative variables.
23. *Who*—students in an MBA statistics class; *What*—total personal investment in stock market ($), number of different stocks held, total invested in mutual funds ($), and name of each mutual fund; *When*—not specified; *Where*—United States; *Why*—The information was collected for use in classroom illustrations; *How*—An online survey was conducted. Presumably, participation was required for all members of the class; *Variables*—There are 4 variables. Name of mutual fund is a categorical variable. Number of stocks held, total amount invested in market ($) and in mutual funds ($) are quantitative variables.
25. *Who*—Indy 500 races; *What*—year, winner, car, time (hours), speed (mph) and car #. *When*—1911–2007; *Where*—Indianapolis, Indiana; *Why*—It is interesting to examine the trends in Indy 500 races; *How*—Official statistics are kept for the race every year; *Variables*—There are 6 variables. Winner, car and car # are categorical variables. Year, time, and speed are quantitative variables.
27. Each row should be a single mortgage loan. Columns hold the borrower name (which identifies the rows) and amount.
29. Each row is a week. Columns hold week number (to identify the row), sales prediction, sales, and difference.
31. Cross-sectional
33. Time series

Solutions to review questions

in Waters

Chapter 3 – Drawing graphs

3.1 A variable whose value is set by the value taken by the independent variable.

3.2 No. Graphs show relationships, but do not suggest cause and effect.

3.3 (0, 0).

3.4 Yes – the distance between the two points is 10.

3.5 It is a straight line with a gradient of −2 that crosses the y-axis at −4.

3.6 (a) 0, (b) 1, (c) −6.

3.7 They correspond to the points where $y > 3x + 5$.

3.8 No – they are the same general shape, but differ in detail.

3.9 The points where the curve crosses the x-axis.

3.10 They are imaginary.

3.11 Because graphs are difficult to draw exactly and calculations give more accurate results.

3.12 A function containing x raised to some power.

3.13 A point where the gradient changes from positive to negative (or vice versa), corresponding to a peak or trough.

3.14 Using the usual procedure to draw a graph of the general form $y = ne^{mx}$, where n and m are positive constants.

3.15 You cannot draw this on a two-dimensional graph. You can draw it on a three-dimensional graph, but the results are generally difficult to interpret.

Chapter 5 – Diagrams for presenting data

5.1 Data are the raw numbers, measurements, opinions, etc. that are processed to give useful information.

5.2 To simplify raw data, remove the detail, and show underlying patterns.

5.3 Unfortunately not.

5.4 Using diagrams or numbers.

5.5 They can display lots of information, show varying attributes and highlight patterns.

5.6 A description of the number of observations in a set of data falling into each class.

5.7 This depends on the nature of the data and the purpose of the table. A guideline suggests between 4 and 10 classes.

5.8 Because they are a very efficient way of presenting a lot of detail. No other format can fit so much information into a small space.

5.9 To a large extent yes – but the choice often depends on personal preference, and a diagram of any kind may not be appropriate.

5.10 To show that they are scaled properly, accurately drawn, and give a true picture.

5.11 No – there are many possible variations and the best is often a matter of opinion.

5.12 Probably some kind of pictogram.

5.13 They are not very accurate, show a small amount of data, and can be misleading.

5.14 Unfortunately, you can find many of these.

5.15 No – it is true for bar charts, but in histograms the area shows the number of observations.

5.16 The average height of the two separate bars.

5.17 Often there is no benefit from histograms and it makes sense to stick with bar charts. Sometimes histograms help with further statistical analyses.

5.18 To show the cumulative frequency against class for continuous data.

5.19 Perhaps – the diagonal line shows equally distributed wealth, but we do not know whether this is fair.

Chapter 6 – Using numbers to describe data

6.1 They give an overall impression, but do not give objective measures.

6.2 A measure of the centre of the data – some kind of typical or average value.

6.3 No. These only partially describe a set of data.

6.4 A measure for the centre of the data or a typical value.

6.5 No.

6.6 The most common measures are: arithmetic mean = $\Sigma x/n$; median = middle observation; mode = most frequent observation.

6.7 $(10 \times 34 + 5 \times 37)/15 = 35$.

6.8 In Excel useful functions are AVERAGE, MEDIAN and MODE.

6.9 We concentrated on range, mean absolute deviation, variance, and standard deviation. Yes.

6.10 Because positive and negative deviations cancel and the mean deviation is always zero.

6.11 Metres^2 and metres respectively.

6.12 Because it gives standard results that we can interpret and use in other analyses.

6.13 210 is nine standard deviations away from 120, and the chances of this are very small. It is more likely that there has been a mistake – perhaps writing 210 instead of 120.

6.14 Useful ones include MAX, MIN, VARP, STDEVP and QUARTILE.

6.15 To give a relative view of spread that can be used to compare different sets of data.

6.16 The general shape of a distribution.

6.17 The coefficients of variation are 0.203 and 0.128 respectively (remembering to take the square root of the variance), which shows that the first set of data is more widely dispersed than the second set.

Solutions

in Croft

Chapter 14

Self-assessment questions 14.1

1. A root is a solution of an equation.
2. A linear equation can be written in the form $ax + b = 0$, where a and b are constants. In a linear equation, the variable is always to the first power only.
3. Adding or subtracting the same quantity from both sides; multiplying or dividing both sides by the same quantity; performing the same operation on both sides of the equation.
4. Equation: The two sides of the equation are equal only for certain values of the variable involved. These values are the solutions of the equation. For all other values, the two sides are not equal. Formula: A formula is essentially a statement of how two, or more, variables relate to one another, as for example in $A = \pi r^2$. The area of a circle, A, is always πr^2, for any value of the radius r.

Exercise 14.1

2. (a) $x = \frac{9}{3} = 3$ (b) $x = 3 \times 9 = 27$
   (c) $3t = -6$, so $t = \frac{-6}{3} = -2$ (d) $x = 22$
   (e) $3x = 4$ and so $x = \frac{4}{3}$ (f) $x = 36$
   (g) $5x = 3$ and so $x = \frac{3}{5}$ (h) $x + 3 = 6$ and so $x = 3$
   (i) adding the two terms on the left we obtain

$$\frac{3x+2}{2} + 3x = \frac{3x+2}{2} + \frac{6x}{2}$$

$$= \frac{3x+2+6x}{2} = \frac{9x+2}{2}$$

   and the equation becomes $(9x+2)/2 = 1$, therefore $9x + 2 = 2$, that is, $9x = 0$ and so $x = 0$

3. (a) $5x + 10 = 13$, so $5x = 3$ and so $x = \frac{3}{5}$
   (b) $3x - 21 = 2x + 2$ and so $x = 23$
   (c) $5 - 10x = 8 - 4x$ so that $-3 = 6x$ finally $x = \frac{-3}{6} = -\frac{1}{2}$
4. (a) $t = 9$ (b) $v = \frac{17}{7}$
   (c) $3s + 2 = 14s - 14$, so that $11s = 16$ and so $s = \frac{16}{11}$
5. (a) $t = 3$ (b) $t = 5$ (c) $t = -5$ (d) $t = 3$
   (e) $x = \frac{12}{5}$ (f) $x = -9$ (g) $x = 24$
   (h) $x = 15$ (i) $x = 23$ (j) $x = -\frac{43}{19}$
6. (a) $x = \frac{1}{5}$ (b) $x = \frac{2}{5}$ (c) $x = -\frac{3}{5}$
   (d) $x = 1\frac{2}{5}$ (e) $x = -1$ (f) $x = -3/5$
   (g) $x = -1/2$ (h) $x = -1/10$

Exercise 14.2

2. (a) Adding the two equations gives

$$\begin{aligned} 3x + y &= 1 \\ 2x - y &= 2 \\ \hline 5x \quad &= 3 \end{aligned}$$

from which $x = \frac{3}{5}$. Substitution into either equation gives $y = -\frac{4}{5}$.

(b) Subtracting the given equations eliminates y to give $x = 4$. From either equation $y = 1$.

(c) Multiplying the second equation by 2 and subtracting the first gives

$$\begin{aligned} 2x + 6y &= 24 \\ 2x - y \ &= 17 \quad - \\ \hline 7y &= 7 \end{aligned}$$

from which $y = 1$. Substitute into either equation to get $x = 9$.

(d) Multiplying the second equation by -2 and subtracting from the first gives

$$\begin{aligned} -2x + y \ &= -21 \\ -2x - 6y &= \ \ 28 \quad - \\ \hline 7y &= -49 \end{aligned}$$

from which $y = -7$. Substitution into either equation gives $x = 7$.

(e) Multiplying the first equation by 3 and adding the second gives

$$\begin{aligned} -3x + 3y &= -30 \\ 3x + 7y &= \ \ 20 \quad + \\ \hline 10y &= -10 \end{aligned}$$

from which $y = -1$. Substitution into either equation gives $x = 9$.

(f) Multiplying the second equation by 2 and subtracting this from the first gives

$$\begin{aligned} 4x - 2y &= \ \ 2 \\ 6x - 2y &= \ \ 8 \quad - \\ \hline -2x \quad &= -6 \end{aligned}$$

from which $x = 3$. Substitution into either equation gives $y = 5$.

3. (a) $x = 7, y = 1$ (b) $x = -7, y = 2$
(c) $x = 10, y = 0$ (d) $x = 0, y = 5$
(e) $x = -1, y = -1$

Self-assessment questions 14.3

1. If $b^2 - 4ac > 0$ a quadratic equation will have distinct real roots.
2. If $b^2 - 4ac = 0$ a quadratic equation will have a repeated root.

Exercise 14.3

1. (a) $(x + 2)(x - 1) = 0$ so that $x = -2$ and 1
(b) $(x - 3)(x - 5) = 0$ so that $x = 3$ and 5
(c) $2(2x + 1)(x + 1) = 0$ so that $x = -1$ and $x = -\frac{1}{2}$
(d) $(x - 3)(x - 3) = 0$ so that $x = 3$ twice
(e) $(x + 9)(x - 9) = 0$ so that $x = -9$ and 9
(f) $-1, -3$ (g) $1, -3$ (h) $1, -4$
(i) $-1, -5$ (j) $5, 7$ (k) $-5, -7$
(l) $1, -\frac{3}{2}$ (m) $-\frac{3}{2}, 2$ (n) $-\frac{3}{2}, 5$
(o) $1, -1/3$ (p) $-1/3, 5/3$ (q) $0, -\frac{1}{7}$
(r) $-\frac{3}{2}$ twice

2. (a) $x = \dfrac{-(-6) \pm \sqrt{(-6)^2 - 4(3)(-5)}}{6}$

$= \dfrac{6 \pm \sqrt{96}}{6}$

$= 2.633$ and -0.633

(b) $x = \dfrac{-3 \pm \sqrt{9 - 4(1)(-77)}}{2}$

$= \dfrac{-3 \pm \sqrt{317}}{2}$

$= 7.402$ and -10.402

(c) $x = \dfrac{-(-9) \pm \sqrt{(-9)^2 - 4(2)(2)}}{4}$

$= \dfrac{9 \pm \sqrt{65}}{4}$

$= 4.266$ and 0.234

(d) $1, -4$ (e) $1.758, -0.758$
(f) $0.390, -0.640$ (g) $7.405, -0.405$
(h) $0.405, -7.405$ (i) no solutions
(j) $2.766, -1.266$

3. (a) $(3x + 2)(2x + 3) = 0$
from which $x = -2/3$ and $-3/2$
(b) $(t + 3)(3t + 4) = 0$
from which $t = -3$ and $t = -4/3$
(c) $t = (7 \pm \sqrt{37})/2 = 6.541$ and 0.459

Worked solutions to review activities

in Smailes & McGrane

CHAPTER 4

Review activity 1

(a) Let percentage mark given for speed = x and percentage mark given for print quality = y. Table S.4.1 is then constructed.

Table S.4.1

x	y	x^2	y^2	xy
20	65	400	4225	1300
45	35	2025	1225	1575
25	55	625	3025	1375
10	85	100	7225	850
30	15	900	225	450
25	25	625	625	625
35	45	1225	2025	1575
30	25	900	625	750
20	55	400	3025	1100
25	35	625	1225	875
$\sum x = 265$	$\sum y = 440$	$\sum x^2 = 7825$	$\sum y^2 = 23{,}450$	$\sum xy = 10{,}475$

Using the data in the table calculate:

$$r = \frac{n\sum xy - \sum x\sum y}{\sqrt{\{n\sum x^2 - (\sum x)^2\}\{n\sum y^2 - (\sum y)^2\}}}$$

$$= \frac{(10 * 10{,}475) - (265 * 440)}{\sqrt{\{(10 * 7825) - 265^2\}\{(10 * 23{,}450) - 440^2\}}}$$

$$= \frac{104{,}750 - 116{,}600}{\sqrt{\{78{,}250 - 70{,}225\}\{234{,}500 - 193{,}600\}}}$$

$$= \frac{-11{,}850}{\sqrt{8025 * 40{,}900}} = \frac{-11{,}850}{18{,}116.912}$$

$$= -0.654 \text{ (to 3 d.p.)}$$

This suggests there is a reasonably strong correlation between the speed and the print quality of the machine. As the correlation coefficient is negative this would suggest that as speed increases then print quality decreases.

(b) Before calculating the rank correlation coefficient, the prices of the machines require ranking. The ranks awarded (where 1 = most expensive) are shown in Table S.4.2. It should be noted that the two cheapest printers share the ranks of 9 and 10 giving them each a rank of 9.5.

Table S.4.2

Overall rank	Price (£)	Price rank	d	d^2
5	410	3	2	4
3	396	6	−3	9
8	350	9.5	−1.5	2.25
7	530	1	6	36
4	399	5	−1	1
10	353	8	2	4
1	430	2	−1	1
2	404	4	−2	4
9	350	9.5	−0.5	0.25
6	375	7	−1	1
				$\sum d^2 = 62.5$

Then calculate:

$$r = 1 - \frac{6\sum d^2}{n(n^2-1)}$$

$$= 1 - \frac{6 * 62.5}{10 * 99} = 1 - \frac{375}{990}$$

$$= 1 - 0.3787878 = 0.621 \text{ (to 3 d.p.)}$$

The correlation coefficient of 0.621 suggests there is a reasonable level of agreement between the overall rank awarded to the printer and its price.

Review activity 2 (a) Phoneyvode:

$y = 15 + 0.5x$ *or* charges = 15 + 0.5 * minutes of calls

Purplecom:

$y = 17.25 + 0.35x$ *or* charges = 17.25 + 0.35 * minutes of calls

In each case y = charges, x = number of minutes of calls made.

(b) Calculations required:

Minutes of calls (x)	0	20	40
Phoneyvode charge	15	25	35
Purplecom charge	17.25	24.25	31.25

This gives a graph as shown in Figure S.4.1.

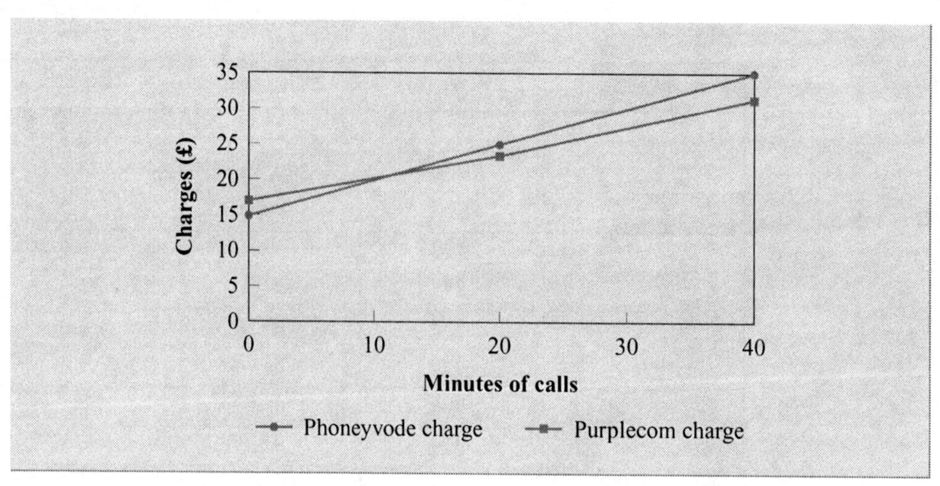

Figure S.4.1 Graph for Review activity 2, showing mobile telephone charges

(c) Purplecom becomes cheaper where the two lines cross. To find this point exactly:

$$15 + 0.5x = 17.25 + 0.35x$$

$$0.15\,x = 2.25$$

$$x = \frac{2.25}{0.15} = 15$$

i.e., if less than 15 minutes of calls per month are to be made, Phoneyvode should be chosen. If the anticipated call level is higher, Purplecom is the cheaper option.

(d) Either equation can be used:

$x = 15$ gives $y = 15 + 0.5 * 15 = 15 + 7.5 = 22.5$

or

$x = 15$ gives $y = 17.25 + 0.35 * 15 = 17.25 + 5.25 = 22.5$

The overall charge for 15 minutes of calls (on either scheme) is £22.50 per month.

Review activity 3 (a) Takings = y and Number of coaches = x.

(b) The calculations needed are shown in Table S.4.3.

Table S.4.3

Day number	No. of coaches	Takings (£)		
	x	y	xy	x^2
1	24	962	23088	576
2	30	1181	35430	900
3	9	578	5202	81
4	48	1429	68592	2304
5	38	1324	50312	1444
6	15	752	11280	225
7	5	542	2710	25
8	38	1355	51490	1444
9	15	788	11820	225
10	24	998	23952	576
11	49	1462	71638	2401
12	10	650	6500	100
13	17	862	14654	289
14	11	719	7909	121
15	16	828	13248	256
	$\sum x = 349$	$\sum y = 14430$	$\sum xy = 397825$	$\sum x^2 = 10967$

The data from the table gives:

$$b = \frac{n\sum xy - \sum x \sum y}{\left[n\sum x^2 - (\sum x)^2\right]} = \frac{15 * 397825 - 349 * 14430}{(15 * 10967 - 349^2)} = \frac{931305}{42704} = 21.80837$$

$$a = \frac{\sum y}{n} - \frac{b\sum x}{n} = \frac{14430}{15} - 21.80837 * \frac{349}{15} = 962 - 507.40807 = 454.5919$$

Hence the regression equation is:

$y = 454.59 + 21.81x$

or

Takings = 454.59 + 21.81 * No. of coaches

(Notice that calculations have been done using a number of decimal places, with rounding only carried out at the very end to avoid errors.)

(c) (i) If $x = 27$, $y = 454.59 + 21.81 * 27 =$ £1043.46

(ii) If $x = 55$, $y = 454.59 + 21.81 * 55 =$ £1654.15

(d) Answer (i) above is likely to be reliable because the forecast has been made using data inside the range used to make up the regression equation (interpolation).

Answer (ii) may be less reliable. The value of 55 coaches is outside the range used to make up the equation, and it is not known whether the model is still valid. For example, there may be limited parking in the town which would lead to problems if larger numbers of coaches arrive.

Answers to even-numbered additional exercises

in Smailes & McGrane

CHAPTER 4

4.2 (a) Spearman's rank correlation coefficient, $r = 0.8929$ (to 4d.p.)

(b) This indicates a high level of agreement

4.4 Weight loss (lb) = –0.8111 + 0.0175 * minutes of aerobic exercise. When 150 minutes of aerobic exercise is carried out the predicted weight loss is 1.814 lb.

4.6 (a) Age when bought has a strong negative relationship with battery life. In the case of price there is little evidence of a relationship with battery life.

(b) Battery life = 15.438 – 0.537 * Age when bought

(c) When batteries are new they have an expected lifetime of around 15½ months. For every month after this lifetime reduces by one half of a month.

(d) (i) 2.55 months; (ii) 12.216 months

(e) d(i) Extrapolation has occurred so the forecast may be unreliable